D1565045

UNIVERSALS OF HUMAN LANGUAGE

VOLUME 1

Method & Theory

CONTRIBUTORS

Alan Bell
Eve V. Clark
Herbert H. Clark
Charles A. Ferguson
Joseph H. Greenberg
Hans-Heinrich Lieb
Edith A. Moravcsik

Universals of Human Language

Edited by Joseph H. Greenberg

Associate Editors:
Charles A. Ferguson & Edith A. Moravcsik

VOLUME 1

Method & Theory

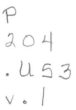

Stanford University Press, Stanford, California
1978

Stanford University Press
Stanford, California
© 1978 by the Board of Trustees of the
Leland Stanford Junior University
Printed in the United States of America
ISBN 0-8047-0965-3
LC 77-89179

Number 8 in this volume, by Clark and Clark, is adapted from "Language and Thought" in *Psychology
and Language: An Introduction to Psycholinguistics,* by Herbert H. Clark and Eve V. Clark, © 1977
by Harcourt Brace Jovanovich, Inc. Reprinted by permission of the publishers.

Preface

The mainspring of the contemporary interest in language universals is the conviction that linguistics as a science must develop broader goals than the description of the structures of the thousands of individual languages which exist in the present or of which we have records from the past. It must be broader even than a body of generalizing theory concerning how such descriptions can be carried out.

Theory of this latter type already existed by the early 1950's, although many defects have since become apparent. As compared with other human sciences of the time, it seemed to possess an evident superiority in methodological sophistication and rigor. Yet a thoughtful and alert observer could raise fundamental problems not evident to the practical purveyor who took for granted the tacit premises of his science.

It fell to the lot of one of the present writers, as a participant in the seminar on psycholinguistics sponsored by the Social Science Research Council in the summer of 1951 at Bloomington, to give an exposition of linguistics for the psychologists present. The task was undertaken with a sense of pride in the accomplishments of the linguistics of the period. One of the psychologists, Charles Osgood, was suitably impressed. He commented, however, to the effect that while linguistics had an admirable and well worked out method, it was being applied merely to the description of individual languages. Could the linguists present tell him anything about <u>all</u> languages? That would be of the highest interest to psychologists. To this the linguistics of the period had no real answer.

The stimulating quality of these remarks and of the other discussions that followed bore fruit in the work of the Social Science Research Council, leading ultimately to the Dobbs Ferry conference on Language Universals in 1961. This meeting played an essential part in inaugurating a period of renewed interest in this topic.

While there were several papers at that conference which stated tentative generalizations of universal scope regarding several aspects of language, it was realized that to extend such studies from these modest beginnings was an enormous task requiring relevant data regarding numerous other aspects of language to be

drawn from adequately large samples of languages. Hence arose
the notion of a research project in which scholars would undertake
concrete research of this sort on a large variety of linguistic
topics.

This took shape at Stanford where the Project on Language
Universals was organized. It began its activities in October 1967
and brought them to an end in August 1976. During its entire nine-
year period it was directed by Charles A. Ferguson and Joseph H.
Greenberg, both professors at Stanford University, as principal
investigators. Its main source of financial support was the National
Science Foundation, which, over the years, contributed slightly
below $1,000,000. In addition to the two principal investigators,
the Project staff included altogether thirty-two part-time or full-
time linguists, some of whom held short-term visiting positions
not spanning more than a few months, while others were with the
Project up to several years. The names of these linguists are as
follows: Rebecca Agheyisi, Alan Bell, D.N.S. Bhat, Jean Braine,
Richard Carter, Eve Clark, Harold Clumeck, John Crothers,
Gilles Delisle, Talmy Givón, Victor Girard, Mary Ellen Greenlee,
Helga Harries-Delisle, Laurence Horn, Charles Jennings, Joan
Kahr, Dorothea Kaschube, Ian Maddieson, James Michael Moore,
Edith Moravcsik, Chris O'Sullivan, Andrew Rindsberg, Merritt
Ruhlen, Gerald Sanders, Philip Sedlak, Susan Steele, Leonard
Talmy, Russell Ultan, Marilyn Vihman, Krystyna Wachowicz,
Werner Winter, and Karl Zimmer. The staff also included Nicholas
Zirpolo on a short-term bibliographer appointment, and Dal
Dresser, Vicky Shu, and Vicki Fahrenholz as successive secretary-
bibliographers for the Project; budgetary questions were attended
to throughout by Jean Beeson. In addition to those mentioned here,
from time to time visiting scholars with outside funding collabor-
ated with the Project for varying periods. Among these was
Hansjakob Seiler.

The original goals of the Project were stated by Greenberg in
his introductory words to the first issue of Working Papers in
Language Universals (WPLU) in November 1969. They were to
formulate cross-linguistic and, if possible, universally valid
empirical generalizations about language structure; generalizations,
that is, which hold true for some significant universe of languages
and which at the same time are capable of being refuted by actual
language data. The fact that such generalizations cannot be verified without reliable cross-linguistic data justifies the other original objective of the Project, which was to collect data from various languages of the world and store them in precise and comparable form. These two objectives were seen as not in themselves

sufficient but nonetheless necessary parts of the long-range goal
of accounting for similarities and differences among human language
in terms of increasingly general laws overarching various apparently unrelated aspects of language structure.

The particular format chosen for the realization of these two
initially conceived goals of the Project was the following. At any
one time the staff consisted of the two directors, a secretary-
bibliographer, and three or four researchers. Although the selection of staff linguists reflected adherence to the basic goals of the
Project, once on the staff, linguists were free to follow their own
philosophies and methodologies regarding research on typology
and universals. The papers in WPLU indeed reflect the resulting
theoretical and methodological diversity. The choice of topics was
similarly left up to the individual investigator, subject in principle
to the veto of the directors -- a power, however, which was never
actually exercised. Middle-range projects were encouraged,
requiring not more and possibly less than half a year to complete.
The rich linguistic resources of the Stanford University library,
as well as Ferguson's and Greenberg's private libraries, provided
most of the basic data. For some studies linguistic informants
from Stanford and the surrounding area were also utilized. Frequent biweekly or weekly meetings of the Project, attended at
times by other linguists from Stanford and from neighboring univer-
sities and by scholars visiting the area, provided opportunities for
reporting on and criticizing ongoing or completed work. The working paper series of the Project ensured informal and rapid dissem-
ination of results to wider circles.

It is in accordance with this mode of organization that the Project progressed toward the realization of its two goals. As far as
data collection is concerned, almost every one of the sixty-eight
working papers that were published in the twenty issues of WPLU
presented data from a variety of languages in comparable terms.[1]
In addition to the actual data, efforts were also made to provide
guidelines for data collection. This was done by "check lists" or
sets of parameters related to specific aspects of language data and
of use both to linguistic fieldworkers and to cross-linguistic re-

---

[1]This includes all full-size working papers published in the series, whether written by Project members (54) or contributed by
linguists not associated with the Project (14). The number does not
include the survey papers and shorter notes contained in WPLU.

searchers. After several years of the operation of the Project,
attempts to archive data on phonetics and phonology, an area which
seemed particularly promising in this respect, took the shape of
an independent research endeavor, the Phonology Archiving Project. This group was also Stanford-based, had the same directors
as the Language Universals Project, and received funding from the
same source. A still ongoing enterprise, the Phonology Archiving
Project has to date computer-stored the phonetic segment inventory of about two hundred languages, as well as phonological rule
information on some of them. [2] Although tentative plans for a
similar large-scale computer archiving project with respect to
grammatical information were made, their realization is still a
matter for the future.

As far as the other aim is concerned, the establishment of
cross-linguistically valid generalizations about language structures,
we believe that substantial progress has been made, as the papers
in WPLU attest, making allowances for the inevitable future revis-
ions and even the abandonment of certain generalizations in the
light of further investigation. It seems reasonable to conclude that
a substantial portion of this work will prove, in the long run, to have
contributed substantially to our understanding of human language.

As the Project's end drew nearer, it was felt that a publication
that is both more formal and also more widely available than the
WPLU series should stand as a summary of our activities. [3] Thus

---

[2] For access to this material, write to Phonology Archiving Project, Department of Linguistics, Stanford University, Stanford,
California 94305.

[3] Copies of issues 11-20 of WPLU nonetheless remain available
at $2.00 apiece. Write to Working Papers on Language Universals,
Department of Linguistics, Stanford University, Stanford, California 94305. A bibliographical list including all references cited in
WPLU papers (about 2,000) arranged according to languages (about
750) is also available from the same address (under the name
"Bibliography") for $1.00 a copy; and so are the proceedings of a
conference on nasals and nasalization held in 1974 at Stanford,
entitled Nasalfest, for $6.50 a copy. Xerox and microfiche copies
of individual papers contained in any of the twenty issues of WPLU
are also available from ERIC clearinghouse in Languages and Linguistics, Center for Applied Linguistics, 1611 North Kent Street,
Arlington, Virginia 22209.

the idea of the present book was conceived. The original intention
of simply summarizing what we have done was then complemented
by the desire to answer the very patent need in the present linguistic literature for a comprehensive statement on where exactly we
are in our knowledge about cross-linguistically recurrent structural properties of language. The "we" in the latter part of this
sentence is not confined to Project members. In the past few years
endeavors to establish and test similar generalizations have been
increasingly initiated by individual scholars and organized projects
in other countries as well as in Western Europe and the Soviet
Union. In addition, even those whose basic methodology and
approach are quite different from that employed for the most part
in the Project have taken note of its results and have felt the need
of accounting for them by incorporating them within their own
theoretical framework, or even modifying that framework to
account for them.

In accordance with these aims, we have sought to make these
volumes as comprehensive as possible, consistent with the current
stage of research and the particular interests and competences of
those scholars who were either active in or basically sympathetic
with our enterprise.

These volumes consist of forty-six papers. Roughly corresponding
to three fundamental aspects of language structure, the data-
oriented papers have been grouped into three classes: those mostly pertaining to phonology, those mostly dealing with morphological
and lexical properties of the word-unit, and those primarily involved with syntactic and related semantic problems. The second,
third, and fourth volumes of the book each contain one of these
three groups of papers. The first volume presents the general
papers which discuss questions of the theory and methodology of
typological and universals research. Each paper in the book is
preceded by an abstract and followed by its own list of references.
At the end of each volume is an author index and a language index
specific to papers in that volume.

Of the forty-six studies included in the book, thirty-five appear
here for the first time. These have been written in part by scholars
who were either members of or associated with the Stanford Project on Language Universals, in part by scholars not formally
associated with the Project who have been invited by the editors to
deal with a specific topic. Among the latter are Elaine Andersen,
Dwight Bolinger, Bruce Downing, Thomas Gamkrelidze, Brian

Head, Larry Hyman, Hans-Heinrich Lieb, Adam Makkai, Yakov
Malkiel, and Elizabeth Closs Traugott. The remaining thirteen
papers are original or revised versions of working papers that
were previously published informally. They were written by members of this group as part of their work for the Project.

In general, the arrangement is topical; it reflects the manner
in which research was actually carried out under the aegis of the
Project and of the typical product as seen in the Working Papers.
This approach has some advantages. In general, it selects areas
of research comprehensive enough not to be trivial and, on the
other hand, not so all-encompassing as to be impractical. It leads
to numerous concrete and testable generalizations. We are also
keenly aware of certain inevitable defects. Since, to begin with,
we did not provide a comprehensive a priori scheme and did not
impose particular topics on investigators, there are necessarily
major omissions. There is also the danger that a somewhat ad
hoc and piecemeal approach will lead to the neglect of topics that
do not easily fall within present classificatory rubrics, as reflected
in the overall organization of this work. For example, there is
much to be learned from the phenomenon of word accent as it
relates to morphological systems. However, this topic does not
easily fall within conventional classifications.

The other defect is more closely tied into the basically, but not
exclusively, inductive nature of this approach. Interconnections
based on the presence of similar general psychological or other principles, or of even more specific factual relevance, may be overlooked through compartmentalization. Still, as an initial strategy,
we believe it to be defensible in terms of its immediate fruitfulness.
This is, however, something for the linguistic community as a
whole to judge. Moreover, many of our investigations, it can be
claimed, have already involved at least an adumbration of more
comprehensive principles -- for example, of marking theory.

In behalf of the authors of the papers included in this work and
in our own behalf, we would like to express our deep gratitude to
all of those who made the appearance of the books possible. Thus,
we would first like to thank Vicky Shu for the competence and genuine care she brought to the editing and typing of the final camera-
ready version of the manuscript. We are furthermore grateful to
Stanford Press and to William Carver in particular for their
guidance in our endeavor to produce a book that is pleasing to the
eye. Our most sincere thanks should go to Stanford University,

especially to the Department of Linguistics and its current chair-
person, Clara Bush, for being such an understanding host to the
Language Universals Project in the past nine years, and to Deans
Halsey Royden and W. Bliss Carnochan, and Provost William
Miller for their generous financial support toward the preparation
of the manuscript in final form. Finally, we thank the National
Science Foundation for its continuing support of the work of the
project.

J.H.G.
C.A.F.
E.A.M.

Contents

Contributors

Alan Bell is Assistant Professor of Linguistics at the University of Colorado at Boulder. He was a member of the Stanford Project on Language Universals in 1968-70 and a visiting member in the summer of 1971.

Eve V. Clark is Associate Professor in the Department of Linguistics at Stanford University. In 1969-70 she was a Research Associate with the Stanford Project on Language Universals.

Herbert H. Clark is Professor of Psychology at Stanford University, with a specialization in psycholinguistics.

Charles A. Ferguson is Professor of Linguistics at Stanford University. He was Co-Director of the Stanford Project on Language Universals and is Associate Editor of these volumes.

Joseph H. Greenberg is Professor of Linguistics and Anthropology at Stanford University. He was Co-Director of the Stanford Project on Language Universals and is the Editor of these volumes.

Hans-Heinrich Lieb is Full Professor of Linguistics in the German Department of the Freie Universität Berlin in West Berlin, Germany.

Edith A. Moravcsik is a Visiting Assistant Professor of Linguistics at the University of Wisconsin in Milwaukee. She was a member of the Stanford Project on Language Universals in 1968-72 and again in 1975-76. She is Associate Editor of these volumes and was the Editor of Working Papers on Language Universals.

UNIVERSALS OF HUMAN LANGUAGE

VOLUME 1

Method & Theory

Introduction

JOSEPH H. GREENBERG

This first volume of <u>Universals of Human Language</u> differs essentially from the remaining three. The others consist of papers almost all devoted to a search for generalizations regarding specific aspects of language based on cross-linguistic data. By language is meant here normal adult spoken language in its thousands of individually variant forms. As the basic vehicle of social interaction and cultural transmission, the centrality of language in this sense for linguistic generalization is obvious, and it is not without reason that when the term language is employed by linguists without qualification this is the meaning intended.

However, there remain matters of fundamental significance in relation to the topic of language universals that cannot be accommodated within such a framework. This volume is intended to treat a number of these and thus help to contribute a more general perspective—historical, methodological, and interdisciplinary—to the work as a whole.

As Ferguson's paper 'Historical Background of Universals Research' points out, the contemporary revival of interest in language universals was preceded by a period in American linguistics in which there was an emphasis on linguistic variability. It was largely devoted to the development of rigorous techniques by means of which each language could be described in terms of its own categories. Much was achieved from this perspective. In particular the enormous accumulation of information concerning a vast range of human languages in accordance with improved and more sophisticated techniques of description provides a large part of our present data base. Moreover, out of this ultimately came the realization that there were limits to this variability and that if linguistics was to progress as a science it must develop a generalizing approach designed to uncover and explain the common properties of language.

As is also made clear in Ferguson's paper, there have grown up over the last fifteen years or so two such approaches, one largely typological, inductive, and empirical, the other more deductive and concerned with the interest in formal aspects of grammar and characteristic of the MIT generative school. The Stanford Project on Language Universals, whose work is largely represented in the

present volumes, essentially represents the first of these
approaches. It does not, however, dogmatically exclude work
more oriented toward the generative approach. Indeed, a fair
proportion of the research sponsored by the Project, as can be
noted in its series Working Papers on Language Universals and
in some of the articles in the present collection, might be termed
eclectic in this regard.

The approach basically represented here, then, grew out of
typology. In a sense this was an unexpected development, although
foreshadowed by Jakobson's now classic work of 1941, Kindersprache,
Aphasie und allgemeine Lautgesetze, 'Child Language, Aphasia and
General Sound Laws.' What was unexpected here was that typology,
historically, had been a pursuit that emphasized language differences
rather than similarities and that sought to characterize the typological uniqueness of individual languages. However, a classification
of languages into types in regard to any aspect of language virtually
always shows that some logically conceivable types do not exist.
For example, as far as we know, there are no languages with the
regular word order object-subject-verb in main clause declarative
sentences. Such negatively expressed restraints on possible types
can be restated positively, often as conditional, or, as they are
frequently called, implicational universals. For example, in this
instance we can state that whenever the object precedes the verb
the subject does likewise. Thus the advantage of a typological
approach is that even differences, among languages where there are
limits to them, become the material for linguistic generalization.
My paper 'Typology and Cross-Linguistic Generalization' is devoted
to a general exploration of this relationship.

Another and more recent trend in linguistics is a revival of
interest in historical linguistics. In connection with universals
research, this arises on a generalizing level, that of process. By
a process is meant here a class of similar but historically independent changes. Thus many languages in different areas and at different historical periods have developed definite articles from
demonstratives. By comparing such developments on a broad
scale it becomes possible to generalize concerning diachronic
processes. My paper 'Diachrony, Synchrony, and Language Universals' is an attempt to explore the methodology for arriving at such
process generalizations and to investigate their interrelations
with cross-linguistic regularities arrived at by synchronic investigation.

Processes are likewise involved in Moravcsik's paper 'Language
Contact,' for changes resulting from language contact necessarily

work themselves out over time. Many linguists tend to think of
basic linguistic changes as generated by purely internal factors.
However, there is much empirical evidence supporting the view
that external linguistic influences play an important role in init-
iating linguistic changes. In spite of the quite large accumulation
of data concerning the results of linguistic influence, little has
been done in regard to generalizing about such change. Moravcsik's
paper is a pioneer effort in this direction, which concentrates on
grammatical categories rather than phonological or semantic ones.

Two main questions here are the following. Are there regularities concerning the relative stability of certain typological features
under contact conditions in comparison with other closely associated
features? Is it true, for example, as has been suspected, that in
regard to word order, subject-verb-object is more easily influenced
by that of adjacent languages than genitive order? Is there indeed
an overarching generalization that the higher the grammatical level
of the construction the greater the susceptibility of word order to
external influence? The second and related question is this. If
languages can be affected in essential ways by contact, by what
mechanisms do the observed synchronic generalizations about
language survive this process unscathed? Consider an example
from phonology. There is an implicational universal that an
alveolar affricate such as ts always implies the presence of s in a
language but not vice versa. Further, there are languages without
s (e.g. some Nilotic languages). Hence there are three types of
languages in regard to this matter: (1) those with both s and ts;
(2) those with s but without ts; (3) those with neither. But there
are no languages with ts that lack s. The question is what happens
when a language of type 3 is influenced by a language of type 1. It
is logically possible that ts would come into the language as a
result but not s, which would produce the 'forbidden' fourth type.
However, one might conjecture that such selective borrowing is
unlikely or that even without a previous s, words from the source
language with ts would be borrowed with s in the place of ts even
in a language which had neither.

Alan Bell's paper 'Language Samples' is concerned with
another neglected and important aspect of universals research, the
methodological problem of language sampling. We are just emerg-
ing from what might be called the pioneering period of universals
research. One of its characteristics has been that in its legitimate
pursuit of linguistic generalizations derived from the examination
of data from a variety of languages regarding any particular aspects of linguistic structure, it has derived samples on an oppor-

tunistic basis, resting on the individual language background of the
investigator, the convenience of source data, the research languages
within the investigator's competence, etc., and without any
systematic notions of the size and composition of a reasonable sample in relation to a particular problem. This situation is to some
extent mitigated by the intuitive realization that such a problem
indeed exists and must be taken into account. Thus no one, say,
investigates relative clauses cross-linguistically by a sample of
30 languages, 29 of which are Bantu. Nevertheless, as Bell's
paper makes clear, the time has arrived both for more theoretical
attention to this problem and for the application of such theoretical
considerations to actual language samples.

    A truly basic set of problems for both the theory and practice of
research on language universals is considered in Lieb's paper
'Universals and Linguistic Explanation.' It is clear that from the
outset a major source of the attractiveness of universals research
was that generalizations across languages could be considered as
akin to laws in the sense in which they exist in the physical sciences.
As such they figure in the scientific explanation of linguistic phenomena. A deeper and more systematic study of this aspect of
universals research clearly cannot be detached from the broader
question of the nature of scientific explanation in general, for which
a sophisticated body of theory has been developed in the philosophy
of science. An important development here has been an extension
of interest in these problems by philosophers of science, from the
paradigm field of physics to a number of other fields including, in
the present context, linguistics. A further evidence of the topical-
ity of this question is the recent appearance of an entire volume
devoted to this topic. The volume, based on a symposium and
edited by David Cohen, is entitled <u>Explaining Linguistic Phenomena</u>
(New York, 1974).

    Ferguson's paper 'Talking to Children: A Search for Universals'
shows that even in an area marginal to 'normal' adult language and
one which suffers from a paucity of material, at least provisional
generalizations begin to emerge. Such results have a significance
beyond the highly restricted aspect of language to which they primarily pertain. To begin with, constants across language in regard
to simplifications of phonetic and grammatical structure in discourse
with children and foreigners are of interest from the psychological
point of view as involving intuitive judgments, regarding relative
complexity of particular aspects of language, and involve implicit
linguistic analysis. For example, in the course of a linguistic
survey of the Jos area of Nigeria in 1955, I discovered that one of
my informants on a language with a complex system of noun class

prefixes had consciously omitted them, as he explained to me
later, because they were complicated for a foreigner and because
one could be understood without them. The further significance of
such a study is for its bearing both on child language acquisition
and for language pidginization, in both of which both morphological
and phonological simplification are essentially involved.

Finally, the Clark paper 'Universals, Relativity, and Language
Processing' illustrates well the benefit of universals research for
the psychology of language, on the one hand, and the role of psychology in uncovering psychological factors underlying language universals, on the other. An interdisciplinary approach can thus make use
of linguistic results at the most general level as material for deeper
generalizations connecting superficially different results. It also
suggests that whatever psychological principles are involved may
be of yet broader application as special instances of regularities in
human behavior of which language is just one manifestation, even
if a particularly important one. This is, of course, relevant to the
ongoing debate regarding 'strong' and 'weak' universals. The former would be purely linguistic. It would seem that a methodological
commitment at least to the possible existence of some of the latter
has the advantage that it leads to the exploration of connections between human linguistic and non-linguistic behavior and thus opens
the possibility of important discoveries, whereas their denial tends
to discourage such research. In this matter, one is reminded of
the extensive discussion generated in late nineteenth- and early
twentieth-century linguistics regarding the proposition that sound
laws have no exceptions. Even though in some instances the proposition is surely not true, a conviction of its validity leads to the
discovery of regularities.

Historical Background
of Universals Research

CHARLES A. FERGUSON

ABSTRACT

Current research in the universals of human language dates
from a) the work of Greenberg in the 1950s and the Conference
on Language Universals, Dobbs Ferry, N.Y., 1961, and b) the
Chomskyan "revolution" in linguistics as exemplified in the Symposium on Universals in Linguistic Theory, Austin, Texas, 1967.
These conferences are representative of two different streams of
research during the 1960s, one oriented to typological analysis of
cross-linguistic data, the other to theories of language and the
form of grammars. The two streams began to interact in the
1970s, and universals research is now widely recognized as a
major concern of linguistics.

Part of the work reported here was done under the auspices of
the Stanford Phonology Archiving Project, supported by the National
Science Foundation, Grant No. BNS 76-16825. I am grateful to
Susan Steele for first calling my attention to the differentiation of
the terms "language universals" and "linguistic universals;" she
has not read this paper, however, and is not to be blamed for what
I have said here about the distinction.

Charles A. Ferguson

CONTENTS

1. Introduction

As soon as human beings began to make systematic observations
about one another's languages, they were probably impressed by
the paradox that all languages are in some fundamental sense one
and the same, and yet they are also strikingly different from one
another. The story of the tower of Babel in Genesis 11, whatever
its original sources and intended moral may have been, reflects
this human bewilderment. "Now the whole earth had one language
..." seemed a reasonable hypothesis about human history; what
needed explanation was the world's linguistic diversity. The Babel
story says in narrative form exactly what Roger Bacon's often
quoted sentence asserted about language in the thirteenth century:
"Grammatica una et eadem est secundum substantiam in omnibus
linguis, licet accidentaliter varietur." (Grammar is one and the
same in all languages in substance, though it may vary in accidents.)
The systematic (read philosophical, scientific, or linguistic) study
of human language has this paradox as its central concern. Students
of language have looked for the oneness in a sacred language, in an
artificially contrived language, or in a comparison of many languages; they have looked for it to set a norm of correctness, to
understand the workings of the human mind, or simply to find general properties of language. At the height of American structural-
ism some were even content to find the universality in the set of
discovery procedures which could be used to make analyses of all
languages. Although the search for oneness may be as old as the
study of language, the expression "universal grammar" dates from
the beginning of the seventeenth century (cf. Padley 1976), and the
expressions "language universals" and "linguistic universals" came
into linguistic terminology in the 1940's and 1960's, respectively
(e.g. Aginsky and Aginsky 1948, Katz and Postal 1964).[1]

2. Two Conferences on Universals

Two important conferences typify much of the work on universals
done during the sixties: the Conference on Language Universals
held in Dobbs Ferry, New York, April 13-15, 1961, and the symposium on Universals in Linguistic Theory held at the University of

---

[1] Although the term "language universals" was introduced in the
Aginskys' article and was used in discussion among some linguists,
it did not become widely used until 1961. The term "linguistic universals" apparently appeared first in print in the Katz and Postal
volume in 1964, was used in Chomsky's Aspects in 1965, and became
a widespread technical term almost immediately.

Texas in Austin, April 13-15, 1967. The Dobbs Ferry conference
was sponsored by the Linguistics and Psychology Committee of the
Social Science Research Council and was attended by linguists,
anthropologists, and psychologists. The Texas symposium was
sponsored in effect by the Department of Linguistics of the University of Texas and was attended almost exclusively by linguists.
Each conference resulted in a published volume that presented
revised versions of the papers and regrettably omitted an account
of the discussions, which were called, respectively, "highly stimulating and productive" and "articulate and vigorous." The books
were Universals of Language edited by J. H. Greenberg (hereafter
UL), and Universals in Linguistic Theory edited by E. Bach and
R. T. Harms (hereafter ULT). As an indication of the rather separate lines of research that were being followed at the time, we
may note that no one who participated in the first conference also
attended the second, and there was almost no overlap in the two
bibliographies. The exceptions in references are instructive: both
books referred to several European theoreticians (Bazell, Hjelmslev,
Jakobson, Martinet, Robins) and the Texas book referred to one
paper in the Dobbs Ferry volume, Greenberg's study of basic word
order (Greenberg 1966b).

   2.1   In several respects, the Dobbs Ferry conference represented a movement at odds with the mainstream of American linguistics at the time. For decades the dominant position had been
to emphasize the diversity of languages rather than their essential
unity; most linguists were very suspicious of attempts at sweeping
generalizations and were opposed to any notion of universal grammar. They believed that each language should be described in its
own terms and not be forced into some common mold, such as that
of classical grammar. The flavor of the times may be conveyed
by two quotations. One is from Bloomfield, cited several times
at Dobbs Ferry, "The only useful generalizations about language
are inductive generalizations" (Bloomfield 1933: 20), which seemed
to preclude the possibility of any general theory of language. The
other is a comment of Joos, generally quoted in recent years to
be ridiculed, "...languages could differ from each other without
limit and in unpredictable ways" (Joos 1957: 96), which seemed to
suggest that there are no constraints on the form of grammars.
The organizers of the conference took a different view, which was
expressed in the "Memorandum Concerning Language Universals"
by Greenberg, Osgood, and Jenkins, which served as the starting
point of the conference, "Language universals...constitute the
most general laws of a science of linguistics" and "...coordinated

efforts beyond the scope of individual researchers will be necessary to establish [them]" (UL xv).

All the linguists who prepared papers for Dobbs Ferry made valiant, honest attempts to identify universals, but it was an unfamiliar task, and, except for Greenberg, their publications during the following decade did not continue the search. Yet much groundwork was laid, and some of the themes that were to emerge in strength in the seventies were already in evidence. One was the notion of typology, the nongenetic, nonareal classification of languages as a valuable means to the discovery of universals; typology had been deemphasized in the American linguistics of the time, but was explicitly supported by Hockett, Greenberg, and Saporta at the conference and referred to by others. Another was the relating of diachronic processes to synchronic universals, a change from the descriptivism of the time and its rigid separation of synchrony and diachrony. This point was made in the Memorandum and echoed by a number of the participants. A third was the need for archiving, the accumulation of comparable data from many languages in a form accessible for researchers. Linguists continue to collect data, writing grammars, dictionaries and technical articles on languages, but they rarely attempt to make such data across languages readily available topically by indexing or other means of information retrieval. At the conference, Jakobson mentioned the desirability of a phonological atlas of the world, which would be a specific kind of archive, but the general need was asserted in the Memorandum: "...the organization of something on the order of cross-cultural files for a large sample of languages would greatly facilitate the establishment of factually well-grounded universals...."(UL xxvi).

In connection with having suitable data on which to establish universals, the question of sampling just barely appeared as a minor point at the conference. Weinreich saw the problem "... we must insist on a ... wide sampling of languages" (UL 149); but he did not see how to solve it, adding that "...we must search for suitable methods of... sampling" (UL 187). Saporta noted the problem and dismissed it: "Indeed, the question of how many languages constitute an adequate sample for a generalization is not a linguistic problem at all, but rather a statistical one" (UL 67). Only Greenberg's paper made a sample of languages explicit and attempted to justify it (UL 74-75).

A theme that recurred repeatedly but inconspicuously was the relevance of the study of child language in connection with universals.

Its marginal role at Dobbs Ferry can be seen in retrospect as
foreshadowing the later trend in which language acquisition assumed a central importance in the issue of universals. Evidence
from child language is cited on pp. xvii (Memorandum), 175 (Weinreich), and 269 (Jakobson), but in each case without giving documentation for the claims; also, Jakobson cited the view on language
of Weinreich's six-year-old daughter in support of an argument
(273), but made no attempt to check this anecdotal material against
evidence from other children.

Finally, the need for links between linguistics and other disciplines, in particular anthropology and psychology, was a recurrent
theme, mentioned by most of the participants and emphasized in
the three final summarizing papers. The flavor of the discussions
was often anthropological, at least in part because of the heavy
representation of that characteristic American phenomenon, the
anthropologist-linguist; Jakobson's suggestion of linkage with philosophy and mathematical thought (UL 276) was an isolated reference, although Weinreich's paper made considerable use of
philosophical literature and notation from mathematical logic.

Three characteristics of the "language universals" proposed
at Dobbs Ferry are significant in contrast to the "linguistic universals" of the Austin conference. The Dobbs Ferry universals
were chiefly nondefinitional, statistical, and implicational. Hockett's
paper listed 16 "design features" of language, and in particular ten
defining or "criterial" characteristics of human language as opposed
to animal communication, but he regarded as especially important
those properties that are "shared by all human languages but are
not obviously necessitated by the presence of the features of the
criterial set" (UL 2), and offered 20 such grammatical and phonological universals. Examples:

1. Among the deictic elements of every human language is one
    that denotes the speaker and one that denotes the addressee
    (UL 21).

2. No phonological system has fewer than two contrasting posi-
    tions of articulation for stops (UL 27).

The papers of Ferguson, Saporta, and Greenberg also referred to
definitional universals and the problem of a metatheory for linguistic
description (UL 53, 62ff., 73-74), but all opted for the discovery
of nondefinitional universals, and they listed 15, 5, and 45 of them,
respectively. Examples:

3. In a given language the number of PNCs [primary nasal consonants] is never greater than the number of series of obstruents (Ferguson, UL 57).

4. In a given language the frequency of occurrence of NVs [nasal vowels] is always less than that of non-nasal vowels (Ferguson, UL 58).

5. For languages with phonemic stress, the presence of n unstressed syllables flanking a stressed syllable implies the presence of n - 1 unstressed syllables (Saporta, UL 68).

6. Languages with dominant VSO [Verb-Subject-Object] order are always prepositional (Greenberg, UL 78).

7. If either the subject or object noun agrees with the verb in gender, then the adjective always agrees with the noun (Greenberg, UL 93).

The authors found near-universals just as interesting as absolute universals and even looked for "generalizations which tend to hold true in more than chance number of comparisons or which state tendencies to approach statistical limits across languages or in one language over time" (UL xvii; cf. also 66-67). The "exceptions" are then to be explained by special conditions or conflicting universal tendencies, or as diachronic transition states. Finally, many of the universals are "implicational universals" of the type "if Y exists in a language, then X must also be present," a type whose importance had been discussed previously by Jakobson (1958). The listing (and numbering) of language universals is a characteristic outcome of this style of research.

It was a psychologist at the conference who seemed most excited about the difference between the usual linguistics of the day and the discussions at the conference. Charles Osgood proclaimed a "revolution," seeing "linguistics taking a giant step from being a method of describing languages to being a full-fledged science of language" (UL 299). In fact, however, a revolution of a different sort was taking place elsewhere, as the ideas of Noam Chomsky spread among linguists and others interested in language (Searle 1972), and that revolution was to have a great impact on the study of universals. Several of the participants at Dobbs Ferry commented hopefully on the results that might come from transformational generative grammar, e.g. "...new approaches like transformational grammar may also bring new principles of importance to an understanding of the

universals of change" (Hoenigswald, UL 51), but only one, Saporta,
had adopted the Chomskyan view of language. Saporta's paper was
an interesting but unsuccessful combination of the "empiricist"
approach that he had previously followed with the "rationalist"
approach of Chomsky.

2.2 The discussions of the Austin conference took place within
the new mainstream of American linguistics, the "consensus on
basic goals and methods of linguistic theory as it [had] developed
in the last decade, especially under the leadership of Noam Chomsky"
(ULT vi). On the place of universals in linguistics, this consensus
differed in striking and important ways both from the earlier consensus and from the viewpoint of Dobbs Ferry. It was taken for
granted that "the main task of linguistic theory must be to develop
an account of linguistic universals" (Chomsky 1965: 27-28) and
these universals that hold for all languages constitute in effect a
definition of human language. Further, it was assumed that every
child has tacit, innate knowledge of these universals, since no other
hypothesis would reasonably explain the rapidity with which the
young child acquires the complex grammar of his or her mother
tongue. The linguistic universals were seen as properties of any
generative grammar of a natural language and were held to be of
two kinds: "substantive," which are the fixed set of technical concepts that the linguist may draw on in constructing a grammar
(e.g. distinctive feature, Noun Phrase), and "formal," which specify the form of statements in a grammar (e.g. that there must
be syntactic and phonological components, that the syntactic component must contain transformational rules, and that the phonological component must have a transformational cycle). The new
"rationalist" consensus looked back on early attempts at universal
grammar with a feeling of kinship, whereas the former "empiricist"
consensus regarded grammaire raisonée as wrong-headed: Bach
cited the Port Royal grammarians for support (ULT 104), Hoenigswald preferred Schwyzer and Grammont (UL 31).

In the Chomskyan framework of assumptions, the papers and
discussion of the Austin conference were devoted to arguments on
the correct form of grammars and generally made use of data
from different languages as evidence for showing that one way to
formulate grammars is better than another. "Surface" universals
of the Greenberg sort were seen only as additional data that might
give support for one proposal or another in linguistic universals
(ULT 2), not as phenomena of any particular interest in their own
right or as requiring any kind of theoretical explanation.

The recurrent themes of Dobbs Ferry reappeared in unexpected ways at Austin. In the consensus of the time, no place was seen for typology as a route to universals; it seemed just the opposite of looking for a universal form of grammar. Fillmore's paper, however, discovered a reason to be interested in typology: given a universal kind of 'deep structure' in human languages, typological classification would help to determine the existence and nature of universal constraints on the derivations of surface forms. In his long section on typology (ULT 51-60), he acknowledged that different word orders across languages are probably of importance from this point of view, but he did not examine them.

The theme of diachronic processes in relation to synchronic universals was taken up by Kiparsky, who described language change as a "window" through which the linguist can study the psychological reality of proposed universals. The bulk of his paper was analysis of diachronic data from SWISS GERMAN dialects, GERMAN, YIDDISH, and ENGLISH. The diachronic arguments were all concerned with phonology, however, and diachronic processes were not to be treated in connection with syntax anywhere in the book.

The theme of archiving and the related question of sampling did not appear. The papers of Bach and McCawley were almost completely limited to ENGLISH although they were discussing universal properties of the deep structure of languages; their examples from other languages were typically based on the author's knowledge, or on the personal communication of students or colleagues. Fillmore had much wider cross-linguistic exemplification, citing data from over 20 languages, mostly from published sources. No attempt was made by any of the authors to justify the sample of languages used, presumably because the universal features are present in any language, and ENGLISH, being the best analyzed and most familiar, was the natural choice for illustration.

The theme of child language might have been expected to occur more often in the Austin papers because of the central role of language acquisition in the Chomskyan view of universals, but this was not the case. Only Kiparsky had much to say about it, and in his several pages on simplification and language acquisition (ULT 192-196) he made claims about child language development rather than adducing child-language evidence for universals hypothesized on other grounds. Kiparsky also discussed connections with other disciplines, in particular the relevance of recent psycholinguistic

experiments for the validation of linguistic universals (ULT 174).
It is noteworthy that there was little or no flavor of anthropology
at Austin, but somewhat more of philosophy and mathematics than
at Dobbs Ferry. This was especially true of McCawley's chapter,
which was dedicated to Weinreich and, like Weinreich's chapter in
UL, was primarily concerned with semantics.

In contrast with the Dobbs Ferry conference, the linguistic universals were definitional, nonstatistical, and nonimplicational, and
they were nowhere listed or numbered. The universals were, in
fact, presented so discursively that if one asks exactly what substantive and formal universals were proposed in the papers, it is
not always easy to determine the answer. Some examples of fairly
clear proposals will serve to indicate the nature of the universals
discussed. As substantive universals, Fillmore proposed such
concepts as "case" and "modality" (ULT 21, 23); Bach, "terms"
and "contentives" (ULT 91); and Kiparsky, "simplification" (ULT
175). As formal universals Fillmore proposed the base rules that
a sentence has two constituents, the proposition and the modality
$(S \rightarrow M + P)$, and that the proposition consists of a verb and one or
more case categories $(P \rightarrow V + C_1 + \ldots C_n)$ (ULT 23, 24). Bach
proposed, among other things, that all nouns derive from relative
clauses based on the predicate nominal constituent and that the universal base component develops sets of semantic and syntactic features that are mapped into phonological shapes after the operation
of transformational rules (ULT 117). McCawley proposed that instead of separate syntactic and semantic components, a grammar
will have a single set of rules that convert the deep semantic representation into surface syntactic representation (ULT 167). Kiparsky
proposed formal universals of language change such as that there
are two kinds of change in grammars: rule addition and rule simplification (including rule reordering) (ULT 174-175).

3. Two Streams of Research

    3.1 During the decade 1961-71 the different streams of research
represented by the two conferences for the most part flowed separately.
Greenberg's own research continued with a series of papers and
overviews, such as his lectures at Indiana University in the summer
of 1964, which appeared in Current Trends III and, slightly revised,
as the monograph Language Universals (see also Greenberg 1966c;
1969a,b; 1970; 1975a,b). The Dobbs Ferry conference volume itself
was widely read in Europe, and many linguists, especially Russian
and East European linguists interested in typology, responded. The
most striking response was that of Uspenskij, a Soviet linguist

who had just published a book on typology. In 1965 he published
a new work, Structural Typology of Languages, which reviewed
the whole field, included references to Dobbs Ferry, and provided
a numbered list of universals that included many from that conference. In due course Uspenskij edited a volume directly devoted to
the Dobbs Ferry conference that contained a lengthy introduction
by him and translations of the Memorandum and six of the papers
(Uspenskij 1970). In 1966 a conference was held in Moscow on the
general topic of typology and universals. It was reported in Voprosy
Jazykoznanija in 1967, and Vardul'(1970) reports the proceedings of
that conference, with over a score of papers and an appendix with
a list of universals. In general the European conferences and books
that incorporated material from Dobbs Ferry were concerned not
only with typology and universals, but also with questions of areal
typology and the characterization of groups of related languages.
Although the original interest in language universals on the American scene derived from cultural universals in relation to areal
characteristics of American Indians, interest in areal typology
and universals has not been much in evidence in American linguistics.

The most direct successor to the Dobbs Ferry conference was
the Language Universals Project at Stanford in the decade 1967-76,
directed by Greenberg and Ferguson, which produced the series
Working Papers in Language Universals, edited by Edith Moravcsik,
during that period. Although the Project had no explicit theoretical
orientation and the researchers associated with it represented a
variety of theoretical approaches, much of its work was in the
spirit and manner of Dobbs Ferry (see the Introduction to this volume).

3.2 The other stream of universals research was, in a sense,
the whole enterprise of developing transformational generative
grammar, since all those doing original work were concerned with
the form of grammars, and even attempts to find the best or "correct" way to account for the phenomena of a particular part of a
particular language, usually ENGLISH, were regarded as explorations of linguistic universals. The title of a paper by Bierwisch
epitomizes this point of view: "Some Semantic Universals of German Adjectivals" (Bierwisch 1967). Looking back over this period,
in an interview published in 1974, Chomsky reaffirmed the distinction between substantive and formal universals, as explained in
Aspects (Chomsky 1965: 27-30) and listed examples of the progress
made in developing theories of universals. For phonology he cited
Chomsky and Halle's Sound Pattern of English; for syntax he

mentioned Bach 1965, 1971 on substantive universals and the dis-
sertations of Ross and Emonds on formal universals; and for semantics the work of Katz, Jackendorf, Fillmore and others on both
sorts of universals (Parret 1974: 42). The optimistic evaluation
of linguistic research he then gave reflected nicely the perspective
of Chomskyan research on universals: "...there has been encour-
aging progress toward a comprehensive and well-founded theory
of language that begins to approach the level of explanatory adequacy in important respects, incorporating explicit proposals concerning formal and substantive universals; and ... work on specific
languages -- ENGLISH in particular -- is progressing toward the
goal of descriptive adequacy" (ibid.). The route to take was to
suggest universals in response to particular problems in grammar
writing and to argue alternatives, making use of whatever examples
(from whatever languages) the researcher's ingenuity could put to
that use. It was felt that the more important kind of research was
to determine the form of grammars (i.e. to establish universals)
rather than merely to describe languages or collect surface characteristics of large samples of languages. J. Moravcsik (1967) made
the point explicitly: nondefinitional "accidental" universals were
"trivial" and the significance of statistical universals was "mini-
mal."[2]

   In 1970 another issue arose, the distinction between "strong" and
"weak" universals. If linguistic universals are viewed in connection
with the acquisition of language (the Innateness Hypothesis), it might
be argued that they are not specific to language but are universal
characteristics of human cognition. McNeill, in The Acquisition of
Language, clarified this issue by proposing two possible kinds of
universals: "A weak linguistic universal is the reflection in language of a universal cognitive ability.... A strong linguistic universal
is a reflection of a specific linguistic ability and may not be a reflection of a cognitive ability at all" (McNeill 1970: 73-74). This distinction
remained in the literature about universals, and those linguists and
psychologists who worked within the Chomskyan tradition generally
argued for the existence of strong linguistic universals, whereas

---

2 Moravcsik actually distinguishes three kinds of universals:
"analytic" which all languages have by definition, "accidental"
which all languages happen to have, and "synthetic" which all languages have, though not by definition, and must have if they are
to be acquired and understood in the normal way by human beings.
Unfortunately, he gives no examples and offers no way to recognize which is which.

a number of other scholars, especially psychologists, argued that few or none of the suggested innate structures would turn out to be strong linguistic universals. An extensive literature grew up around this issue in psychology, philosophy, and linguistics, much of the experimental literature focusing on child language development and on the teaching of sign language to chimpanzees.

4. The Streams Move Toward Each Other

The two streams of research represented by Dobbs Ferry and Austin began to interact, and a convenient date for the beginning of the interaction is the Linguistic Institute in Buffalo in the summer of 1971, when a set of public lectures on universals represented sharply differing points of view. In 1972 two events on the international scene marked the broadened interest in universals research: the establishment of the Universalienprojekt at the University of Köln under the direction of Hansjakob Seiler, and the provision of a plenary session and other papers on universals at the XIth International Congress of Linguists in Bologna.

4.1 The Köln project was in some respects modeled on the Stanford project -- Seiler had visited and worked with the Language Universals Project; and Russell Ultan, a research associate at Stanford, joined the Köln project for two years.

The staff members of the Köln project agreed, for the most part, on an approach that combined some of the interests of both streams of American universals research. They were not satisfied with searching for a "universal base" or some other direct characteristic of the form of grammars, and they did not want to catalog similarities among many (or all) languages. They were concerned with universal principles that would connect communicative functions with the very varied structural means which languages use to fulfill them. The series of publications and working papers they issued (Linguistic Workshop I-III, Arbeiten des Kölner Universalien-Projekts 18-) revealed both the collection of data from many languages and great concern with linguistic theory.

4.2 At the Bologna Congress there were important contributions by Greenberg, Kurylowicz, Coseriu and Seiler at the session on universals. The Greenberg and Seiler papers each offered detailed analysis of one topic as an exemplification of universals research, along with a general statement of the author's position. Kurylowicz, a distinguished Polish scholar in historical and general linguistic theory, presented a highly idiosyncratic but suggestive paper.

Coseriu's presentation was an analysis of what he called "universals of language" (universaux de langage) of the Dobbs Ferry type and "universals of linguistics" (universaux de linguistique) of the Austin type. In clarifying many issues, he was continuing some of his own previous work and also reacting directly to publications in the two streams of American research. The discussion at the close of the session was lively in spite of the disadvantage of so large an audience. Many other papers at the Congress touched on universals and showed the importance and timeliness of the topic. One such paper by Paul and Carol Kiparsky, on semantics and language acquisition, which was in the generative tradition, abandoned almost completely the Chomsky-McNeill kind of innate syntactic universals. A number of papers combined the two approaches (e.g. A. Lehrer, and Coyaud and Hamou).

An American event of 1972, the "Chicago Which Hunt," a parasession of the Chicago Linguistic Society, was also an indicator of future directions. Here, papers were invited on any aspect of relativization, particularly descriptions of relative clause structures in different languages. This Relative Clause Festival of over 20 papers filled a long day (April 13, 1972) and afterward a book (Peranteau et al. 1972) with data, analyses, and suggested typologies. It was the forerunner of other "festivals" with similar format, in effect conferences on universals with a focus on particular topics.

A number of factors combined to move the two streams toward one another. One was the fragmentation of the transformationalist approach to linguistics. For a lively period, roughly 1967-71, there was heated debate between two major points of view, interpretive and generative semantics, but this subsided into an uneasy coexistence of very varied models of grammar, and practitioners looked eagerly for fresh evidence to support their particular model. Another factor was the rapid expansion of transformational models to linguists in other countries, many of them native speakers of languages other than ENGLISH. This fact, coupled with increased interest in Native American and other languages on the part of American linguists, led to more of a cross-linguistic perspective. Third, a renewed interest in diachronic syntax, typified by Traugott (1964), Klima (1965), Lehmann (1970), and Givón (1971), led to the recognition of Greenberg's diachronic-synchronic universals of word order as a useful focus for research.

A factor of change from the other side was the increasing interest in discussing cross-linguistic statistical and implicational

universals in more theoretical terms. At the Stanford Project
this was shown in such papers as Bell 1971, which explicitly discussed models of grammar and goals of linguistic theory and
attempted to show a relationship between the two kinds of universals. Outside the Project, as well, scholars began to subject
papers of the Greenberg type to analysis of their form and goals;
for example, Lieb, in a whole series of publications, rejected the
Chomskyan framework as such, but attempted to give a theoretical
foundation to universals research.

Also, a number of empirical anthropological studies of semantic
universals focused attention on possible biological substrates for
the lexical organization of categories. The most dramatic of these
was the discovery of a universal hierarchy of color terms (Berlin
and Kay 1969 and subsequent literature). Although at first this
seemed to suggest a very specific "wired-in" visual-perceptual
and linguistic capacity in human beings comparable to strong linguistic universals, subsequent research in other semantic fields
suggested a broadly cognitive capacity more like weak linguistic
universals (Brown 1977). In any case, these Greenberg-like typologies and hierarchies established links with the theoretical arguments of the Chomskyan tradition.

Beginning with occasional use of Greenberg universals, usually
taken from his basic word-order paper, transformational theorists
themselves moved toward an increasing use of these as evidence
for arguments, as clues to what form grammars should take, or
even as phenomena ultimately to be explained by a theory of language. The kind of universals cited in argumentation began to
shift, so that in a paper defending the Innateness Hypothesis at
least two of the three putative universals cited as examples of
"strong universals" were surface universals of the Greenberg
type (Wasow 1973). By the time of the symposium on Explanation
in Linguistics, held in Milwaukee in 1973 (reported in Cohen 1974),
a number of well-known transformational linguists acknowledged
the importance of the Greenberg kind of universals as something
to be explained and as a source of possible formal constraints on
transformational grammar, e.g. Sanders (Cohen 1974: 19) and Bach
(Cohen 1974: 161). Bach's textbook Syntactic Theory which appeared
in 1974 had a final chapter on universal grammar in which a whole
section (253-259) was devoted to "substantive universals in syntax"[3]

---

[3] The distinction between substantive and formal universals
seems unclear and of doubtful utility. Many interpret substantive

by which he meant similarities in syntax across languages, of the
Greenberg type, and he asserted that such facts must be "described
in an account of universal grammar."

5. Universals Research Today

5.1 Increasingly, the major themes of Dobbs Ferry are appear-
ing side by side with formal arguments on formal grammars. The
Causative Festival organized by Shibatani at the University of Southern California in 1974 is a typical example. About half the papers
were called Theoretical Foundations; these were tightly argued
polemics with almost exclusively ENGLISH examples. The other
half were called Universals and Language Particular Studies; several of these presented interesting points from single languages
(sometimes with implications for general treatments of causatives
in language), and the others were explicitly cross-linguistic and
typological in orientation. Shibatani's own view was that "we need
to work out the details of the theoretical devices employed, and we
need more detailed syntactic and semantic descriptions of causative
constructions of various languages" (Shibatani 1976: 39).

The cross-linguistic **archiving** theme appeared in the paper by
Comrie at the Causative Festival. Comrie's paper was remarkably
like Dobbs Ferry in orientation, but with the benefit of a decade's
worth of added sophistication in syntactic analysis. He claimed
that his study had general implications for linguistics, especially
for what he called "universal grammar": "by which I mean the comparison of parallel areas of grammar in a large number of languages
from different genetic, geographical and typological groups, rather
than the construction of wide-ranging hypotheses on the basis of
English data" (Shibatani 1976: 303). He drew from a sample of 17
languages that had been examined in detail and gave occasional examples from others, but apologized for inadequacies in the sample.
In Chomskyan terms, his paper may be seen as a proposal for a
substantive universal "case hierarchy" and some formal universals
associated with it. He himself viewed it as a contribution to a "syntactic typology [which] has an important role to play in the identification of linguistic universals, in a theory that is both constrained

---

(ftnt. 3 cont.)
as referring to concrete surface data of languages as opposed to
formal characteristics of grammars, and some universals (e.g.
universal rules or Bach's substantive constraints) do not fit into
either category. The distinction often seems to be invoked ritually
and then not applied.

enough to make interesting predictions and flexible enough to accommodate the range of variety that we in fact find in human languages"
(307).

The typology theme appeared at the Causative Festival, sometimes as an incidental interest, e.g. "It would be a fascinating
study in typology to investigate how languages encourage or discourage the derivation of objects from underlying subjects" (Binnick,
in Shibatani 1976: 227). It also appeared, however, as a major consideration, as in the Comrie paper cited above. Already in the
Chicago Which Hunt (see above), a number of the papers had been
typological in orientation, especially those of Perlmutter and Keenan,
which proposed typologies of, respectively, Shadow Deletion and
syntactic strategies of restrictive relative clause formation. These
two transformational papers proposed universals (Perlmutter used
the expression "universals of human language") based on a selected
sample of the world's languages. This kind of microtypology has
so far not been linked closely with the extensive typological studies
being carried out in the older, European tradition (cf. Greenberg
1974), but these two streams are bound to interact.

Diachronic processes in syntax also had a significant place at
the Causative Festival. The Li and Thompson paper on the history
of causatives in CHINESE brought into focus several generalizations
about diachronic processes in all languages, and the Givón paper
on BANTU made a crucial point on the diachronic origins of causative constructions in general. The increasing recognition of the
importance of diachrony along with typologizing of large numbers
o f languages in the search for universals became evident in later
topical conferences, such as the Conference on Word Order and
Word Order Change in Santa Barbara and the Conference on Nasals
and Nasalization in Berkeley, both held in 1974 and both dedicated
to Greenberg. In the book reporting the Santa Barbara Conference
(Li 1975), out of 12 papers only those by Bach and Sanders were
completely synchronic. In the Nasals book (Ferguson et al. 1975)
a number of papers were diachronic, and the one by Hyman was
explicitly related to the Greenberg state-and-process model of
language.

The connection of child language and universals of language has
persisted, but the linguistically informed study of child language
acquisition has expanded to such an extent that "developmental psycholinguistics, " as it is often called now, is a recognized field in
its own right, with a journal, the Journal of Child Language, large
semiannual professional meetings (the Stanford Child Language
Research Forum in the spring and the Boston University Conference

on Language Development in the fall), and an international organization with a congress every four or five years (Florence 1972, see
Engel and Lebrun 1976; London 1975, see Waterson and Snow forthcoming). The question of linguistic universals as such is only one
aspect of the study of language development, and the Innateness
Hypothesis has become a small specialized area of study (for a
recent review see the section Universals and Relativity in Clark
and Clark 1977, reprinted in this volume).

The area of child language and universals has been joined by two
other fields that have also expanded rapidly: the study of pidginization and creolization processes and the study of the sign language
of the deaf. Leading studies in both these fields treat universals
explicitly, both as a theoretical framework for the new fields and
as a body of knowledge to which the new research can contribute
(Kay and Sankoff 1974; Bickerton 1977; Bellugi and Fisher 1972;
Fisher forthcoming). These fields have generated professional
newsletters ("The Carrier Pidgin," "Sign of the Times") and jour-
nals (Journal of Creole Studies, Sign Language Studies); they remain linguistically informed, and linguists are finding in them new
testing areas for hypotheses about universals. The "visibility" of
these three new fields of language research led Greenberg to comment about them in a public lecture at the 1976 Linguistic Institute.
He said jokingly that he was unable to respond to questions about
child language, sign, or pidgins on the topic of his lecture, since
he had not yet considered them in his research, but in all serious-
ness he had to acknowledge their relevance.

Finally, there have been connections with other disciplines. The
Dobbs Ferry link to psychology has grown dramatically, and may
be typified by the Dingwall volume, which regarded linguistic theory
as most obviously valid if confirmed by psycholinguistic experimen-
tation (Dingwall 1971).[4] The tie with philosophy and mathematics,
more evident at Austin, has also grown dramatically, and may be
typified by the volume Approaches to Natural Language (Hintikka
et al. 1973), which, like a number of other volumes of 1967-77,
joined linguists, philosophers, and mathematicians in the effort

---

[4] Strangely, this book, in spite of its return to empiricism and its
broad coverage, ignored the earlier efforts of the SSRC Committee
on Psychology and Linguistics, which coined the term "psycholinguistics" and established the field (cf. Osgood and Sebeok 1954) and
also sponsored the Dobbs Ferry conference. Such was the power of
the intervening period of emphasis on formal structure, innateness,
unverifiable universals, and ENGLISH.

to devise formal structures equal to the task of representing natural human language. The connection with anthropology, which had seemed much weakened, has now returned in full force, as witness the large sections on language in the meetings of the American Anthropological Association and the theme of the 1977 Georgetown Round Table (cf. Ferguson 1977).

5.2 Research on universals of human language is flourishing. In the short space of 15 years American linguistics has moved from a time when the very mention of universals was suspect to a time of general agreement with the position expressed by Bach and Harms: "What is linguistic theory itself if not the attempt to discover what is common to all languages, what is essential to the notion "natural language," what are the limits within which language can vary, what are the (universal!) terms by means of which this variation can be described?" (ULT vi). That this change has taken place is due in no small measure to the efforts of Joseph Greenberg and his associates, along with the impetus of the Chomskyan "revolution" and favorable changes in the intellectual climate of neighboring disciplines.

The events of 1976 were special signs of the place of cross-linguistic universals research. At the Linguistic Institute in the summer of 1976 at the State University of New York at Oswego, the notion of universals was one of the main emphases. Greenberg held the Linguistic Society of America professorship, Ferguson taught for a three-week period, and three former Research Associates of the Language Universals Project were faculty members: Bell, Steele and Givón. A weekly Universals Seminar heard an outside speaker each session, and one of the four Visiting Lecturers was Comrie, who spoke on ergativity. Lehmann, the Associate Director of the Institute, discussed diachronic universals of word order in his courses, and there was a three-day workshop on the Stanford Phonology Archive. This kind of concentration is not likely to recur, since each annual Institute tries to offer a unique combination of emphases to attract faculty, student and visitors. What is significant is that cross-linguistic universals research rated sufficiently high in interest and activity that it was selected as an emphasis for an Institute.

On October 4-8, 1976 a Research Conference on Language Universals was held at Gummersbach, Germany. The Köln project sponsored this international conference in order to assess the present state of universals research and to enter into dialogue with other scholars on the basic questions addressed by the Project. Papers prepared by staff members of the Project were

distributed in advance, participants were invited from a number
of countries including the U.S., and informal proceedings of the
conference are available in Seiler 1976 (another volume of papers
to appear later).

Perhaps the most surprising aspect of the current universals
research is the heavy inertia that retards the development of adequate archive resources in linguistics. The need is urgent for
reliable, detailed, comparable cross-linguistic data, accessible
to researchers by topic. The archiving need is twofold. On the
one hand there is a need for creating archives that take their data
from existing published sources. On the other hand there is a
need for the preparation of "check lists" of topics that field work-
ers should attempt to cover in writing new description of languages.
Every researcher in the field of cross-linguistic universals has
felt the frustration of failure to find a single crucial fact about a
language in a well-known grammar or highly regarded descriptive
study.

The Stanford Project was concerned with both these problems,
and it made an important advance in the creation of archives: over
a four-year period it brought into operation a Phonology Archive
with basic phonetic and phonological data on segment inventories
of over 200 languages, selected by criteria of genetic affiliation,
geographic distribution, and availability of descriptions. This
archive is actually one unit of a larger operation, the Stanford
Computer Archive of Language Material, which includes textual
and lexicographic data as well, but an obvious lack is a computer
archive of syntactic/semantic data. The Stanford Project produced
checklists on a few topics, but made little progress on this other
aspect of the archiving need. Recently, an important step has been
taken under other auspices: the preparation of a volume of papers
on selected topics in linguistics (Shopen forthcoming), so arranged
that fieldworkers — or general linguists -- can see what an expert
in a particular subfield sees as the important information in his
area of specialization, which should be found in any adequate description. We may hope that the Stanford Phonology Archive and
Shopen's Language Typology and Syntactic Fieldwork Project will
be forerunners to a massive organization of language data, so that
universals research can progress more rapidly as a part of a cumulative science of human language.

BIBLIOGRAPHY

Aginsky, B.W. and E.G. Aginsky. 1948. The importance of language universals. Word 4.168-172.

Bach, Emmon. 1965. On some recurrent types of transformations. Sixteenth Annual Round Table on Linguistics and Language Studies (Monograph Series on Languages and Linguistics 18), ed. by C.W. Kreidler. Washington, D.C.: Georgetown University Press.

_____. 1971. Questions. Linguistic Inquiry 2.153-166.

_____. 1974. Syntactic theory. New York: Holt, Rinehart and Winston.

_____, and Robert T. Harms (eds.) 1968. Universals in linguistic theory. New York: Holt, Rinehart and Winston.

Bell, Alan. 1971. Acquisition-significant and transmission-significant universals. WPLU 5. U1-9.

Berlin, Brent and Paul Kay. 1969. Basic color terms: their universality and evolution. Berkeley: University of California Press.

Bickerton, Derek. 1977. Pidginization and creolization: language acquisition and language universals. Pidgin and creole linguistics, ed. by A. Valdman. Bloomington, Ind.: Indiana University Press.

Bierwisch, Manfred. 1967. Some semantic universals of German adjectivals. Foundations of Language 3.1-36.

Bloomfield, Leonard. 1933. Language. New York: Holt.

Brown, Cecil H. 1977. A theory of lexical universals: color categories and folk botanical taxa. Twenty-Eighth Annual Round Table on Languages and Linguistics (GURT 1977), ed. by M. Saville-Troike. Washington, D.C.: Georgetown University Press.

Chomsky, Noam. 1965. Aspects of the theory of syntax. Cambridge, Mass.: M.I.T. Press.

_____, and Morris Halle. 1968. Sound pattern of English. New York: Holt.

Clark, Herbert H. and Eve V. Clark. 1977. Psychology and language; an introduction to psycholinguistics. New York: Harcourt Brace Jovanovich.

Cohen, David (ed.) 1974. Explaining linguistic phenomenon. New York: John Wiley and Sons.

Coseriu, Eugenio. 1975. Les universaux linguistiques (et les autres). Proceedings of the XIth International Congress of Linguists, ed. by L. Heilmann, 47-73. Bologna: Mulino.

Coyaud, Maurice and Kaled Ait Hamou. 1974. Les quantificateurs dans les langues naturelles. Proceedings of the XIth International Congress of Linguists, ed. by L. Heilmann, 593-600. Bologna: Mulino.

Dingwall, William O. (ed.) 1971. A survey of linguistic science. College Park: University of Maryland Press.

Engel, Walburga von Raffler and Y. Lebrun (eds.) 1976. Baby talk and infant speech. Lisse, Belgium: Swets & Zeitlinger.

Ferguson, Charles A. 1977. Linguistics as anthropology. Twenty-eighth Annual Round Table on Languages and Linguistics (GURT 1977), ed. by M. Saville-Troike. Washington, D.C.: Georgetown University Press.

_____, Larry M. Hyman and John J. Ohala (eds.) 1975. Nasálfest; papers from a synposium on nasals and nasalization. Department of Linguistics, Stanford University.

Givón, Talmy. 1971. Historical syntax and synchronic morphology: an archaeologist's field trip. Papers from the Seventh Regional Meeting of the Chicago Linguistic Society.

Greenberg, Joseph H. (ed.) 1966a. Universals of language. Cambridge, Mass.: M.I.T, Press (2nd ed., original ed. 1963).

_____. 1966b. Some universals of grammar with particular reference to the order of meaningful elements. In Greenberg 1966a.

_____. 1966c. Synchronic and diachronic universals in phonology. Language 42. 508-517.

Greenberg, Joseph H. 1966d. Language universals with special reference to feature hierarchies. The Hague: Mouton.

————. 1969a. Some methods of dynamic comparison in linguistics. Substance and structure of language, ed. by J. Puhvel, 147-203. Berkeley and Los Angeles: University of California Press.

————. 1969b. Language universals; a research frontier. Science 166. 473-478.

————. 1970. Some generalizations concerning glottalic consonants, especially implosives. International Journal of American Linguistics [IJAL] 36. 123-145.

————. 1974a. Language typology: a historical and analytic overview (Janua Linguarum series minor 184). The Hague: Mouton.

————. 1974b. Numeral classifiers and substantival number: problems in the genesis of a linguistic type. Proceedings of the XIth International Congress of Linguists, ed. by L. Heilmann, 17-38. Bologna: Mulino.

————. 1975a. Research on language universals. Annual Review of Anthropology 4. 75-94.

————. 1975b. Dynamic aspects of word order in the numeral classifier. In Charles N. Li, ed. 1975: 27-45.

Hintikka, K.J.J., J.M.E. Moravcsik, and P. Suppes. 1973. Approaches to natural language. Dordrecht, Holland: Reidel.

Holenstein, Elmar. 1976. 'Implicational universals' versus Familienähnlichkeiten. Linguistik, Semiotik, Hermeneutik, 125-133. Frankfurt: Suhrkamp.

Jakobson, Roman. 1958. Typological studies and their contribution to historical comparative linguistics. Proceedings of the VIIIth International Congress of Linguists, 17-25. Oslo.

Joos, Martin (ed.) 1957. Readings in linguistics; the development of descriptive linguistics in America since 1925. Washington, D.C.: American Council of Learned Societies.

Katz, Jerrold J. and Paul M. Postal. 1964. An integrated theory of linguistic descriptions (Research Monograph 26). Cambridge, Mass.: M.I.T. Press.

Kay, Peter and Gillian Sankoff. 1974. A language-universals approach to pidgins and creoles. Pidgins and creoles: current trends and prospects, ed. by D. De Camp and I. Hancock. Washington, D.C.: Georgetown University Press.

Kiparsky, Paul and Carol Kiparsky. 1974. Semantics and language acquisition. Proceedings of the XIth International Congress of Linguists, ed. by L. Heilmann, 289-292. Bologna: Mulino.

Klima, Edward. 1965. Studies in diachronic transformational syntax. Doctoral dissertation, M.I.T.

Kurylowicz, J. 1972. Universaux linguistiques. Proceedings of the XIth International Congress of Linguists, ed. by L. Heilmann, 29-46. Bologna: Mulino.

Lehmann, Winfred P. 1970. Proto-Germanic syntax. Toward a grammar of Proto-Germanic, ed. by F. van Coetsem and H.L. Kufner. Tübingen: Max Niemeyer.

Lehrer, Adrienne. 1974. Universals in a culture-bound domain. Proceedings of the XIth International Congress of Linguists, ed. by L. Heilmann, 769-773. Bologna: Mulino.

Li, Charles N. (ed.) 1975. Word order and word order change. Austin, Texas: University of Texas Press.

Lieb, Hans-Heinrich. 1975. Universals of language: quandaries and prospects. Foundations of Language 12. 471-511.

McNeill, David. 1970. The acquisition of language. New York: Harper and Row.

Moravcsik, J.M.E. 1967. Linguistic theory and the philosophy of language. Foundations of Language 3. 209-233.

Osgood, Charles E. and Thomas A. Sebeok (eds.) 1954. Psycho-linguistics; a survey of theory and research problems. Baltimore: Waverly Press.

Padley, G.A. 1976. Grammatical theory in Western Europe 1500-1700; the Latin tradition. Cambridge: Cambridge Univ. Press.

Parret, Herman. 1974. Discussing language (Janua Linguarum series maior 93). The Hague: Mouton.

Peranteau, Paul M., Judith N. Levi and Gloria A. Phares (eds.) 1972. The Chicago which hunt; papers from the relative clause festival. Chicago: Chicago Linguistic Society.

Searle, John. 1972. Chomsky's revolution in linguistics. New York Review of Books, June 29, 1972.

Seiler, Hansjakob. 1972. Universals of language. Leuvense Bijdragen 61. 371-393.

_____. 1973. Das Universalienkonzept. Linguistic Workshop, ed. by H. Seiler, I. 6-19.

_____, (ed.) 1976. Materials for the DFG International Conference on Language Universals held at Gummersbach, October 4-8, 1976 (= AKUP 25). Köln: Universalienprojekt.

Shibatani, Masayoshi (ed.) 1976. The grammar of causative constructions. New York: Academic Press.

Shopen, Timothy (ed.)(forthcoming) Variation in the structure and use of language. New York: Winthrop.

Traugott, Elizabeth C. 1969. Toward a theory of syntactic change. Lingua 23. 1-27.

Uspenskij, B.A. 1965. Strukturnaja tipologija jazykov. Moscow: Nauka.

_____, (ed.) 1970. Jazykovye universalii (Novoe v Lingvistike V). Moscow: "Progress."

Vardul, I.F. (ed.) 1969. Jazykovye universalii i lingvističeskaja tipologia. Moscow: Nauka.

Wasow, Thomas. 1973. The innateness hypothesis and grammatical relations. Synthese 26. 38-56.

Waterson, Natalie and Catherine E. Snow (eds.) (forthcoming) The development of communication: social and pragmatic factors in language acquisition. New York: Wiley and Sons.

Typology and
Cross-Linguistic Generalizations

JOSEPH H. GREENBERG

ABSTRACT

The logically possible kinds of typology are surveyed in terms of three main variables: 1) the number of dimensions; 2) the nature of the attributes (e.g. categorical, comparative, quantitative); 3) the distribution of languages over classes defined by a typology either as statistically non-random or as constituted by presence or absence of languages exemplifying each type. Each sort of typology is discussed in terms of logical convertability into a particular form of cross-linguistic generalization. One of the results is to suggest that the term <u>universal</u> is not always appropriate since, for example, absences of certain phenomena lend themselves to generalization and are not appropriately termed universals.

In the recent period, typological studies have come to be generally associated with the quest for linguistic generalizations.
Courses are given to the titles of which typology is linked to language universals as a kindred topic. Historically speaking, explicit
recognition of this connection is relatively recent. By a singular
turn of fate, a method which in the past has been used to characterize and define differences among languages has become a major
methodological tool in the investigation of linguistic generalizations.[1]

One result of the relative recency of this view of linguistic cross-
generalizations as the major goal of typological studies and typology
in turn as a basic method in the study of language universals is the
absence of a systematic analysis of the relations between the two.
It is the basic aim of this paper to explore the possibilities of a
broader and more systematic framework than has hitherto been
available for the study of these connections.

The treatment here is essentially synchronic. However, it requires supplementation in certain respects by bringing into consideration diachronic factors as well. Hence, this paper should be
read in conjunction with that on synchrony, diachrony and universals
in the present volume, a study in which the dynamic aspects of type
play a central rôle.

The connection between typology and universals can be perhaps
most easily seen by considering the relationship between any implicational universal and what might be called its associated typology.
This particular instance can be considered a "paradigm" case in
that it is the one most frequently encountered in actual research and
so dominates contemporary research oriented along typological lines,
that is has tended to obscure the fact that it is, from the logical point
of view, but one of a broad range of possibilities.

It will be convenient as a point of departure to consider this particular case by means of a concrete instance and then to show, from
it, what are the significant ways in which typologies can differ and
how, in turn, such variation is associated with generalizing statements of different logical forms.

---

[1] For historical treatments of typology, the reader is referred to
Horne (1966), Greenberg (1974) and the standard histories of linguistics. The historical aspects of typology, while of considerable inherent interest and possessing relevance for contemporary studies,
are treated here only in an incidental manner.

Consider the following implicational universal regarding consonant clusters. For all languages the existence of initial consonant
clusters implies the presence of medial clusters, but not vice versa.
The same fact about languages can be stated by means of a typology
involving two attributes: the possession of initial clusters and the
possession of medial clusters. For each of these we can have either
presence or absence in a language, the latter being indicated by the
negation sing (-). The distribution of languages over these types is
shown in Fig. 1. (A plus in the table indicates the existence of at
least one language of the given type while a minus sign indicates its
absence.)

	Medial clusters	-Medial clusters
Initial clusters	+	-
-Initial clusters	+	+

Figure 1

The logical equivalence between the universal implicational statement and the associated typology can be stated in the following terms.
The statement that for all languages the existence of initial clusters
implies the existence of medial clusters is equivalent to the statement
that there is no language of the type which possesses initial clusters
and lacks medial clusters. The typology classifies languages of the
world into four possible types of which three only find empirical
exemplification:

a. languages in which both initial and medial clusters are
found (e.g. ENGLISH),

b. languages with medial clusters but without initial clusters
(e.g. TAMIL),

c. languages with neither initial nor medial clusters (e.g.
HAWAIIAN),

d. languages with initial clusters but without medial clusters
(none).

One thing to note about this example is that it is but one of an
indefinitely large number of examples all of which exhibit the same
logical form. If we symbolize the property of having initial clusters
by Φ, and having medial clusters as Ψ, then the implicational statement takes the form $\Phi \rightarrow \Psi$ (read, Φ implies Ψ). This is equivalent
to the denial of the existence of the class $\Phi.\sim\Psi$ (read, Φ and not Ψ).
This equivalence can be stated as a logical tautology $(\Phi \rightarrow \Psi) = \sim(\Phi.\sim\Psi)$.

There is a certain value in stating such tautologies once and for all. We can now automatically convert implications into statements about typologies and vice versa, treating as variables to be substituted any properties between which these relationships hold.

Reverting to the examples set forth in Fig. 1, we may note a number of characteristics of this particular typological scheme which define parameters along which typologies may themselves vary. We may specify three such properties of typologies, dimensionality, the logical nature of the attributes, and the distribution of languages in relation to the "attribute space."

The typology of Fig. 1 has two dimensions. Each dimension is defined by an attribute, in this case possession or non-possession of initial clusters and possession or non-possession of medial clusters. Essentially, a dimension is such because of its logical independence from the other dimensions in the same typology. The attribute which defines a dimension may be said to have certain values (always two or more). In the present instance each attribute has two values, presence or absence. By logical independence is meant that any value of an attribute on one dimension may combine without contradiction with any value of any attribute on the other dimensions which form the total attribute space. Hence, the number of typological classes in a typology of this sort is the product of the number of values on each dimension. In the present instance it is, of course, four, since there are two dimensions on each of which the attribute has two values.

A one-dimensional typology is of course possible. It is associated with unrestricted universals. For example, the universal that all languages have some phonetic segments which are vocalic has a corresponding one-dimensional typology with the attribute vocalicity and the two values, presence and absence. There are thus two classes, to one of which all the languages of the world belong, and to the other of which no language belongs. Thus, the unrestricted universals can be seen to be the limiting case involving the most simple logically conceivable typology. The logical tautology involved in such cases in $\Phi = \sim(\sim\Phi)$. We shall see later that many more complex and interesting single dimensional typology schemes exist.

The two-dimensional typology is frequently encountered in typological research, since, as we have seen, it corresponds to a very commonly encountered form of implicational universal. However, typologies of larger and even theoretically infinite numbers of

dimensions are possible and some of these possess viability.
As an example of a typology with a infinite set of dimensions, let
us consider consonant clusters once more. As presented earlier,
the property of having initial clusters or having medial clusters
each formed a single dimension with two values, presence or absence of clusters. It is a basic factor in the manipulation of typologies that they may often be usefully simplified in the sense that
distinctions present in finer-grained typologies are obliterated by
positing more complex properties, with corresponding diminution
of the number of categories, and typological classes. Thus the
category 'cluster,' as earlier treated, was an overall consolidation
of the properties, 'having initial sequences of two consonants, '
'having initial sequences of three consonants,' etc. In a typology
of initial clusters where these cases are treated as separate types,
since the property of having clusters of two consonants is independent of the property of having three consonants, etc. each constitutes a separate dimension.

If, for the moment, we posit that there is no <u>logical</u> limit to the
length of consonant clusters, then the number of dimensions is infinite and, in any typology, restricted to clusters of maximum
length $\underline{n}$, the number of typological classes will be 2^n.

Whether this is indeed a logical infinity is an interesting question,
but one of more concern to logic than to linguistics. There is apparently an intuitive tendency to identify physical limits with logical
limits, no doubt because of the common use of the term 'impossibility' for transgressions of either. I believe this is mistaken.
For example, if (and it remains to be empirically determined what
this limit is) a cluster of more than six consonants is physically
impossible to pronounce, this is probably not a logical limit. At
any rate, where psychological factors are involved, it somehow
seems more plausible to admit as logical possibilities structures
which are surely beyond psychological performance capabilities,
e.g. embeddings of indefinitely large size. It seems inconsistent
to treat physiological and psychological possibilities in different
ways since they are both empirical.

Another perhaps less disputable example of an infinite set of
dimensions occurs in regard to numeral systems. Let us suppose
that all cardinal numbers in particular systems have been analyzed
in terms of mathematical functions so that, for example, in ENGLISH
twenty four has been analyzed as $2 \cdot 10 + 4$. A linguistically unanalyz-
able morpheme, e.g. 'eight' in ENGLISH, is simply a limiting case
of the identity function. Now any particular number can be expressed

by an infinity of expressions, even limiting ourselves to arithmetical functions. For example, some languages use subtraction, as
in LATIN duodēvīginti, literally 'two from twenty,' for eighteen.
Even with subtraction alone, 'six,' for example, can be expressed
as (7-1) or (8-2) or (9-3), etc. Each of these possibilities gives
rise to a logically possible type of language which expresses 'six'
in this manner.[2] Since the number of cardinal numbers is itself
infinite, in this instance we have a typology in which each of the
infinite set of numbers constitutes a dimension with an infinite set
of values (a "Hilbert-space") and the total number of typological
classes in an uncountable infinity, aleph-null to the aleph-null
power.[3]

The question of the relations of the attributes in a multidimensional typology raises further issues than the mere definition in
terms of logical independence. It is possible to construct an indefinitely large number of multidimensional typologies which, on
a common sense basis, will appear to unite in an arbitrary manner
attributes among which there is no reason to believe that any significant connection exists. This is the traditional problem of the
arbitrariness of typologies. For example, there is no purely
logical reason which prevents us from constructing a two-dimensional typology based on the presence or absence of phonological
tone and the presence or absence of noun classes.

However, in such cases we would expect that in the presumed
absence of any causal connection between the two, languages of the
world would be distributed fairly randomly among the four possible
typological classes. It is certainly unlikely that we would find a
complete lack of empirical exemplification of one or more of these
classes, but is not unlikely that the distribution would in some

---

[2] It is in fact plausible to assert that all languages have cardinal numerical systems (i.e. those based on counting) with a finite
upper limit. However, there is clearly no logically given upper
limit. An infinite number system can, of course, be constructed
by utilizing the place concept and zero, but no such system exists
in natural languages. This question is considered in detail in my
paper 'Numeral Systems' in Vol. III of the present publication.

[3] Aleph-null is the cardinal number of the set of natural numbers,
the model of a countable infinity. Aleph-null to the aleph-null power
is an uncountable infinity. An example is the set of all real numbers.
This number is called aleph.

instances depart considerably from randomness. This is because of areal and genetic factors. Certain genetic stocks or geographical areas may have, for example, both sex gender and tonalism as characteristics, in spite of an absence of causal connection between these properties. It is at this point that the problem of language sampling becomes a serious factor. For a detailed discussion, the reader is referred to the paper by Bell on sampling in the present volume.

Note that in the example of initial and medial consonant clusters, while these two attributes are logically independent, they both refer to consonant clusters so that it seems "sensible" to combine them in a single typology. Most multidimensional typologies are of this nature, even those involving an infinitude of dimensions as described earlier. In many instances diachronic factors may furnish a justification. For example, when compounding takes place, even if a language has no initial or final clusters, if it has closed syllables as well as universally present CV type syllable, syllable clusters will arise medially. If a language has initial clusters, medial clusters will inevitably develop in compounding if the second member begins with such a cluster, even if the language has no closed syllables, and if not eliminated by other processes, will produce a confirmatory case for the generalization mentioned earlier.

It may be noted in passing that the earlier example of an arbitrary typology combining tone and sex gender was, in fact, at least implicitly present in a formerly widely accepted typological-evolutionary scheme of AFRICAN language classification; the most primitive type was supposed to be monosyllabic, isolating, tonal, non-inflectional, and lacking in noun classification. The advanced inflectional polysyllabic type was supposed to be characterized by sex gender (e.g. INDO-EUROPEAN, SEMITIC, "HAMITIC"). Hence, languages with tone and sex gender were not to be expected. The inevitable exceptions, e.g. IJO, were explained as the result of secondary contact ("mixture") between pure types.

The commonest kind of typology encountered is the sort of two-dimensional in which the two attributes, although logically independent, are so closely connected empirically that it seems prima facie a good candidate for the discovery of generalizations.

It is characteristic of such typologies that each seems to embrace a small and factually independent "world." For example, there is no reason to assume that if a language is classified in a particular way in a typology having to do with orality and nasality in vowels,

that this assignment increases the probability that the same language will belong to a particular class in other, even phonologically
based typologies. In this respect the results are characteristic of
most present day typology, when contrasted with earlier typological
approaches. This earlier approach may be called "individualizing"
in that its main interest was the characterization of individual languages for their own sakes. In effect, it sought to answer questions
such as these: what is Japanese like, what is French like? On
the other hand, contemporary typologizing which in relation to individual languages may be called part-language typology has a "generalizing" goal. If we typologize relative clauses, for example,
the center of interest is the answer to the question: what are relative
clauses like? The assignment of a language to a particular typological class becomes merely an incidental by-product and is not of
great interest for its own sake.

Insofar, however, as we do find empirically that there are connections among typologies so that the results for a particular language in one typology is relevant for its classification in another
where the two are non-trivially different, we have advanced towards
the legitimate, though difficult, goal of characterizing languages
typologically in a more global way. But this becomes essentially
the construction of multidimensional typologies involving attributes
whose differences are more than trivial. For example, in addition
to the implicational relationship cited earlier, namely that initial
clusters imply medial clusters, we may note that there is likewise
an implicational relationship in accordance with which final clusters
imply medial clusters. It is possible, and entirely legitimate, given
these more complex relationships, to construct a three-dimensional
typology involving initial, medial and final consonant clusters. However, the connection here is once again obvious and will not lead,
therefore, to any broader characterization of languages. Such
multidimensional typologies might be called homogeneous in that
the properties which define the different dimensions have terms in
common (e.g. consonant cluster in the example just mentioned) or
are otherwise very similar. These contrast with heterogeneous
ones, though the difference is not an absolute one.

There seems, at the moment, to be just one example of a typology of more than two dimensions which are sufficiently heterogeneous
so that it characterizes individual languages in regard to an extensive
set of interconnected attributes, namely word order.

For example, if I know that a language is VSO, it can be predicted
that it will be prepositional, and such a relationship is clearly

between attributes that one would a priori attribute more independence to than final and medial clusters.

Given that there exists a variety of connections of this kind,
mainly in the form of implicational universals, some of which have
exceptions, the notion of typicality in regard to individual languages
arises in the following way. Stated abstractly, if there are a series
of properties Φ, X... all of which separately imply some other more
"fundamental property" Ψ, and also possibly implicational chains
of the sort $\Phi \rightarrow X$, $X \rightarrow \Psi$, then the absence of Φ where Ψ is present
does not refute the implication, only its presence in the absence of
Ψ, e.g. if VSO $\rightarrow$ Prep, then it is possible for a language to be
SVO and prepositional without violating the implicational relationship.

A "typical" language will then be one which possesses most or
all of the implying properties Φ, Ψ.... Particularly regarding
such languages, we will seem to be saying something significant
and of an overall nature if we characterize it in relationship to such
a multidimensional typology, e.g. if we say that JAPANESE is a
"typical" SOV language.

Other typological clusterings than those relating to order
may well exist, although they have not been demonstrated. One
area of possible exploration is that of the traditional nineteenth century morphological typology. It is possible that the internal structure of the word, which is the essential basis of this typology and
which was intuitively seized upon as characterizing language in a
broad manner, may furnish a basis for a significant multidimensional typology. For example, the notion of a typical isolating
language may involve such properties as complex tonal systems,
use of a verb 'to give' to express the indirect object relation, absence of markers for direct cases, significant word order, etc.[4]
In spite of the enormous literature on morphological typology, these
questions still remain for objective investigation.

From the problem of dimensionality of a typology, we now move
to a consideration of the nature of the attributes used in any particular dimension. It will be recalled that our initial example, that

---

[4] For an interesting attempt to characterize agglutinative language
by what amounts to a heterogeneous multidimensional typology, see
Skalička 1965. However, the traits listed by him are largely associated with each other in Northern Asia rather than on a worldwide
scale.

of initial and medial clusters, exhibits two values on each dimension,
namely presence and absence of the attribute which defines the dimension. The term used generally by logicians for an attribute of
this sort is a predicate because it can be expressed by means of a
propositional function containing a predicate as a one-place argument.
Thus 'x is red' is a propositional function in which 'red' is a predicate. All the objects in the given universe of discourse which, when
substituted for the variable x give a true statement, e.g. 'blood
is red,' generate one class , while all those for which the statement is false generate a second class. In the present context, I
shall use the term 'category' rather than predicate as being closer
to the normal usage of linguists. A categorical attribute, then, will
always result logically in just two classes, one of which may naturally fail to receive empirical exemplification.

We may note how similar such categories are to the binary features of contemporary phonological and grammatical analysis.
However, the typological usage is clearly broader. For example,
it is unlikely, in any model of contemporary grammatical theory, a
feature such as [± initial cluster] will figure.

Nevertheless, given this resemblance between categorical attributes in typology and feature analysis in general linguistic theory,
it will prove useful for the moment to carry out our analysis further
along these lines. For example, Trubetskoy's classic analysis of
phonological features into privative, equipollent and gradual will be
found to be applicable, with some modifications, to categorical attributes in typology (Trubetskoy 1939).

The privative features are those involving the values of presence
and absence of an attribute. The peculiarity of privative features
lies in their representing the paradigm case for marking relationship. The situation stated in general terms is that the category is
so defined that the value '+' or 'presence' represents the marked
value, and '-' or 'absence' the unmarked. Strictly speaking, the
difference between privative features in which presence and absence
has an external empirical basis and equipollent relations in which
they are not is not a matter of logic per se.

Thus, while it seems "natural" to designate voicing as a predicate category (say ϕ) so that its presence is marked plus and its
absence is assigned the value minus, from the purely logical point
of view, it could be possible to call absence of vocalic segments an
attribute and the negation of its absence (i.e. presence) the negative value.

Such a manoeuver will allow us in certain cases to state, in a
paradoxical way, certain non-occurring items as linguistic universals. For example, the sound type "unvoiced velar lateral pharyngealized affricate," as far as I know, does not occur in any language.
By setting up the categorical attribute "not possessing a sound segment which is unvoiced, lateral, pharyngealized, and an affricate, "
it is possible to construct one-dimensional two-valued typology in
which it is true of all languages that they belong to the type having
the attribute which has just been defined, while no language possesses its negation. In other words it becomes an unrestricted universal.

The option of expressing a universal absence as an unrestricted
universal is simply the most extreme and dramatic instance,which
suggests that it might be advisable to abandon the current term
'universal' as being misleading and substitute for it some such
expression as 'cross-linguistic generalization.'

The question at issue is not merely a terminological one, resulting from logical game-playing. Even if it is possible to exclude
typologies based on negative properties by some viable reformulation of the notion of linguistic attribute, the real question at issue
is whether such items are of interest to the linguist in his capacity
as a scientist seeking to discover general principles. From this
point of view, such an example as the preceding is relevant insofar
as it has reference to a general theoretical problem, the limits of
phonological complexity. In this and other instances of non-existent
but pronounceable sound types, such 'negative' low-level generalizations can play their part in disengaging more general principles
concerning the limitations in possible complexity in the sound features of language in general.

Categorical attributes, while always binary, need not, however, involve a clear hierarchy of presence or absence of a marked feature.
We often find instances that might be assimilated to the general
rubric of equipollent as defined by Trubetskoy, i.e. cases in which
the asymmetry which leads to a natural assignment of positive and
negative values is absent.

Consider, for example, typologies of word order insofar as they
refer to the order of two elements. Disregarding for the moment
problems due to variant orders or the existence of subclasses with
differing orders, there are two possibilities. For example, regarding adjective noun order with the foregoing provisos, there are two
possibilities: AN or NA. However, the relation is equipollent.

There is no reason to assign priority to one or the other. In fact
the two types are usually designated as AN and NA, not, for example,
[+NA] and [-NA].

This does have one interesting consequence for the form in which
implicational relationships based on such typologies are stated.
Where the category is privative, as in our basic example, it would
probably never occur to anyone to state the implicational relationship
in any other form than the following. The presence of initial clusters
implies the presence of medial clusters. We may state this symbolically as [+IC] → [+MC]. However, every implication of the
form Φ → Ψ is logically convertible with and logically equivalent
to a reversal of order with change of signs, i.e. ~Φ → ~Ψ. In the
present instance, the absence of medial clusters implies the absence
of initial clusters.

Where the category is equipollent, however, such equivalent
statements are more likely to be made and it is important to be
aware of this. For example, with very few exceptions, if a language has basic AN order, cardinal numbers will also precede the
nouns they modify. We may call this latter QN order. This implicational relationship can be stated as AN → QN. However, the
very same typological facts are stateable -- alternatively as ~QN →
~AN and this in turn is equivalent to NQ → NA.

Since the implied is in general the more fundemental, the first
statement AN → QN might suggest a dependence of adjective-noun
or quantifier-noun order. However, the second alternative shows
that this is not involved or at least is not legitimately deducible
from it, although it might be true on other grounds.

The third type of Trubetskoyan feature is the 'gradual.' These
involve a continuum, e.g. vowel height, pitch, etc. within which
there is a theoretical infinity of points based on the principle of
indefinite divisibility, that is, the principle of an infinitesimal infinity. Moreover, within this continuum any language might once
more choose any number of points, depending on whether there are
2, 3, 4... levels of vowel height, pitch, etc. The number of possible language types here is infinite, although not uncountably infinite.
As with consonant clusters, it is $2^{\aleph_0}$, that is, for every point there
is a categorical decision as to whether a language possesses a vowel
of that height or pitch, and the number of such points is theoretically
infinite.

In practice, of course, there are severe limitations in that the
number of points which can occur is limited by the perceptual

indistinguishability of points which are very close to each other, the psychological factor JND (just noticeable differences). Even within this finite, though large, set, there are again drastic limitations in that the systems found in languages rarely display more than three values for vowel height or tone.

Prague theory in the case of phonetic continua of this sort introduced a notable and fruitful simplification by defining properties relationally. Viewed in absolute phonetic terms, the number of empirically occurring language types will be very large, even though finite, and virtually every language will constitute a type in itself. Prague theory developed a typology with a small number of types by abstracting from everything but the number of vowels and their height relative to each other and, for pitch, the number of levels and their relations in terms of fundamental frequency, the number of levels being further reduced by grouping together allophonic variants in terms of Prague phonological theory.

It is clear that the general tendency of Prague theory, as embodied most notably in the work of Jakobson and his associates, was to analyze all phonological attribute spaces on the model of the privative features, that is, to make them binary with marking relationship. For gradual features which in practice often show three significantly contrasting points on a continuum, this involved a further reduction beyond that just described, so that there were only two values. This is gained at the cost of increasing the number of dimensions and of the introduction of redundant 'impossible' combinations, e. g. [+high]·[+low] for vowel height.

Continua based on the indefinitely small probably only occur in phonology. Cases of an infinity of types based on the indefinitely large have already been mentioned in regard to consonant clusters and cardinal number systems in language. Whether based on the infinitely large or the infinitely small, these attributes differ in a fundamental way from predicates or categories which, it will be recalled, can be viewed as determined by substitutions in a propositional function with one argument position of the form, $\underline{x}$ has the property Φ. In place of categorical attributes, we have numerical attributes; that is, to every language is assigned a number or set of numbers. The logical form is that of a functor. An example from the physical sciences is temperature. Let $\underline{x}$ be a variable whose range is a set of objects; then, $T'x = n$ will assign to every object $\underline{x}$ a number $\underline{n}$ as its temperature. T is here a functor.

Such numerical attributes differ in certain important ways from categories. Thus, among numerical attributes we can distinguish

those which are discrete from those which are continuous. This
has already been exemplified from consonant clusters and vowel
height (when viewed purely phonetically), respectively. Another
important distinction in this area is between pragmatic (textual)
attributes and systemic attributes.

The various measures proposed in quantitative morphological
typology as e.g., the morpheme-word ratio as a measure of the
degree of typological synthesis and the very common measurements
of relative text frequencies of phonemes or other linguistic elements,
belong here. Such measurements all involve an underlying continuous rather than discrete mathematics. Examples of systemic numerical attributes are such items as the number of noun classes in
a language and the relative dictionary frequency of individual phonemes. These probably always have an underlying discrete mathematics.

Typological characterization on the basis of a continuous numeral
attribute differs in two fundamental ways from that of categorical
attributes. It does not segregate languages into mutually exclusive
classes, i.e. it does not lead to a classification in the usual sense.
The second characteristic is that of ordering. We may illustrate
both of these from the index of synthesis, defined for any particular
language as the text ratio M/W where M is the number of morphemes
and W the number of words over a given sample of texts.

The result for any language is a number expressing this ratio.
For any two languages which will, in the general case, differ in
regard to the ratio, we cannot, as in a categorical typology, say
whether, relative to that typology, the languages are assigned to
the same or different classes. Instead of dividing languages into
mutually exclusive classes, it assigns them a relative place on a
continuum, and thus involves ordering. We can say that ESKIMO
is more synthetic than VIETNAMESE and that GERMAN lies somewhere between them.

The associated generalizations about language which arise from
a typology of this sort are also different in their form from the unrestricted and implicational generalizations, which, as we have
seen, are logically equivalent to certain assignments of presence
or absence in a typology based on categorical attributes. What results is not a division of languages among the types which can be
represented, for example, where there are four logically possible
types by the familiar tetrachoric tables, but a frequency distribution
across languages. The associated generalizations involve such

statistical properties as measures of central tendency, e.g. averages and medians, numerical limits and measures of dispersion, the most familiar of which, statistically, is the standard deviation.

It is important to realize this because many discussions of typology have treated it primarily as a method of classifying languages in contrast to such other methods as the genetic and areal. In the light of the present discussion, this seems an arbitrary and confining restriction. In fact, various statistical properties of language have in the past been unquestioningly accepted as relevant typological criteria (e.g. Menzerath 1954, Greenberg 1954).

If the mathematics is a discrete one, that is, one which assigns a particular cardinal number to each language, unlike the case of continuous numerical predicates, a classification into mutually exclusive classes does result. For example, we may have a classification of languages based on the number of noun classes defined by the existence of grammatical agreement, in which absence of noun classes may be viewed as a limiting case in which there is just one noun class. This will produce, of course, a discrete classification of languages, but it will also give rise to an ordering which is lacking in the case of categorical attributes. Hence, there will also be a frequency distribution which is appropriately represented by a histogram rather than a continuous curve. If will also, like continuous distributions, produce cross-linguistic generalizations referring to measures of central tendency, range (i.e. upper and lower limits), and measures of statistical dispersion.

We have noted in this section three main types of attributes: categorical, discrete numerical and continuous numerical. An important relationship among these, already illustrated from the Prague treatment of gradual features, deserves more explicit treatment. We may call it reduction, and it always goes in the order continuous numerical, discrete numerical and categorical. By the process of reductions, typologies are simplified, thus in many instances providing the possibilities for relevant generalization which may be difficult or impossible to read directly from unreduced data. A continuous numerical attribute can be reduced to a discrete one by setting up intervals in terms of which classes are defined. For example, by using class intervals of .2 we might classify languages with M/W rations of 1–1.19 into one class, 1.2 –1.39 into another, etc., as is often done with data of this kind in statistical studies. By further reduction to two or three main classes, we can produce categorical typologies, although evidence of the underlying numerical basis will appear in the presence of an ordering principle and in the

arbitrariness of the boundaries as compared to true categorical
attributes. Thus, we can define an analytic language as one with
an M/W ratio of less than 2.00, a synthetic language as one with
the values within the limits 2.00 - 2.99, and a polysynthetic language
as one with an M/W $\geq$ 3.00.

This reduction involves a fundamental change in the logical and/or
mathematical nature of the attribute. It is to be distinguished from
those operations of simplification which do not involve such a change.
One of these is the merging of classes in a typology based on categorical attributes, as when consonant clusters of varying lengths
are all put in a single class, namely that which contains two or more
consonants.

These procedures are to be distinguished from another reducing
operation, subtypologizing. The typologies we have been considering
up to now involve properties of languages of universal applicability
so that, insofar as the criterion is stated with sufficient clarity, it
always produces a decision so that any language of the world can be
assigned to one of the classes defined by the typology. A subtypology
of a given typology may be said to be contained in it as a proper part,
in that the entire set of languages to which the typology is applicable
is but one class of the larger typology.

For example, in a typology of oral and nasal vowels, we take the
class of languages with both nasal and oral vowels as a subuniverse
and in turn typologize it on the basis of the number of nasal vowels,
or on the basis of the presence or absence of round and unrounded
nasal vowels.

The types just enumerated do not exhaust either the logical possibilities or the sorts of typologies actually encountered. A further
type might be called combinatorial. It is encountered especially in
the analysis of semantic domains. Particularly clear examples are
furnished by kinship terminologies. Consider, for example, the
typology of kinship terminology first independently suggested by
Kirchoff and Lowie (Lowie and Eggan 1929). Three kin types are
defined in an etic metalanguage: father, father's brother and mother's
brother (symbolized as Fa, FaBr and MoBr respectively). We assume that all terminologies provide designations for these kin-types
without overlapping designations, e.g., a language will not have one
term for Fa and FaBr and another for FaBr and MoBr. The number
of possible types is the number of partitions where n is 3. This
turns out to be five, of which one is never found, namely a system
with two terms, one which designates FaBr and the other Fa and MoB

The mathematics for determining the number of partitions for a specific value of $\underline{n}$ is recursive and highly complex. As an example, for n = 4, the number of types is 15, after which it increases very rapidly.

Note that we cannot say, on the basis of our definition that, for example, in the instance of n = 3, the five types provide a five-dimensional typology, because the putative dimensions are not logically independent. Thus, if a language has a term which designates FaBr and MoBr, this logically excludes any type in which FaBr combines with Fa under the hypothesis of non-overlapping. Hence, these typologies are to be considered one-dimensional, and in the absence of any ordering relationship, can perhaps be considered to be of the same general kind as the categorical with, however, some properties which differ from those with binary attributes.

We now consider in more detail the sorts of generalizing statements to which the various sorts of attribute spaces just considered give rise. It is not merely the logical form of the typological framework as such which enters here as a factor, but also the nature of the distribution of languages within the typology.

This can be illustrated once more from our earlier example of initial and medial consonant clusters. An implicational universal only results if one, and just one, of the four fields in the 2 x 2 table has a minus while the rest have pluses. As a general convention, the unmarked feature will be displayed horizontally and the marked vertically, as in Fig. 2. Given this arrangement, for private features by definition the field with the minus value is the one in the upper right hand corner, as shown in Fig. 2.

	U	~U
M	+	–
~M	+	+

Figure 2

With one minus and three plus values, other positions for the minus do not represent significantly different cases, but merely different arrangements of the same primary data in accordance with different conventions from the one adopted here.

Where the attributes are equipollent, even though binary, it was noted that two logically equivalent, so to speak, as it were "psychologically" different implicational statements are possible. We can

Joseph H. Greenberg

illustrate this by the example earlier cited of the almost exceptionless relation between AN and QN word order. Since the disfavored
order is the combination of NQ and NA, the least arbitrary decision
is to symbolize QN as ~NQ and AN as ~NA. However, there is no
unarbitrary way of deciding whether NA/AN should be the horizontal
and NQ/QN the vertical dimensions, and vice versa. In either case,
however, we get a minus in the lower right field rather than the
upper right field, as in Fig. 2. These alternatives are shown in
Fig. 3.

	NA	~NA			QN	~QN
QN	+	+		NA	+	+
~QN	+	−		~NA	+	−
	(a)				(b)	

Figure 3

    Instances in which two pluses and two minuses occur are also
quite frequent and often here give rise to generalizing statements
which seem implicational in form but, for reasons which will immediately appear, such instances should be clearly distinguished
from those in which a single minus value occurs.

    Take, for example, the well known fact about the relationship
between nasal and oral vowels, namely that there are no language
with nasal vowels which do not also have oral vowels. However, since
all languages have oral vowels, the resulting tetrachoric table takes
the following form (Fig. 4).

	Oral	~Oral
Nasal	+	−
~Nasal	+	−

Figure 4

    It is true, of course, that if a language has nasal vowels, it also
has oral vowels, but given the universality of oral vowels as shown
by the two pluses in the first column, it is also possible to assert
that if a language has twenty-seven genders, it also has oral vowels.
Any property whatever will imply the presence of oral vowels. This
is an example of one of the "paradoxes of material implication" already known to the Stoic logicians, which results from defining implication as a function of the truth value (i.e. truth or falsity) of the
constituent propositions alone, without regard to possible causal
connections. Any proposition implies a true proposition. This

difficulty has been noted in Howard 1971, who expresses himself in rather strong terms on this matter:

"It might be pointed out that some implicational universals are only trivially so. What appears at first to be a legitimate inference, namely, that if a language has nasal vowels, it must also have oral vowels, is merely a consequence of the statement that all languages have oral vowels. We could just as well say that if a language has subject-verb inversion, it has oral vowels. I trust that such an implicational universal would be viewed with scepticism."

There is a twin paradox, namely that a false proposition implies any proposition. It is obtained from the above by reversing signs and the order of the propositions. It is illustrated by such expressions as "if..., then the moon is made of green cheese." As alternative statement of this form based on the universality of oral vowels could be: if in any language oral vowels are not found, the language has sex gender, or just as easily, the language does not have sex gender. This kind of statement derives from the facts of the second column in Fig. 4.

Still, statements of the kind "nasal vowels imply oral vowels" can be justified, although the implicational form is not really appropriate. This is because there is an obvious causal connection between the two, most easily shown diachronically in that nasal vowels come from oral vowels, and not vice versa. Another form for statements involving distributions of the kind indicated in Fig. 4 is the following. Whereas there are languages in which WH words are always initial, there are no languages in which WH words are always final. This form of statement is of course more appropriate than the implicational one, and brings out the empirical connection between the attributes. A corresponding statement about oral and nasal vowels would be: although there are languages without nasal vowels, there are no languages without oral vowels. The assertion regarding WH words takes a somewhat different form than that of Fig. 4, because it is a universal absence which is being asserted, namely the nonoccurrence of languages in which all question words are final. This can be seen from Fig. 5.

	QI	~QI
QF	–	–
~QF	+	+

Figure 5

Joseph H. Greenberg

There are two other distributions of plus and minuses involving
two pluses and two minuses which are of interest. One of these
is the arrangement shown in Fig. 6.

	U	~U		M	~M
M	+	–	U	+	–
~M	–	+	~U	–	+
	(a)			(b)	

Figure 6

Two versions are given here. It will be noted that the distribution
in (b), which contravenes our convention for arrangement in regard
to marking, states exactly the same facts as those of (a). In this
instance, because of the symmetry of the distribution, there is in
fact no hierarchical relationship based on facts internal to the typology itself. The determination of sign may also be arbitrary in equipollent cases. Here again, as shown later in Fig. 7, either arrangement
of an equipollent case will produce the same distribution of pluses
and minuses.

The arrangement of Fig. 6 is associated with statements of logical
equivalence, or what is tautologically the same, mutual implication
of properties of language. The following is an illustration based on
an assertion which is merely conjectured to be true. If a language
expresses the relation 'under' by a preposition, it also expresses
the relation 'over' by a preposition. One possible labelling is
shown in Fig. 7.

	under-prep.	under-post.
over-prep.	+	–
over-post.	–	+

Figure 7

Statements of this type are hardly ever encountered, perhaps
because of their obviousness. They are probably worth more attention in that they involve a very strong relationship, stronger than
that of a unidirectional implication. They are not subject to any
of the paradoxes of material implication.

By sign reversal, it is also possible to state the same relation
negatively. If a language has 'over' as a postposition, it never has
'under' as a preposition, and if it has 'over' as a preposition, it
never has 'under' as a postposition. There is still another logically
possible arrangement of two pluses and minuses, as shown in Fig. 8.

```
        U      ~U
  M     -      +
 ~M     +      -
```

Figure 8

This would be applicable if, for example, the facts were that whenever 'over' is expressed by a postposition, then 'under' is expressed by preposition, and vice versa. I am doubtful as to whether such cases actually occur.

Thus far all the distributions dealt with have either two or three pluses in the cells of the tetrachoric table. Instances involving a single plus entry are related to the examples just discussed, but with the important additional proviso that the attributes which define both dimensions are universally present. We thus get an assertion of the universal coexistence, i.e. mutual implication of two properties. In these instances we encounter what might be called the paradox of mutual implication, parallel to the paradox of unidirectional implication discussed earlier. Any two properties, regardless of possible causal connection which are universal, will be connected by such statements. This is illustrated in Fig. 9, where once more the arrangement of marking relationships is arbitrary. Consider the properties: a) having some vocalic segments; b) having demonstrative adjectives.

```
        Dem    ~Dem
  V      +      -
 ~V      -      -
```

Figure 9

Whether there are real connections here cannot, as in the earlier case, be shown by diachronic factors, since ex hypothesi both are always present and therefore do not change into something else. Similar considerations are involved in instances in which the plus is the lower right hand corner (mutual implication of universally present and universally absent properties), or in one of the remaining cells, e.g. right upper. This latter type is associated with an assertion of the universal presence of one property and the absence of another.

When dealing with equipollent properties, however, plausible instances of causally significant relations involving universally coexistent properties are conceivable. If we disregard a few exceptions

and also languages which do not use intonation for statements or
questions, we have the situation shown in Fig. 10, in which R is
rising, F is falling intonation, S is a statement and Q is a question.

	RQ	FQ
RS	–	–
FS	+	–

Figure 10

The remaining cases are those with four pluses and those with
no pluses. The former distribution occurs quite frequently. It
indicates that all possible cases actually occur so that no exceptionless generalization is possible. However, there might be non-
random statistical distribution of languages over the cells. So-called
near universals or statistical universals exhibit this logical form.

The final type is one with no pluses, i.e. four minuses. This
type is of no empirical interest. We normally construct typologies
with categorical attributes applicable to all languages, but such a
distribution would imply that there are no languages with any combination of such properties. This would only hold if no languages
existed, or possibly, if we used a property which is irrelevant to
language, e.g. physiologically nourishing. We could say that all
languages are neither nourishing nor non-nourishing.

Analyses similar to the foregoing and even more complex ones
would be carried out in regard to typologies based on categorical
attributes of more than two dimensions but are not attempted here.
One special case, however, deserves mention, namely that of the
implicational chain. An example is that of agreement of major
constituents with the verb, as noted in Moravcsik 1974. Denoting
agreement of the verb with subject, object, indirect object and ad-
verbial elements by S, O, I and A respectively, we have A → I →
O → S.

Since four dimensions are involved, we cannot use the method
of representation which we have been employing up to now. Such
relationships can, however, be conveniently represented by a Venn
diagram, showing the inclusion relationship of classes of languages
as is in fact done by Moravcsik. More complex relationships can
also be shown by this technique. It, of course, can be summarized
by a set of generalizing statements of the sort we have been dealing
with up to now.

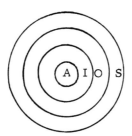

Figure 11

However, where we are dealing with an infinity of classes, there is no way of displaying the totality of possible arrangements either by tables or Venn diagrams. More importantly, the generalizations cannot be "read off" from a table of fixed form by applying some known tautology, as was illustrated from the example of a tetrachoric table with three pluses, with the arrangement associated with an implicational relationship.

To deal with an infinity of types, a convenient method is that of a set of postulates which can be viewed as forming a set of logically independent generalizations whose conjunction coincides exactly with the set of all languages. That is, all existing languages will be satisfied by the postulates and there will be no non-existent types which satisfy them.

An example which I have treated elsewhere (Greenberg 1970) is that of the category of number in the noun, excluding, however, the construction with numerals themselves, which may show special peculiarities. We may consider the category of number to be defined by a mapping into the set of natural numbers 1, 2, 3.... Each grammatical category of number is associated with a part or whole of this set. For example, a language with singular, dual and plural maps these respectively into (1), (2), and (3, 4, 5...). The types actually found are 1) no category of grammatical number, 2) singular and plural, 3) singular, dual and plural. A set of postulates satisfied by these and only these mappings is the following: 1) every language has one and just one infinite set, 2) every finite set is a unit set (i.e. it contains just one cardinal number), 3) if n̲ is the number of a unit set, n-1 is always a number of a unit set (this is to be applied recursively until 1 is reached), 4) the largest unit set is 2.

There are other instances in which, while the number of possible types is not infinite, it is extremely large. An example is kinship terminology. Here the logically generated set of possibilities is truly vast, far larger than the number of known systems. This means the non-existence of some particular system might be "accidental," due to the small size of the sample of existent systems. Under these circumstances a more modest goal seems reasonable. All existent systems should conform to the postulates, but not all systems which satisfy them need actually be found.

A more drastic departure from the form of generalizing systems thus far considered is appropriate where we are dealing with a frequency distribution involving numerical predicates. This was mentioned earlier in the course of the discussion concerning logical types of attributes. Measures of mean values for continuous numerical attributes which have not been reduced, and modal values for discrete numeral attributes are appropriate in these cases. For systemic discrete attributes, e.g. numbers of tone levels, maximal values are also important. Thus, the largest number of tone levels thus far discovered is five. Such limits may be called inevitable universals. The discovery of a language with six tone levels would overthrow the previous generalization only to replace it by a new one. Their importance is in exhibiting psychological and physiological limits to human performance capabilities and as a challenge to the production of a more general theory within which they can be deduced.

There is a basic issue regarding typology which is not within the scope of this paper, but which requires at least passing mention. What is to count as an attribute of language? The notion of typology is broad enough to encompass a variety of responses. In every historical period, the prevailing mode of conceiving language has quite naturally and inevitably exercized an influence on typology. In the present period, the conception of language as a set of rules is prevalent as a result of the dominance of the generative approach.

Hence, properties of grammars are involved rather then properties of language as such. However, insofar as particular rules, e.g. transformation are widespread but not universal, it is possible to typologize in terms of them. Languages with grammars containing a particular rule would belong to a particular type, and those not containing them to a different type. Implicational relations may obtain among the rules themselves. These possibilities were apparently first pointed out and explored by Bach (1965) and Ross (1967) and characterize much present work.

Insofar as transformations are formulated on the basis of certain relationships among classes of sentences, alternative statements including direct reference to these data will be possible. Indeed, it will make no real difference whether one states a generalization in terms of a question-word-fronting rule or in terms of languages which have initial question-words corresponding to statements with a different word order.

There are advantages in both. Contemporary grammatical theory allows for the convenient statement of complex relationships of this sort and provides a heuristically valuable method of uncovering them. On the other hand, there are typologically relevant characteristics of language usually excluded from contemporary models of grammars, e.g. textual frequency properties. There is therefore no reason in principle to confine ourselves to one approach or the other.

One kind of typologizing in relation to language has been tacitly ignored in the entire preceding discussion. There has been no room for such types as literary language, pidgin language, language of wider communication, etc. Yet such classifications have been called typologies, and Stewart (1962) for one has developed a sociolinguistic scheme which embraces some of these phenomena.

In a broader sense than just the exclusion of sociolinguistic typology, one may say that the treatment and the example of this paper as has generally been the case in linguistic typology, have been confined to "internal attributes" of language. Some philosophers have talked about internal and external predicates. Examples of external predicates are: "spoken by more than 5,000,000 people, extinct, having an orthography based on the LATIN alphabet, spoken by pre-industrial people," etc. In some instances, e.g. pidginization, a basic source of disagreement has been whether the attribute is internal or external. Are pidgins to be defined in terms of internal properties, e.g. morphological simplicity, or external, e.g. "spoken by no one as a first language?" If both are true, then we have an example of the possibility of typologies in which both internal and external attributes figure. We might even have an implicational generalization of the sort "if a language is spoken only as a second language, it is always morphologically simple, but not necessarily vice versa," with morphological simplicity to be determined in some manner left unspecified in the present context.

Some genuine questions regarding linguistic evolution belong here. For example, the following is a plausible implicational relation linking

58   Joseph H. Greenberg

an internal with an external predicate. "If a language has a system
of cardinal numbers which makes no use of arithmetical functions
(e.g. addition, multiplication), it is spoken by a hunting, food-
gathering people."

We may summarize the conclusions of the present paper as follows. A theoretical analysis of basic typological concepts helps us
to broaden our conception of cross-linguistic generalization, while
its application provides a useful methodology for discovering such
generalizations at the lower empirical levels and thus providing
the materials for broader and deeper conclusions about the nature
of human language. The special contribution that the generalization
associated with typology makes is that it allows us to explore even
properties in regard to which languages differ from each other for
the purposes of developing significant linguistic generalizations.
It thus "makes sense" out of a large group of linguistic phenomena
which are neither found in all languages nor are language particular.
As will be shown in the companion paper on diachrony, the introduction of this latter factor into typological theory permits us in many
instances to account for rules which, on the face of it, are so language particular and idiosyncratic that they might seem impervious
to generalizing theory.

BIBLIOGRAPHY

Bach, Emmon. 1965. On some recurrent types of transformation.
    Georgetown Series on Language and Linguistics 18. 3-18.

Greenberg, Joseph H. 1970. Language universals: a research
    frontier. Science 166. 473-478.

_____. 1974. Language typology: a historical and analytic
    overview. The Hague: Mouton.

Horne, Kibbey M. 1966. Language typology, 19th and 20th century
    views. Washington: Georgetown University Press.

Howard, Irvin. 1971. On several concepts of universals. Working
    Papers in Linguistics 3.4. 243-248 (April). University of Hawaii.

Lowie, R.H. and F.R. Eggan. 1929. Art. kinship terminology.
    Encyclopedia Britannica (14th ed.).

Menzerath, P. 1954. Architecktonik des deutschen Wortschatzes. Bonn: Dümmler.

Moravcsik, E. 1974. Object-verb agreement. Working Papers on Language Universals 15. 25-140. Stanford University.

Ross, John R. 1967. Constraints on variables in syntax. Doctoral dissertation, M.I.T.

Skalička, V. 1968. Über die Typologie der finnisch-ugrischen Sprachen. Congressus Secundus Internationalis Fenno-Ugristarum. Helsingiae habitus 23-28, VIII. 1965. Helsinki: Societas Fenno-Ugrica.

Stewart, William A. 1962. An outline of linguistic typology for describing multilingualism. Study of the role of second language in Asia, Africa and Latin America, ed. by Frank A. Rice. Washington D.C.: Center for Applied Linguistics.

Trubetskoy, N. 1939. Grundzüge der Phonologie. Travaux du Cercle Linguistique de Prague 9.

Diachrony, Synchrony, and Language Universals

JOSEPH H. GREENBERG

ABSTRACT

The question whether a typological approach to universals is in principle confined to synchrony is discussed and answered in the negative. A general framework for a typological treatment of universals through change of type is presented in the form of a state-process model. Extensions of this model allow for multiple processes between states and a probabilistic interpretation of transitions between states. A section on methodology is devoted to a discussion of a number of types of dynamic comparison, this being the overall term for research methods associated with a state-process approach. The final topic is the place of diachronic universals within the overall structure of explanatory theory in linguistics.

62   Joseph H. Greenberg

CONTENTS

1. Diachrony and the Typological Approach to Language Universals

The study of universals has until the last few years been almost entirely synchronic.[1] This does not mean, of course, that dia-chronically oriented studies relating to universals must start from a pristine state of ignorance. Just as the descriptive linguist brings a body of implicit hypotheses concerning possible language states from a broad experience concerning what actual languages are like, so the historical linguist operates with numerous hypotheses about probable changes based both on his experience with attested cases and, to some extent, by deduction from more general principles. As with synchronic linguistics, there is in practice a constant interaction between the explanation of specific cases and deductive hypotheses. Thus, given the commonly attested process of vowel nasalization of vowels adjacent to nasal consonants and other known instances of assimilatory changes involving marked features, the linguist concerned with languages without recorded historical documentation and dealing with sounds not found in the better studied linguistic stocks is prepared to consider other, not directly evidenced assimilations as plausible processes, e.g. the laryngealization of vowels adjacent to a glottal stop or a glottalic pressure consonant.

The absence, until very recently, of an explicit recognition of the study of general diachronic principles in its connection with the topic of language universals is the result of a number of factors. One of these is that on a nontypologic view of universals as con-sisting exclusively of unrestricted universals to be found in all languages, no corresponding facts seemed to be observable in the crucible of linguistic changes. What Weinreich, Labov and Herzog (1968) have called the principle of actuation seemed to rule out such a possibility. Given that a change is possible, why does it appear in one dialect of a language and not in another or at an earlier historical period in one case and a later in another? Secondly, the assumption that synchronic states provide the basic material for linguistic generalization is fundamental to struc-turalism and the modern study of typology and universals arose in a structuralist milieu. These assumptions were essentially reinforced by the nature of historical linguistic work itself, which has been to a high degree particularistic, referring to

---

[1] Several of Ferguson's generalizations about nasals (Ferguson 1963) are diachronic though not explicitly stated to be such. This seems to be the first occurrence of such statements in the context of contemporary interest in universals.

specific languages and language families and positing specific
changes and reconstructions. This is even true of those generalizations in historical linguistics which traditionally went by the
names of law, such as Grimm's Law, Grassmann's Law, etc.
Historical linguists were never tired of repeating that such "sound
laws" were bound to specific languages and only valid within certain chronological limits. One has only to ask the questions whether
there are any languages known to be exceptions to Grimm's Law
to realize that such formulations lack one of the most elementary
requirements of a scientific law, that the limits within which it
applies be stated in general terms. That is, it should not mention
specific times or places or employ proper names.

If the things called "laws" were of this nature, then a fortiori
there could be no true laws in historical linguistics.

With specific reference to typology there was still another factor.
Typology was itself conceived to be, by definition, a synchronic
concept. For example, the definition of typology given by Marouzeau
(1961) in his dictionary of terminology was the following: "the typological study of languages is that which defines their characteristics
in abstraction from history." There was indeed something like an
opposition between typology and historical linguistics. They issued
in different, and in the view of some, conflicting forms of classification. Further, typology provided, as it were, a residual and
distinct mode of explanation for certain resemblances which historical comparison could not account for, e.g. tonalism as found in
Southeast Asia and Africa.

Hence, it was only natural that the first attempts to relate historical linguistics to typology (e.g. Ivanov 1958 and Jakobson 1958)
took a basically synchronic point of departure, namely, that reconstructed linguistic systems should not violate other universally
valid synchronic structural norms. This is a legitimate and fruitful
suggestion. It is indeed a suspicious circumstance if precisely
those language states which are the most indirectly attested by
complex processes of inference, turn out to be just those which
violate synchronic norms.

Jakobson's observation that the generally accepted reconstruction
of PROTO-INDO-EUROPEAN consonantism as consisting of three
series of stops: unvoiced unaspirated, voiced unaspirated, and
voiced aspirated, violates the synchronic implicational principle that
the presence of a voiced aspirate implies the presence of unvoiced
aspirates is a particularly influential instance of the application of

this principle. It has provided a powerful stimulus towards recent attempts at drastically revising the previously accepted system. (See, for example, the paper by Gamkrelidze in volume II of this work.)

However important this point is, it is but a single aspect of a complex and many faceted relationship, in fact, the one which emphasizes the most undiachronic aspect of historical linguistics, the reconstruction of earlier synchronic language states.

The points just raised concerning the contradictory nature of the notion of a diachronic universal and the inapplicability by very definition of typological concepts to the diachronic aspect of language are all subject to challenge.

Starting from an approach to universals from the perspectives provided by typology, we can look on diachronic generalization as involving constraints on changes just as synchronic generalization can be considered to involve restraints on synchronic states through the specification of logically possible but empirically non-occurring type. Moreover, as we shall see in much greater detail in the course of this paper, synchronic typology itself provides a very natural framework for much of the study of general principles of change, namely that provided by limitations on change of type. In fact, they imply each other. If there are limitations on synchronic linguistic types, then change must proceed from lawful type to lawful type. But this suggests that there must be corresponding limits on change.

Further, no contradiction arises from the notion that typology is in Marouzeau's terms "an abstraction from history." What is significant here is not that typology should only have reference to synchronic attributes of language. The more basic point is that the objects classified should be historically independent cases. But changes can be historically independent just as states are. For example, languages have again and again in an independent manner undergone such changes as palatalization, merger of morphological classes, grammaticization of phonologically developed alternations, etc. The difference is that we are dealing with types of change, rather than types of languages. The traditional name for such types is process. Palatalization, for example, is a process, that is, a class of changes with common characteristics which have occurred in numerous historically independent instances. These instances are then themselves subject to comparison and generalization.

Without explicitly formulating any theory of diachronic universals, much recent work shows a strong tendency to encompass the dia - chronic dimension within the framework of typology and universals.[2] Examples are to be found in Li (1975) as indicated by its very title "Word order and word order change," and is characteristic of much of the recent work of such linguists as Givón, Comrie, Ed. Keenan, Hyman and Bell, to mention just a few. The same tendency is ob - servable in the rather different European typological tradition (e.g. Sharadzenidze 1970 and Skalička 1968). The latter observes that "the typological description of languages has two sides, namely, synchronic and diachronic. Hence, the thesis that typology is identical with synchronic description is false." (Skalička 1968: 444).

It is no doubt a healthy sign when a particular development arises, as it were, naturally out of the specific problems which concern linguists. There is, however, a real value in an explicit concern with theory in such cases. In the present instance, the problem is that of broadening the by now traditional synchronic emphasis of typology and universals to include the diachronic dimension. In this paper the attempt is made to incorporate some of my own earlier efforts in this direction (e.g. Greenberg 1966, 1969) in a more general and integrated framework. Some of the questions that may be broached in this connection are the following. What is a diachronic universal? What, if any, is the role of typology? How are diachronic generalizations related to synchronic generali - zations? What part does diachronic generalization play in the overall explanatory structure of linguistics?

---

[2] A historical review is not within the scope of the present paper. It is well to point out, however, that much earlier work is more or less directly relevant to present day diachronic generalizing studies. The nineteenth century Neo-grammarians in particular not only provide important individual studies of change but devel - oped a framework of processual terminology which is still in certain respects basic. Explicit attention to diachronic generalization has been characteristic of much French work, e.g. the pioneering efforts of Grammont in phonology, of Meillet concerning parallel processes in different branches of INDO-EUROPEAN and in a more structuralist context the investigations of Martinet in dia - chronic phonology. Mention should also be made of the attempts of Kuryłowicz and, recently, Mańczak on general laws of analogical change; many others, of course, might have been mentioned.

2. The State-Process Model

2.1 Basic concepts

Foundamental to much of what follows is the notion of a state-process model of language. A particular instance of the state-process model is based on a synchronic typology. Each of the logically possible types within the typology which finds empirical exemplification constitutes a state. All languages of the world that belong to the given type may be said to be in that state. We consider, with regard to any two of the states, whether there are processes by which a language in one state can change into the other, or vice versa. For any pair of states there are four possible answers. If we call these states A and B, then: 1) It may be possible for a language in state A to change to state B and vice-versa. 2) It may be possible for a language in state A to change to state B, but not vice versa. 3) It may be possible for a language in state B to change into state A, but not vice versa. 4) It may not be possible either for a language in state A to change to state B or, when in state B, to change to state A. It is convenient to show these possibilities by means of diagrams in which states are represented by quadrilaterals and changes by arrows. The four possibilities just mentioned are represented in Figure 1.

1   2   3   4

Figure 1

If n is the number of states, then the total number of different possible state-process diagrams can be shown to be $2(n^2-n)$. In the above example, since n is 2, the result is $2(4-2) = 4$.

Diagrams of this sort can be handled by a branch of mathematical topology called graph theory which deals with points connected by either directed lines or non-directed lines.[3] Certain questions can

---

[3] Graph theory is not the only branch of mathematics which deals with structures of the sort discussed here. For example, the theory of relations first developed in its modern form in the Principia can also be applied. One has only to represent "A --> B" as "a R b" (read "a has the relation R to b") as a starting point in order to make statements isomorphic with those in the text. For a standard treatment of graph theory, see Berge 1973.

68   Joseph H. Greenberg

be raised in terms of such theory regarding the empirically derivable properties of state-process diagrams in linguistics which
can lead to generalizations regarding such systems in general.

Consider the following hypothesis. In every state-process diagram in which there are at least two states, there is some way in
which a language can move into each state and out of it. This does
not require that every pair of states be connected even indirectly,
but that every state have at least one arrow going towards and at
least one going away from it.

It is likely that this is a true hypothesis. Among the possibilities
excluded by it is the following. There are eternal properties which
are not universal. Consider, for example, a simple typology of
two types defined by the presence or absence of a tonal system.
The situation shown in Figure 2 would, of course, violate the
hypothesis just stated.

Figure 2

This would mean that a language which is non-tonal could never
become tonal and one which is tonal could never become non-tonal.
There would then be two eternal properties which are not universal.
Its truth would be an effective refutation of linguistic monogenesis
since there must then be at least two original languages of mankind, one tonal and one non-tonal to give rise to the present languages. There could, of course, be more than two. This hypothesis
concerning tone is known to be false, but it is a tacit premise of
some historical linguists in denying possible genetic affiliation of
a non-tonal language to a genetic family otherwise marked by tonalism or of a tonal language to an otherwise non-tonal stock.

A second possibility excluded by the general hypothesis is shown
in Figure 3. Ferguson (1963) once conjectured that there were no
sources for nasal consonants whereas there were processes by
which they could be lost.

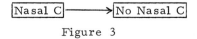

Figure 3

This sort of possibility is the one called a sink in general systems
theory. If there is one state which has no egress and which is

connected directly or indirectly with every other state, ultimately
everything in the system must end up in this state.

It has since been shown that there are sources for new nasals
(e.g. voiced implosives). If Ferguson's hypothesis were true,
however, it would have interesting consequences for our views
regarding certain near-universals. In this case the near-universal
status of nasal consonants, which are found in all the languages of
the world, except a few AMERINDIAN languages of the northwest
coast, would seem a mere accident resulting from the fact that
the first human language happened to have nasals and these have
persisted almost everywhere. If this language chanced not to
have nasals, since by hypothesis there would be no source for
them, they would be universally absent.

The indications are, then, that in every language type in a typology with at least two existent states, there is at least one process
which leads to it and one which leads from it. A stronger hypothesis,
however, can be conjectured to hold, namely that every diagram is,
in the terminology of graph theory, strongly connected. This means
that for any two existent states A and B there is at least one path
which leads from A to B and at least one which leads from B to A.
In other words every type can ultimately change into every other
type even if not directly.

That this hypothesis is stronger than the previous one can be
shown in the following way. Suppose there is a typology with four
existent states A, B, C, D and a process-state situation as shown
in Figure 4. This will satisfy the first hypothesis but be excluded by the second.

Figure 4

An example conjectured to be true which illustrates this refers
to the category of number in the noun. The three types are
type A without the category of number, type B which has singular,
dual and plural, and type C which has a singular/plural dichotomy.
This is illustrated by the diagram in Figure 5:

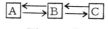

Figure 5

It is likely that the hypothesis of strong connection is true in this and every other case though it cannot, of course, be proven on the basis of our present knowledge.

The combination of the notion of marking relationships in the underlying typology with that of process-state leads to theories of origin and loss. Where the change is most naturally stated as that from a type defined by the absence of a property to one characterized by its presence, we may talk of acquisition and in the opposite case loss. For example, an answer to the question regarding the processes by which a language that is non-tonal becomes one which is tonal may be called a theory of the origin of tone. It is well to qualify such theories by the term relative, since we are not after the manner of cultural evolutionary theory positing the existence of a period in which no language in the world had tone followed by a stage in which it existed, but rather that in diverse language families, at different historical periods and in different parts of the world, languages have changed type in this manner.

How are questions of this sort to be answered? The method to be employed may be called dynamic comparison. It is, as it were, the ordinary comparative-historical method which is employed within the confines of a single genetic group, raised to a higher plane in which each instance among those to be compared is itself the subject of comparative-historical investigation in the conventional sense.

By comparative-historical investigation is meant the employment of all the methods at our disposal for inferring the occurrence of changes in language, e.g. internal reconstruction, the direct historical method which compares the same language in different stages, the comparison of related languages and even, in phonology, the data provided by transcriptions from and into foreign languages or by the adoption of foreign systems of writing.

2.2 Multiple origins

The process-state model just presented in terms of graph theory is a very simple one. It can be usefully elaborated in two general directions. One of these is based on the fact that the underlying assumption represented by the choice of either no-connection between two states or, at the most, a single arrow running in either or both directions often does not adequately portray the situation. There may be several different processes by which a language changes from one state in a given typology to another. If it is a question of origins, we may say that if there is only known to be one process, we are dealing with a single-origin theory, otherwise with a multiple-origin theory. An example of multiple-origin is the following. A process-state model corresponding to a static typological classification into languages with definite articles and those without definite articles will show an arrow from the class of languages without such articles to one with such articles. It is sometimes stated that definite articles always arise from demonstratives. However, further investigation will show at least three far less frequent origins: from possessive third person pronouns, from independent person pronouns, and from numeral classifiers. We should then have at least four arrows going from the state defined by the absence of a definite article to the one defined by its presence.

One way of looking at situations of this kind is to look on each stage of the process of change as itself constituting a type. A theory of typological change can be looked on as interpolating a succession of types between the two types with which we originally started. If there is more than one process, each will result in a different set of such types giving rise to separate paths. The result will be once more a single arrow model but one which has elaborated in a significant manner our original typology.

As a concrete illustration let us take the example of languages changing from the type which has only oral vowels to the type which has both oral and nasal vowels. The dominant but perhaps not exclusive process is through the allophonic nasalization of oral vowels by adjacent nasal consonants and subsequent phonologization through loss of the nasal consonant. The sequences of stages can be presented schematically as V,N $\rightarrow$ Ṽ,N $\rightarrow$ Ṽ, where either order of V in relation to N is symbolized as V, N. What this amounts to is the interposition of an additional type between the two original types as shown in Figure 6.

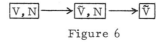

Figure 6

However, such a view of the matter raises the following question. Our original typology was one of four logical possibilities based on the two dimensions of vowel orality and vowel nasality each with two values: presence or absence of the given attribute. It was predicated on the assumption that all languages of the world could

be distributed among these four classes and it was found that only
two of them received empirical exemplification. How, then, can
a new interposed type arise if our initial typology was in theory
exhaustive in assigning all languages of the world to one or other
of the types defined by its criteria? If this holds, then the transitional type must belong to one or the other. These two alternatives
are shown in Figure 7.

(a)   (b)

Figure 7

In Figure 7(a) languages with allophonic nasal vowels are assigned
to the class of languages with nasalized vowels while in 7(b) they
are assigned to the type without nasal vowels. The first of these
alternatives rests on a typology in which vowel nasalization is
defined as a phonetic attribute while in the second, the defining property is surface phonemic contrast. If our typology was explicit
on this point in the first place, no problem arises, but in either
case we now have a subtypological division of one or the other of
our original classes.

It is quite often the case, as in the present instance, that the
assignment of a processually transitional state in one way or the
other raises questions concerning the nature of the definitions
employed in the typology. It is also frequently the case that this
issue is of a more general nature. In the present instance this
more general question is: should phonological typologies be based
on phonetic or phonological criteria?[4]

---

[4] The problem presented here can also be stated in terms of
generative phonological theory. In almost all earlier and many
recent generative treatments of languages with phonetic vowel
nasality, they are treated as surface phenomena, ultimately deriv-
ing from underlying sequences of oral vowels and nasal consonants.
This is no doubt because nasal vowels are usually historically so
recent that their origin can be reconstructed from synchronic
evidences. A universal theory of single origin would take the following form. In any language with a rule in which ([+vocalic],
[-consonantal], [+nasal]) is the output, the input will contain a
sequence, in either order, of ([+vocalic), [-consonantal], [-nasal])
and ([-vocalic], [+consonantal], [+nasal]).
     A phonetically based typology will classify languages merely
into those with or without this rule. A phonemically based typology

It is a basic contribution of a diachronically oriented typology that it serves to put many definitional questions in a new light. The border line cases that cause difficulty both for synchronic typologies and synchronic general linguistic theory are often transitional stages in the process of typological change. But these transitional types, however we assign them in terms of our original typology, can themselves be considered the basis for a subtypology in which, as in any typology, we will be likely to find certain logical possibilities not to be empirically exemplified and thus to furnish the basis for further generalizations.

This point can be elucidated by another example. One of the dimensions of word order typology is the relative order of the cardinal numeral and the noun which it modifies. This is most simply typologized by setting up two alternative basic orders QN and NQ. However, some languages have rules by which certain numerals precede the noun while others follow. It is precisely such cases that make classification difficulties for synchronic typology. However, from the processual point of view, they are opportunities leading to further generalizations and fuller understanding. We may make our criteria more precise by considering languages with unequivocal QN and NQ orders as extreme types within a typology which has an infinite set of logically possible classes which can be interpolated between them. Thus, a language in which 7, 8 and 11 precede and the others follow is an example of a logically possible type. The actually occurring types of this kind, however, are limited in certain ways. They all involve a continuous sequence of numerals beginning with 'one' with one of the orders, and all the numerals with a numerical value larger than some specified number with the other, with a possible sequence involving free variation in between. An example is CLASSICAL ARABIC in which 'one' follows, 2-10 may precede or follow and the numerals greater than 10 generally precede, but may follow when the numeral phrase is definite.

In these and other instances various kinds of evidence show that such systems are in the process of changing from QN to NQ or vice versa and that the smaller numbers, which are the most unmarked, are the most resistant to change. It is then precisely

___

(ftnt. 4 cont.)
will segregate languages into those which have the above rule, followed at some point by a rule of nasal consonantal loss in the appropriate environments as against those which do not have both these rules.

the "border line" cases, those which are the most resistant to
synchronic typologizing, which lend themselves to generalizations
about change, and the processual mode of comparison can help us
to make sense out of what otherwise appear to be highly particu-
larized language specific rules. Once we have done this our efforts
will tend towards developing an understanding of general principles
underlying such limitations on change and the problem of synchronic
definition in some instances becomes a matter of relatively secondary interest.

Similar considerations apply to the example of vowel nasalization
discussed earlier. Recently, there has been considerable discussion
of a possible order of nasalization of individual vowels (e.g. Chen
1975). The evidence seems to be that low vowels nasalize before
high vowels.

The intermediate type of Figure 7 can itself become the basis
of a subtypology. What these data show is that in such a typology
vowel height figures as a significant dimension. In this way diachronic considerations help in the construction of "reasonable"
non-arbitrary typologies among the infinity of possible typologies.

Figure 8 embodies a very simple revision of Figure 7 which
will illustrate schematically how one may typologize a transitional
state in accordance with the hypotheses stated earlier regarding
the priority of high vowels in vowel nasalization.

$$\boxed{\text{VN}} \rightarrow \boxed{\tilde{\text{V}}\text{N (low vowels only)}} \dashrightarrow \boxed{\tilde{\text{V}}\text{N (high and low vowels)}} \rightarrow \boxed{\tilde{\text{V}}}$$

Figure 8

Note that the two intervening types are themselves members of
a subtypology with two dimensions: phonetic presence and absence
of high nasalized and presence and absence of low nasalized vowels.[5]

Considerations of this kind lead in a natural way to the formulation of the notions of implicational universal as applied in the diachronic sphere. For example, we can say that the nasalization of
high vowels implies the previous nasalization of low vowels but not
vice versa. Such generalizations are related to state-process

---

[5] This, of course, represents only the simplest cases. There
will, for example, be further complications if the high vowels
become contrastive before the low vowels become phonetically
nasalized.

models in that, as can be seen from Figure 6 which is a special case, if $\phi \rightarrow \psi$ diachronically, then all paths to ϕ must first go through ψ.

2.3 A probabilistic approach

Besides the possibility of allowing more than one arrow from one state to another, the state-process model can also, and more drastically, be modified by the introduction of numerical probabilities regarding each specific transition. Probably the simplest way in which this can be done is by adopting a Markov Chain Model. This requires a basic simplifying assumption that what happens to a particular language in one state is independent of the states in which it has previously been, i.e. the system is memoryless. Over some fixed arbitrary period of time the total of the possibilities of a language in a given state remaining in that state or changing to one or more other states is 1. There is a theorem that no matter what the assigned distribution of the items over the states, a steady state will ultimately be reached which is determined by the transitional and rest probabilities of each item. The relative frequencies of the items in this equilibrium state can be calculated from the transitional and rest possibilities. Of course, what we are given is the present distribution from which assumptions can be made about the transitional and rest probabilities such that the equilibrium is deduced, unfortunately, in an infinite number of ways.

The only attempt of which I am aware to apply this model is that of Bell (1970b, 1971) in relation to syllabic structure. The actual attempt to do this is fraught with many difficulties. Ideally, however, one would have explained, for example, the universality of CV by the number of other states from which it can arise, the high probabilities of transitions from these states, and its own high rest probabilities as against its probabilities of moving to other states. This does mean that in the general case, the probability of any state is never 1.00, though it may be so high that it remains unlikely that an exception will in fact ever be encountered. Although some universals may thus be, as it were, demoted from absolute certainty, they still remain significant. One must still explain the diachronic conspiracy, as it were, in regard to the processes of change which are involved.

In general one may expect that certain phenomena are widespread in language because the ways they can arise are frequent and their stability, once they occur, is high. A rare or non-existent phenomenon arises only by infrequently occurring changes and is unstable once it comes into existence.

The two factors of probability of origin from other states and
stability can be considered separately. If a particular phenomenon
can arise very frequently and is highly stable once it occurs, it
should be universal or near universal. This could be true of front
unrounded vowels. If it tends to come into existence often and in
various ways, but its stability is low, it should be found fairly
often but distributed relatively evenly among genetic linguistic
stocks. A possible example is vowel nasalization. If a particular
property rarely arises but is highly stable when it occurs, it should
be fairly frequent on a global basis but be largely confined to a few
linguistic stocks, e.g. vowel harmony. If it occurs only rarely
and is unstable when it occurs, it should be highly infrequent or
non-existent and sporadic in its geographical and genetic distribution, e.g. velar implosives.

3. Dynamic Comparison

The state-process model is the central concept in a typological
approach to diachronic generalizations about language. As can be
seen from the exposition thus far, it incorporates within the same
model both historical-comparative and synchronic typological
factors. Given this complexity it is possible to distinguish a number of different methods which are to some extent only pragmatically
distinct, insofar as in particular investigations there may be differences of goals or of the available kind of data. The relative
probability of origin and stability of the phenomenon itself is also
a factor which affects the methodology of investigation, as will be
indicated later.

The underlying structure of a process-state model, insofar as it
involves an interplay of genetic and typological factors, may be
envisioned in the following way. Consider a set of parallel branch-
ing structures. Each symbolizes a specific linguistic stock within
which instances of the phenomenon to be investigated is assumed
to be historically independent. Intersecting this is a set of states
within a typology. Every portion of the lines in the genetic branch-
ing diagram is assigned to one or another of these states on a typological basis.

Such a diagram does, however, omit one important factor which
has not been considered up to now, but whose omission is not a
matter of principle, namely language contact. If a language changes
typologically from one state to another through the effects of contact, such a change involves both typological states and a process
which unfolds over time. It thus involves both process and state.

Moreover, it is susceptible to diachronic generalizations including implicational ones. For example, it may be conjectured that a change of genitive order due to contact implies the previous change of subject, verb, object order through the same factor.[6]

I have elsewhere (Greenberg 1969) discussed four such methods. The present purpose is not to illustrate them in detail but to show their place in the overall structure of the process-state model as just outlined.

The first of these, the dynamicization of a typology, is in a sense simply the state-process method itself. Its pragmatic applicability as compared to the other methods to be outlined is that we start with a typology within which we have already ascertained, at least in a general way, the distribution of the world's languages. For example, corresponding to the almost exceptionless word order implication NQ → NA there is a typology of two dimensions each with two values: 1) NQ, QN, 2) NA, AN. If the implication is valid, the type NQ, AN is rare. We also assume that a language will not simultaneously change both noun-quantifier and noun-adjective order. These possibilities are shown in Figure 9, in which (A), (B), (C) and (D) refer to distinct processes of change.

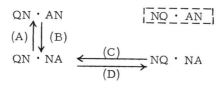

Figure 9

This suggests that the possibilities shown by the arrows are at least candidates for frequent occurrence while those not included should be rare and, in some instances, perhaps non-existent. Further, the existence of the implicational relationship suggesting, as it does, a causal relation between numeral-noun and adjective-noun order leads to other questions which tend more easily to occur to us once we have systematically diagrammed the possibilities. Does a change in adjective-noun order trigger a corresponding change in that of quantifier-noun rather than the other way around? It is a stronger assumption if only one of these two holds. Each

---

[6]Of course, the implication will hold even if the change of genitive order never takes place. What is excluded is that the genitive order will change first.

produces a different set of consequences regarding the relative
frequency of particular transitions. For example, if adjective-
noun order is the independent variable, then the change QN · AN --→
QN · NA (B) is a likely one and should bring fairly soon in its train
the further change back to a harmonic state NQ · NA (D). On the
other hand, if numeral-noun is the more dynamic factor, then a
change NQ · NA --→ QN · NA (C) followed by QN · NA --→ QN · AN
(B) becomes more likely. Further, given the putatively greater
independence of adjective-noun order, languages of the exceptional
type NQ · AN should come from NQ · NA languages rather than
QN · AN languages.

All of this, of course, gives us no automatic answers, but it
does produce a framework of questions to be asked within which
we are better able to judge the adequacy of any theory regarding
change in adjective-noun and numeral-noun order. It can also
happen that we may have empirically noticed certain idiosyncratic
rules in our synchronic survey and we now see that they are evidence for one of the changes of type to which we have been alerted.

The second method is that of dynamicization of a subtypology.
By a subtypology is meant one in which the set of possible languages
included in the typology is a proper part of the set of all languages.
This subset is defined itself by some typological characteristics.
For example, within a typology which classifies languages into
those with or without implosive stops and into which, therefore,
all languages of the world potentially enter, we select one of the
two for subtypologizing. Where marking relationships exist, it
would seem reasonable to base our subtypology on the set of languages, presumably a minority, which possesses this characteristic.
This has a certain obvious advantage in reducing our task to manage-
able proportions. Ideally, an exhaustive sample is advisable here,
since virtually every new case can teach us something. Even this
is in practice not always sufficient for reasons to be indicated later.

We cannot tell a priori what will be a relevant subtypology (or
set of subtypologies). By dynamicization is meant that our overall
goal is to construct as it were a life-history of the defining property
of the subtypology, the process by which it arises, develops along
certain lines and is eventually lost. Two basic methods are involved.
One is the formulation of synchronic generalizations concerning the
trait under investigation and their translation into diachronic hypotheses where this is possible. For example, from a study of languages
with voiceless vowels, we can produce the synchronic universal that
the presence of voiceless low vowels implies the presence of voiceless

high vowels. This can also be viewed diachronically in that it allows for two possibilities for languages in which every voiced vowel has a corresponding voiceless partner. Either all the vowels became voiceless under certain conditions at the same time, or first the high vowels became voiceless and then this spreads to the low vowels. What is excluded is that low vowels should become voiceless first, since this would produce a non-existent type. The other major method is that of comparative-historical linguistics. Internal reconstruction and comparison with closely related languages or generational differences in speech, or stylistic variations based on speech tempo may give independent evidence that, in some instances, languages in which all vowels occur voicelessly have passed through a stage in which only high vowels were voiceless.

All the synchronic data are embedded in a genetic framework. The study of linguistic stocks in which some languages possess the feature being investigated and others do not is particularly strategic for the very initial and very final stages of the development. Hence, where these conditions obtain, languages which do not possess the defining feature of the subtypology can become relevant.

For example, languages with a system of noun-classes can be considered the basis for a subtypology and our study should ideally include all languages of the world with this typological property. However, often in linguistic stocks within which this is an inherited feature, e.g. NIGER-CONGO, NORTH-CAUCASIAN, there are languages in which these classes no longer function so that synchronically, they do not belong to the type. Nevertheless, the existence of "petrified," no longer functioning class-markers in such languages make them relevant for such a study. They provide evidence regarding the very last stages of the process. Further, from such examples, we can derive generalizations concerning the nature of typical survivals and by the application of such methods, we derive clues regarding the former existence of such classes in the more remote past of linguistic stocks which were in this final stage at the earliest reconstructed period. Where the processes unfold with greater rapidity, the former existence of the feature in a historically attested language may be reconstructed, even where related languages do not have it.

Note that the stability of the trait itself enters here as a factor. In those which, unlike nominal classification, have a short "half-life" as, for example, voiceless vowels, the comparative dimension as such becomes correspondingly less important while internal reconstruction based on synchronic data approaches sufficiency.

Although both the methods considered up to now employ the historical-comparative method as a basic ingredient, the next method to be considered, intragenetic comparison, brings in this factor in an essentially different and more central manner. In this method we confine our study to a single linguistic stock. It leads to the construction of a typology confined to languages within that stock on the basis of linguistic traits which are sometimes so idiosyncratic that they cannot lead to a typology which is in principle applicable to all languages. A great advantage is that by starting from a single directly attested or reconstructible base, it becomes possible to follow in detail a set of developments from a given set of initial conditions. The difficulty is in disengaging the presumably more general principle involved so that these can be tested in other independent instances. An example is Bell's study of the BANTU noun prefixes of classes 1, 3, 4, 5 and 18 (Bell 1970a). These are mu-, mu-, mi-, ma- and mu-, respec- tively. In many BANTU languages the vowel is apocopated, leading first to a syllabic consonant and sometimes further to loss of syl- labicity and/or regressive homorganic assimilation to a following consonant. A form like *mi-ti 'trees' might go through the stages m̩ti > ṋti > nti or m̩ti > mti > nti. The following implication chain holds, as far as known, without exception in BANTU. The syncope of vowel in ma → syncope in mi → syncope in mu. The first never occurs. It is then possible to draw up the usual tetrachoric table based, for example, on the two attributes syncope of mu or its absence, and syncope of mi and its absence. The distribution of BANTU languages which results is associated with the implication syncope of mi → syncope of mu as shown in Figure 10.

	mi	m̩
mu	+	−
m̩	+	+

Figure 10

Further generalizations are possible. For example, syncope in stressed syllable → syncope in unstressed syllable and syncope before non-labial consonants → syncope before labial consonants.

The distinctness of this method from the previous ones is that the typology is neither in principle applicable to all languages nor, as in a subtypology, all the languages with a certain non-universal typological feature. In fact "to have mi- as a prefix in Class 4" is not in the usual sense a typological trait, yet it makes sense to talk of a division of BANTU languages into types based on the

presence or absence of this trait. It thus opens up to generalizations a further mass of highly specific traits beyond those non-
universal typological traits in the usual sense which become
susceptible to universal statements by means of synchronic typology.

In the case of the BANTU prefixes the general proposition is
fairly obvious and can be tested from other instances of the development of syllabic consonants, particularly nasals.

Sometimes the problem may be more difficult. Consider the
following case in SLAVIC verb morphology. The first person
singular of the present in all RUSSIAN verbs except the irregular
dam 'I will give' (perfective present) and jem 'I eat' ends in -u,
e.g. délaju 'I do,' berú 'I take,' slýšu 'I hear.' In SLOVENE
every verb has -m in the first singular. Corresponding to the
RUSSIAN forms just quoted, we find in SLOVENE delam, berem
and slišim. Other SLAVIC languages show an intermediate situation, e.g. POLISH, which has dziełam, biorę and slyszę in these
same three verbs. The evidence of OLD CHURCH SLAVIC and
older forms of the SLAVIC languages shows that it is RUSSIAN
which is closer to the earlier situation, since first person -m, is
only found in OLD CHURCH SLAVIC damĭ 'I give,' jamĭ 'I eat,'
vĕmĭ 'I know,' imamĭ 'I have,' and jesmĭ 'I am.' In languages
like SLOVENE this m has spread at the expense of the various
reflexes of the first person nasalized vowel ending (OCS -ǫ, RUS-
SIAN u, POLISH ę, SLOVENE u).

It is beyond the scope of this paper to discuss this matter in
detail. The basic question is why a form confined to five verbs
in the earlier language should have spread so widely at the expense
of a form found in all the other verbs. In Figure 11 the presence
of m in the various main classes of present stem in the SLAVIC
standard languages is indicated by a plus.[7]

---

[7] The parentheses around the plus entry in the second column
for POLISH is meant to indicate that there are only three verbs
in POLISH which have first person -m while most have a reflex
of older SLAVIC -ěj-ǫ. The sequence of events posited here is
that generally accepted by Slavicists. For details see Vaillant
1966, especially 21-27, Vondrák 1928: 111-119 and especially
Nahtigal 1963: 323-325.

	aj-	ej-	e-	i-
OLD CHURCH SLAVIC	–	–	–	–
RUSSIAN	–	–	–	–
UKRAINIAN	–	–	–	–
BYELORUSSIAN	–	–	–	–
POLISH	+	(+)	–	–
CZECH	+	+	–	+
SLOVAK	+	+	+	+
UPPER LUSATIAN	+	–	–	–
LOWER LUSATIAN	+	+	+	+
SLOVENE	+	+	+	+
SERBO-CROATIAN	+	+	+	+
BULGARIAN	+	–	–	–
MACEDONIAN	+	+	+	+

Figure 11

From this table we see that every SLAVIC language in which
the m forms have spread beyond the few irregular verbs in which
they are found in OCS, has them in the aj- stems. From here the
next conjugational class to be affected is the ěj- stems. This
relationship can be stated in the form of an intragenetic implicational generalization. It suggests that the spread of first person
singular m begins with the aj- stems. Historical evidence from
individual SLAVIC languages with -m in several classes shows
in fact that it appears here earliest.

The OLD CHURCH SLAVIC present tense paradigm for the
three main classes of -aj, -e and -i stems is shown in Figure 12,
from which the dual has been omitted (˜ indicates palatalization of
the previous consonant).

	Singular			Plural		
	1	2	3	1	2	3
-aj-	-ajǫ	-aješi	-ajetŭ	-ajemŭ	-ajete	-ajǫtŭ
-e	-ǫ	-eši	-etŭ	-emŭ	-ete	-ǫtŭ
-i	-ǫ	-iši	-itŭ	-imŭ	-ite	-ętŭ

Figure 12

In regard to the -aj stems there is an additional fact not shown in the tables. In OCS, under certain conditions, j was lost inter-vocalically, followed sometimes by vowel assimilation. Thus, alongside of -aješi, we find -aeši and -aaši, but this loss and contraction does not take place before -ǫ. Thus, OCS always has dělajǫ (first singular) and dělajǫtŭ (third plural).

The languages in which -m spreads are precisely those in which the contracted forms of the -aj verbs triumphed. Here, the pres-ence of even the single common OCS verb dami 'I give' (second person singular dasi) and sometimes also imami 'I have' (second person singular imaši), with its clear marking of m versus s for first and second singular, was enough to produce dělam in place of dělajǫ in the first singular. Where, however, as in RUSSIAN the contraction did not occur (cf. RUSSIAN delaješ 'thou dost'), this did not happen. The reasons behind the further spread of -m to other stem classes are not considered here.

There was also contraction in the verb stems in -ej-, and here also, prior contraction is connected with the appearance of -m forms in these verbs.

	(a)		(b)
dělajǫ	dělam	delam	delamV
dělas	dělate	delas	delate
dělat	dělajǫt	delat	delajǫt

Figure 13

The general appearance of the "disliked" SLAVIC conjugation which does not occur is shown in Figure 13 (a) and the preferred form in (b).

In contrast to the BANTU example, the general principle at work is not so easily stateable in general terms, although it clearly has some relation to marking theory. Note that with the loss of final jers in SLAVIC (i.e. ĭ and ŭ), those languages with -m in the first singular no longer distinguished the first singular from the first plural. The result everywhere was an additional vowel on the marked plural which differs from language to language, e.g. POLISH dziełamy 'we do,' SERBO-CROATION delamo, etc. In this way the plural as a block opposed disyllabic endings to the singular monosyllabic endings.

The value of the intragenetic method is that given a common base, we have the closest that we can get to a laboratory situation. History manipulates our variables. We can sometimes discover

84   Joseph H. Greenberg

that in those languages in which a particular development took place,
e.g. aje > aa, a certain result ensued and where it did not, this
result did not ensue.

   In the intergenetic method our interest is in verifying a particular
reconstruction in terms not only of its synchronic typological plaus-
ibility but also in regard to the diachronic sequence of changes that
we posit from the reconstructed form to its later reflexes. We do
this by comparing other historically independent cases which had
had similar outcomes. An example is the testing of the hypothesis
that the second segments of PROTO-INDO-EUROPEAN vowels
first posited by DeSaussure were phonetically laryngeal and pharyn-
geal consonants. A study of the changes undergone by these sounds
in other language families may help both in verifying this hypothesis
in general and identifying more specifically the phonetic specifications
of each individual sound (cf. Greenberg 1969).

   This method is related to the dynamicization of subtypologies.
Thus, in regard to the previous example, a study of the subtype of
languages with pharyngeals and laryngeals should lead to diachronic
generalizations and which would then be applied to the case of PROTO
INDO-EUROPEAN. The difference is one of goals and interest. The
former is employed by the general linguist in search of cross-
linguistic diachronic regularities, the latter by the historical linguist with a specialization in a particular linguistic family.

   The intergenetic method can, on the other hand, be distinguished
from the intragenetic method by the presence in the latter of a presumed common genetic base from which all the developments to be
compared proceed. It is not that the intragenetic method deals with
related languages and the intergenetic method with unrelated languages. A comparison of the genesis of nasal vowels in ROMANCE
and INDIC is an intergenetic comparison because the systems of
oral vowels from which they started were at that point quite different
from each other. Nor would a discovery of a deeper relationship
between INDO-EUROPEAN and the CAUCASIAN languages make
an intergenetic comparison of the changes of laryngeals and pharyngeals any less intergenetic unless it could be shown that they both
arose from an identical earlier system. Different linguistic phenom
ena will therefore correspond in general to different genetic depth
in regard to the point at which the intragenetic method becomes
applicable.

   The areal method should also be included as a fifth type of
dynamic comparison. In principle it enters as a factor in all of

the methods just mentioned and it, also, is capable of application
on an intergenetic plane leading to generalizations about the role
of contact in diachronic change.   For example, THAI languages
are almost all SVO, prepositional and have NG order.   These and
other associated word order properties are in general very stable
within the THAI group.   However, KHAMTI and AHOM have SOV
order, and along with this, show variability in the genitive construction.   It can hardly be accidental that these languages are geo-
graphically isolated from the main body of THAI languages and in
contact with SINO-TIBETAN languages.   One can compare this
case with others that involve similar contact factors, e.g. AMHARIC
and other SEMITIC languages (cf. Ferguson 1971, especially p.15).

We can at least hypothesize that under these circumstances SVO
order is the first word order property to be affected, and that the
genitive order is then affected, but that a change from preposition
to postposition is a much slower development marked by the occurrence of constructions in which old prepositions are accompanied
by historically recent postpositions on the noun in much the same
way that, with the opposite order of elements, INDO-EUROPEAN
case suffixes are in many languages accompanied by prepositions.

4.   Diachronic Universals and Explanatory Theory

At a number of points in the previous exposition, the intimate
relationship of synchronic and diachronic factors was evident.
This relationship also holds at higher explanatory levels.   For
example, marking theory involves a whole cluster of by now familiar characteristics of marked and unmarked properties of languages,
and this in turn leads to a structure of generalizations from which
we can, in individual cases, deduce more specific generalizations
for testing.   The relation to diachronic origin theories regarding
the marked category has thus far been mostly applied in phonology.

Attention to diachronic factors not only helps to account for
specific synchronic generalizations, it also helps in explaining the
cooccurrence of some of the characteristics of marked as against
unmarked properties.   For example, in phonology, marked features most often arise as conditioned variants of their corresponding
unmarked features.   This origin factor can be called in to explain
why, for example, the marked feature is both textually less frequent
and why it is the implicans in implicational relationships.   It tends
to be less frequent because it arises in limited environments, and
it is always accompanied by the unmarked feature because the
latter was the precondition for its occurrence and usually continues

in the remaining environments which were not part of the conditions
for the change.

The diachronic factor also plays an important role in the explanation of exceptions to synchronic generalization. This occurs at
a number of distinguishable levels. There are individual language
exceptions to low level generalizations. For example, word final
position is a favored environment for vowel devoicing. In general
the occurrence of word internal voiceless vowels implies the presence of final voiceless vowels. However, there are exceptions.
Of these most involve the synchronic factor of regular stress in
the word final syllable. In the case of JAPANESE, however, the
absence of final voiceless vowels is because they appeared so early
in this position that they have gone on to the next stage for voiceless vowels, namely, vowel loss.

An instance of an exception on a higher level is the following.
In general the number of phonemes exhibiting a marked feature
is less than or equal to the number of those characterized for the
unmarked feature. For example, there appear to be no exceptions
to the generalization that the number of nasalized vowel phonemes
is never larger than the number of oral vowel phonemes. Length
in vowels exhibits in general the characteristics of a marked feature. However, if anything, the number of long vowels tends to be
equal or even larger than the number of short vowels. In this case,
so to speak, an entire generalization is missing from the structure
of marking generalizations. Diachronic origin theory shows that
long vowels often arise by a process of vowel contraction or the
monophthongisation of diphthongs, which results in vowels with
phonetic qualities different from those of any previously existing
vowel of the system.

This example can be used to illustrate another point in relation
to synchronic marking theory. In the case of relational features
it makes no synchronic sense to assert the implicational relationship that usually holds in a marking hierarchy. Thus, we cannot
assert that the presence of long vowels implies the presence of
short vowels but not vice versa, since by definition there can be
no long vowels in the phonological sense without there being short
vowels.

However, the same diachronic factor which corresponds to the
implicational relationship in other instances holds here. Historically
the short vowels continue the original vowels, while the long vowels
arise by conditioned changes, e.g. intervocalic consonant loss and

subsequent contraction of the resulting vowel sequences. Hence, the short vowels may be expected to exhibit also the other synchronic properties characteristic of segments which continue the earlier segments not found in the environment in which the conditional changes occur, which gave rise to the marked features.

The previous statement regarding vowel length requires a qualification. In some instances the short vowels exhibit the general characteristics of a marked feature. MASSORETIC HEBREW had several short vowels, the shwas, which were in the Tiberian tradition, four in number, while there were seven "long vowels."[8] These latter show all the usual characteristics of an unmarked category. In this case it is the long vowels which continue the older vowels with relatively unchanged phonetic qualities while the shwas result from conditioned changes in certain unstressed open syllables.

We see from this and similar examples that it is the nature of the process that gives rise to them that is decisive in producing marked and unmarked status rather than the inherent nature of the features as such. Thus, a synchronic typology based on vowel length as such will put together systems in which short vowels result from conditioned change of certain of the older vowels of a non-quantitative system and those in which it is the long vowels which result from conditioned changes. Systems with these two different origins will show not only different marking relationship, but also other characteristic differences. In a sense, much as in synchronic grammar the notion of deep structure allows us to distinguish superficially similar surface structures, so in typology

---

[8] Three of the shwas in general only occurred after laryngeal consonants and had vowel colors a̱, e̱, or o̱. The fourth is the so-called moveable shwa (e̱) which was indicated by the same sublinear symbol as that placed under a syllable closing consonant and which is traditionally considered present in unstressed open syllables. Long vowel is put in quotes because, in the traditional Massoretic interpretation, those which were morphophonemically unchangeable were considered long while the others were considered short. It is now generally accepted that these quantitative differences did not exist phonetically for the period of HEBREW described by the Massoretes. The theory of distinctions of vowel length among the unreduced, non-shwa vowels was first enunciated by David Kimhi, ca. 1200. When, in the Middle Ages, the Jews imitated ARABIC quantitative prosody, they equated all the shwas with short vowels and all the non-shwas with long vowels.

the diachronic dimension supplies a similar factor of depth which
distinguishes, in terms of different origins, superficially identical
synchronic types.

In the entire exposition of this paper a central rôle has been
assigned to typology in the investigation of diachronic generalizations and, in particular, to the concept of change of type. However,
in certain respects, the study of universals of change is not coin-
cident with the possibilities provided by a typological framework.
We have already seen, in the case of intragenetic universals, that
it turned out to be useful to include properties of a kind which do
not usually figure in typologies. Some further consideration of
this matter will show both apparent and real instances in which a
typological approach is not sufficient.

Consider first the sort of typology associated with unrestricted
universals. Since all languages belong to one type in such a typology, it would seem that the question of change of type does not
arise. A state-process diagram would show a single state containing all languages and the possibility of change from this state
state would be excluded. We may take the universality of phonetic
vowels as an example. Now the absence of change from this single
universal type does not, of course, rule out the existence of processes which maintain this state and of generalizations about such
processes. Though vowels as such are always present, nevertheless individual vowel systems come and go. This is, however,
only an apparent inadequacy. Any state-process diagram is relative to some particular synchronic typology, and typologies are
capable of indefinite increase in complexity by specifying sub-
properties, e.g. vowel height. Such finer-grained subtypologies
provide a basis for posing questions about the processes by which,
through all the changes in vowel systems, vowels as such are
maintained.

More serious is the problem raised by the following example.
It seems that all languages have abstract terms, and this will then
be an unrestricted universal. Such terms seem to be constantly
recruited from concrete terms by certain characteristic metaphorical changes. In principle there appears to be no reason for excluding the possibilities of various generalizations in relation to
these processes. However, it is hard to see how, in this case,
any changes in type are involved. One might argue that there is
a possible multidimensional typology in which one of the dimensions
would be the existence of a verb meaning 'to understand' with a
derivational or other overt relationship to a verb meaning to 'seize'

or 'grasp,' and so on, with numerous other dimensions. However, such a typology would have so many possible types that each language would in general represent a unique type. If this holds, then no generalizations based on type are possible.

There is another area of generalization about language change in which it is clear that typology, even if based on rules as properties, will not suffice. This is exemplified by the topic of sporadic sound changes such as distance assimilation and dissimilation. This field, pioneered by Grammont, does permit generalizations, although some of them are statistical, e.g. that only certain sounds affect each other (e.g. liquids and nasals),that dissimilation is more frequent than assimilation, that n dissimilates to l (not d), although m dissimilates to b, etc. However, the individual instances which provide the material for generalization cannot be regarded as involving changes of type in any useful way. Moreover, such individual cases are not even examples of rule change, except in a Pickwickian sense, by which any linguistic change whatever is a change of rule. Even this fails, when, as often in the process of borrowing a word from another language, the same characteristic changes occur when compared to the form in the source language.

A similar limitation exists in regard to typology as a basis for synchronic generalization. For example, there are generalizations about sound symbolism in languages which do not appear to be related in any useful way to typologies or to emerge naturally from the typological classification of languages.

The basic purpose of this paper has been to consider the ways in which the scope of the study of universals can be broadened to include the diachronic dimension in an essential manner. The contributions of such an approach would seem to be manifold. Diachronic principles are involved in the explanation of both low and higher level synchronic generalizations. In so doing they often explain exceptions. They also go even further than synchronic typology in subsuming under general principles not only non-universal typological traits, but often even highly idiosyncratic language-specific rules which can be treated as evidence of transitions between less complex, more widely occurring types.

BIBLIOGRAPHY

Bell, A. 1970a. Syllabic consonants. Working Papers on Language Universals 4. B1-B49.

Bell, A. 1970b. A state-process approach to syllabicity and syllabic structure. Doctoral dissertation, Stanford University.

_____. 1971. Some patterns of the occurrence and formation of
syllabic structure. Working Papers on Language Universals
6. 23-138.

Berge, C. 1973. Graphs and hypergraphs, translated by Edward
Minieka. Amsterdam: North Holland Publishing Co., New
York: Elsevier Publishing Co.

Chen, M. 1975. An areal study of nasalization in Chinese. Nasál-
fest, ed. by C.A. Ferguson, L.M. Hyman, and J.J. Ohala, 81-131.
Language Universals Project, Department of Linguistics,
Stanford University.

Ferguson, C.A. 1963. Some assumptions about nasals. Universals of language, ed. by J.H. Greenberg, 42-47. Cambridge:
M.I.T. Press.

_____. 1971. A sample research strategy in language universals.
Working Papers on Language Universals 6. 1-22.

Greenberg, J.H. 1966. Synchronic and diachronic universals in
phonology. Language 42. 508-17.

_____. 1969. Some methods of dynamic comparison in linguistics.
Substance and structure of language, ed. by J. Puhvel, 147-203.
Berkeley and Los Angeles: University of California Press.

Ivanov, V.V. 1958. Tipologija i sravitel'no-istoričeskoje jazykoz-
nanije. Voprosy jazykoznanija 7.5. 34-42.

Jakobson, R. 1958. Typological studies and their contribution to
historical comparative linguistics. Proceedings of the Eighth
International Congress of Linguists (Oslo) 17-25.

Li, Charles. 1975 (ed.) Word order and word order change.
Austin: University of Texas Press.

Marouzeau, J. 1961. Lexique de la terminologie linguistique.
Paris: Genthner. 3rd ed.

Nahtigal, R. 1963. Slavjanskije jazyki. Moscow: Izdatel'stvo
Inostrannoj Literatury. (Russian translation of the second
Slovene edition, 1952.)

Sharadzenidze, T.S. 1970. Language typology, synchrony and diachrony. Theoretical problems of typology and the North Eurasian languages, ed. by L. Dezsö and P. Hajdú, 35-44. Amsterdam: B.R. Grüner.

Skalička, V. 1968. Über die Typologie der finno-ugrischen Sprachen. Congressus internationalis Fenno-Ugristarum Helsingiae habitus I. 494-8. Helsinki: Societas Fenno-Ygrica.

Vaillant, A. 1966. Grammaire comparée des langues slaves, III: Le verbe. Paris: Klincksieck.

Vondrák, W. 1928. Vergleichende slavische Grammatik, II: Formenlehre und Syntax. Second ed., revised by O. Grünenthal. Göttingen: Vandenhoeck and Ruprecht.

Weinreich, U., W. Labov, and M. Herzog. 1968. Empirical foundations for a theory of language change. Directions for historical linguistics, 97-195. Austin: University of Texas Press.

Language Contact

EDITH A. MORAVCSIK

ABSTRACT

A general rationale of language contact studies is provided by
showing how such studies contribute to the basic task of linguistic
research. The substance and application of constraints on borrowing is discussed and some such constraints are proposed as consistent with all known facts.

I wrote this paper as part of my work for the Stanford Project
on Language Universals. I am grateful to members of the Project
for discussions and particularly to Charles Ferguson and Joan Kahr
for detailed comments on a previous version of the paper.

94   Edith A. Moravcsik

CONTENTS

1. Introduction

I will assume that the basic purpose of linguistic research is to explain why human beings communicate by means of orally and nasally articulated sounds the way they can be observed to communicate and not some other ways. The primary data to be explained are, therefore, linguistic utterances; and the task of linguists involves establishing the total set of actual linguistic utterances; establishing what the logically possible set of linguistic utterances is; determining what the inclusion relation is between the set of logically conceivable linguistic utterances and the set of actually observable ones; and, if the latter is properly, rather than improperly, included in the former, explaining why exactly that particular subset of the logical possibilities is actually manifested that is in fact manifested, rather than some other subset. Since the number of actual linguistic utterances used by people is apparently infinite, and so is, of course, the number of logically possible linguistic utterances, the comparison of these two sets can be effected only by representing each in terms of a finite set of statements that can generate all and only that infinite number of utterances that are included within the set in question. The above task characterization can therefore be restated as involving the observation of linguistic utterances, writing a grammar that can generate all of them and only those, writing another grammar that generates all logically possible utterances, observed or not, and only those, comparing the two grammars, and explaining why they differ from each other the way they do. As this characterization reveals, grammars, as all scientific generalizations, serve both as explanations and also as things to be explained. By token of its statements being restricted within the set of logically possible grammatical statements, a grammar of some set of actual utterances is able to explain why particular linguistic utterances are the way they are as opposed to ways they could be; but the very fact that its statements are a proper subset of the set of logically possible grammatical statements constitutes itself a further explanandum.

Writing one single grammar for the set of all human utterances would characterize the concept "human linguistic utterance." However, characterizing and explaining the properties of this concept would not accomplish characterizing and explaining all logically non-necessary facts that we can observe about the linguistic communication of humans. This is because not all human beings naturally use all linguistic utterances that all other human beings use. Rather, what turns out to be the case is that whereas all normal adult human beings are capable of expressing and understanding the same infinite set of meanings that all other human beings are, systematically characterizable subgroups of humans consistently utilize only subsets of the set of synonymous sentences that comprise the total of all sentences used by all human beings; and that, furthermore, the sentence sets used by such groups have some recurrent properties. In other words, members of the set of all human utterances have a particular distribution over the members of the class of all human beings and this distribution is furthermore principled in that both the people using restricted subsets of the set of all human utterances, and also these utterances within each subset themselves, have shared properties that delimit them within the class of all people and within the class of all human utterances, respectively. Now, if linguistic theory characterized only what is a possible human linguistic utterance, then any distribution of the members of this set over the members of the set of human beings would be equally consistent with the theory. In order, therefore, to account for all logically non-necessary facts about how human beings communicate linguistically, the theory has to describe and explain not only what is expressed and how by people but also who says the same thing how.

The most obvious fact about how synonymous sets of linguistic utterances are distributed over people is that there are classes of people that not only prefer to use certain subsets but are in fact only capable of expressing and understanding thoughts through such subsets. Users of such mutually unintelligible synonymous sentence subsets, or languages, constitute age-wise and sex-wise heterogeneous groups whose members in most cases also differ from each other in knowledge, beliefs, habits, physical characteristics, and material means and whose members nonetheless all interact in their creative and social activities to form individual societies. The characterization and the explanation of the recurrent properties of such societal language communities as against properties of random human groups, and of the recurrent properties of such languages, as against properties of random sentence sets, is thus part of the task of linguists.

Unique temporal and spatial coordinates defining language communities (commonly abbreviated as proper names such as "English" or "Hungarian") are not, however, the only property type that correlate with the distribution of synonymous sentence sets. First of all, any single one language also includes a number of synonymous expressions for all sentential meanings; and the use of at least some of these variant expressions is also systematically correlated with interlocutor properties. Furthermore, it also appears that both the particular interlocutor properties that are relevant, and even some properties of the sentence sets in question, are recurrent across language communities and languages. Thus, interlocutor properties with which the use of synonymous sentences within any language may correlate include properties related to area of residence, sex, age, education, religion, financial level, and social level, whereas they appear to exclude others such as climate or diet. Crosslinguistically recurrent ways in which such dialects and styles deviate from each other within the same language have been found at least for some, such as for "baby talk" or "foreigners' talk."

Describing and explaining the non-necessary properties of the set of all linguistic utterances and language-, dialect-, and style-size subsets of these sets, however, still does not account for all logically non-necessary observations that we can make about how human beings communicate with each other linguistically. The fact that has remained unmentioned thus far is that the distribution of language-size sentence sets over the past and present language communities of the world is also non-random. In particular, there are special relationships among some languages that do not obtain among others just in case the speakers of these languages have a particular temporal or spatial relation to each other; and, furthermore, languages spoken by similarly related speakers show recurrent similarities. No observation about such distinctively and systematically related languages would of course be accounted for by a theory which only characterizes the concepts "possible human utterance," "possible human language," "possible areal dialect of a language" and the concepts of various styles: any random spatial and temporal distribution of the languages themselves in the world would be consistent with such a theory. A language labelled TWELFTH CENTURY ENGLISH, for example, and a language labelled TWENTIETH CENTURY ENGLISH may differ from each other, in terms of such a theory, in any way permitted by the limits that the theory defines as determining differences between any two random members of the set of human languages; and, similarly, languages such as SPANISH and YAQUI whose speakers have interacted for centuries would be allowed to differ as much as SPANISH and ESKIMO whose speakers have not been in contact. But since such predictions are counterfactual -- we do know that two such time-sequentially or interactionally related languages cannot differ from each other in any way in which two languages not so related can -- linguistic theory must further be endowed with the ability of characterizing such subsets of human languages as "two distinct languages in immediate temporal subsequence relation" or "two distinct languages whose speakers interact."

In sum: given the basic assumption that linguistic theory is to explain all the logically non-necessary facts about how human beings communicate in terms of orally articulated sounds, it follows that linguistic theory has to be able to characterize the concept "actual human linguistic utterance" within the class of logically possible human linguistic utterances, to impose constraints on various subsets of human linguistic utterances such as those constituting a language, a dialect, and some particular style, and to impose constraints on various subsets of human languages correlated with the temporal and interactional relations of their speakers. Referring to the familiar division of linguistics, general linguistic proper, sociolinguistics, and developmental linguistics define what can and what cannot be a human linguistic utterance, a human language, a dialect of a language, and some style of a language; historical linguistics defines what can and what cannot be a pair of languages whose speakers are time-sequentially related in a particular way; and language contact research defines what can and what cannot be two languages whose speakers are interactionally related. The basic similarity that underlies each of these tasks is that in each case the goal is to determine the membership of some subclass of communicative means used by some systematically characterizable class of human communicators. For "general linguistic proper," the relevant class of human communicators is that of all human beings; for "sociolinguistics" and "developmental linguistics," it is some subclass thereof defined in terms of particular interlocutor properties such as social status, sex, or age; for "historical linguistics," the relevant class of human communicators is that of two tautolingual language communities in some time-sequential relation with each other; and for "language contact research," the relevant class of communicators is that of two contemporaneous non-tautolingual language communities in some interactional relation with each other. The various subfields of linguistics, including the subfield of language contact research, thus all receive justification from contributing to the single purpose of describing and explaining how human beings communicate by means of orally and nasally produced sounds.

The purpose of this present paper is to focus in particular on generalizations about language contact and to explore the nature and use of such statements. Section 2.1 will discuss the form and content of generalizations about language contact; section 2.2 will demonstrate their explanatory use; and section 2.3 will probe into how such statements can themselves be explained.

2. The Substance and Use of Generalizations about Language Contact

2.1 Constraints on borrowing

The term "borrowing" will be understood to refer to a process whereby a language acquires some structural property from another language that is contemporary to it. The acquiring language will be called "borrowing language," the language from which the property is acquired will be called "source language," and the structural feature that is initially the property of the source language but not of the borrowing language and that comes to be shared by both will be called "borrowed property."[1] Given these basic definitions, the term "constraint on borrowing" will apply to a statement that excludes some subset of the set of language-structural properties from membership in the set of possible borrowed properties. All such constraining statements will therefore have to have the following form: "A P_x cannot be borrowed from an L_1 into an L_2 (where P_x is a (possibly unary) class of language-structural properties and L_1 and L_2 are each a structurally or non-structurally characterized class of human languages that may or may not be distinct from each other and that may be properly or improperly included subsets of the set of all human languages)." The immediate purpose of language contact research is to formulate and test particular hypotheses that fit this schema; and my purpose in this section is to present some such hypotheses that, according to the testimony of that portion of the vast literature on borrowing that I am familiar with, stand so far unrefuted.

Since, as the above formulation reveals, formulating hypotheses about constraints on borrowing really involves substituting constants

---

[1]Needless to say, this use of the term "borrowing" is very different from the way the term is used in everyday language. Whereas, according to everyday usage, an object is borrowed if it passes from the use of the owner into the temporary use of someone else and thus at no point in time is it being used by both, according to linguistic usage the source language may continue to include the particular property that has been "borrowed" from it. Thus, what the latter implies is 'permanently acquiring a copy of an object,' rather than 'temporarily acquiring an object itself.' It should be noted that the term "borrowing" can also be applied to instances of intra- rather than inter-linguistic borrowing; such as to borrowing from one dialect, or style, or idiolect, into another. The nature of such processes is not considered in this paper.

for the variables P_x, L_1, L_2 in the above schema, it will be useful to first
survey the range of possible such constants -- that is to say, to
establish what exactly is the range of logical possibilities that we
are attempting to restrict. Let us first consider the logically
possible range of P_x. P_x, as stated above, is any structural property of languages -- with one restriction that follows necessarily
from the concept of borrowing. Since the concept of borrowing
involves a process whereby one language <u>acquires</u> a structural
feature from another one; and since the concept "acquiring" means
'coming to possess something that one did not have before,' it must
be that the borrowed property, P_x, is not a universal property of
all human languages. The total range of P_x that is logically available will therefore be characterized by enumerating the total set
of all language-structural properties that are non-universal. Assuming that all properties of language structure are reflected by
some properties of grammars[2] and assuming the concept of grammars suggested by Sanders (see especially Sanders 1972), the following is a complete list of possible grammar properties and thus
a complete characterization of language properties as well:

1. properties of interpretable phonetic representations:
    a. membership of the phonetic feature set involved;
    b. well-formedness conditions on their simultaneity and
       precedence relations

2. properties of interpretable semantic representations:
    a. membership of the semantic features involved;
    b. well-formedness conditions on their grouping relations

3. properties of the mapping relation between interpretable
    phonetic and interpretable semantic representations:
    a. syntactic, phonological, and lexical equivalences of
       the additive-deletive or substitutive types (or "trans-
       formational rules");
    b. non-equivalences (or "derivational and trans-deriva-
       tional constraints");
    c. rule-applicational principles.

---

[2] The only aspect of language use which falls outside the concept
of language structure and thus also outside the concept of grammar
is frequency differences in the use of synonyms. Although it is of
course conceivable that a language will be affected by another one
in this respect, this type of language contact phenomenon is considered insignificant here and will be left out of discussion.

Of these, I will conservatively assume the universality of only one class of properties as a whole — namely properties of interpretable semantic representations.[3] The range of possible P_x-s is thus taken to be characterized by the properties listed under 1. and 3. above.

Turning now to the logically possible ranges of the other two variables in our schema, L_1 and L_2, as stated above, are any two subclasses of languages, whether distinct or not, structurally or non-structurally defined, and exhaustive of the class of all languages or not. In an optimally general instance of the statement schema, both L_1 and L_2 will refer to the class of all languages; the statement will then exclude some structural properties as borrowable with respect to any source language and any borrowing language. Alternatively, and less generally, L_1 and/or L_2 may be restricted to some properly included subclass of human languages that is structurally defined. The most obvious type of such restriction would hold for borrowing languages and would pertain to the absence of some other borrowed property in that language. Thus, a statement may stipulate that a property P_a cannot be a borrowed property from L_1 into L_2 such that L_2 does not already have the

---

[3] The empirical nature of this claim is being questioned by some linguists and philosophers; compare, for instance, J. Moravcsik 1975: 73. Although, given the fact that it is the synonymy of infinite sets of sentences or discourses that is being claimed, the truth of the claim can never be demonstrated, I take the claim to be empirically refutable. Refutation of the claim will be constituted by the discovery of a sentence or discourse in a language which has no synonymous expression in some other language. The actual test conditions under which such a refutation could be established would include the availability of an individual fully competent in at least two languages. The particular behavior on his part that would establish the refutation of this claim would be his recognition that the meaning of a particular sentence or discourse S_1 in language L_1 indeed presupposes and entails the meanings of appropriate sets of sentences in language L_1 that have been independently established as jointly accounting for the total meaning of S_1; and his subsequent inability to recognize any sentence or discourse in language L_2 whose meaning would presuppose and entail all and only those meanings. Apart from interpretable semantic representations, the only other class of grammatical properties whose universality as a whole has been proposed is 3.c., rule-applicational principles; see, for instance, Sanders 1972.

property P_b borrowed from L_1 into L_2 -- or, in other words, that
a property can be borrowed into a language only if that language
has already borrowed another property from the same source.
Thirdly, it is also conceivable that L_1 and/or L_2 will be defined
non-structurally. The most likely such non-structural stipulations
will pertain to the mutual relations of speakers of the two languages.
Thus, for example, one may hypothesize that some particular structural property -- such as the phonetic form of stressless lexemes --
cannot be borrowed from L_1 into L_2 if L_1 is a non-prestigious language for the speakers of L_1.

Having now at least roughly conceptualized the total range of
logically possible constraining hypotheses on borrowing, let us
turn to the question whether any of them are empirically true at all.
In view of the many instances of borrowing documented in the literature, it would first appear that there are perhaps no constraints
at all on what can be borrowed and between what kinds of languages.
This seems to be initially the case since a number of plausible hypotheses concerning such constraints are multiply refuted by evidence. I will briefly survey some of these first.

It appears, first of all, that the range of borrowable properties
is not coterminous with any of the three major types into which
grammatical rules fall from the point of view of the mode of interpretation of the constituents involved in them: there are well-
attested cases of borrowing both syntactic and phonological and
lexical rules (for examples of all three types, see Weinreich 1966:
14-36). Furthermore, there is also ample evidence to indicate that
borrowed meaning-sound-equating -- or lexical -- rules are not
restricted to lexical rules proper -- that is, to the kind which provides for the substitution of an ordered phonetic segment sequence
for a semantic constituent -- but also include ordering and supra-
segment-assigning rules. The borrowing of syntactic constituent-
ordering rules has been conjectured for instance in the following
cases: ETHIOPIAN SEMITIC languages borrowing "Modifier precedes Modified"-type ordering rule(s) from CUSHITIC languages
(Leslau 1945; cf. also Bach 1970, Hudson 1972, Little 1974); ĀHOM,
a THAI language, borrowing "Modifier precedes Modified"-type
ordering rule(s) either from ASSAMESE, an INDOEUROPEAN language, or from some TIBETO-BURMESE language (Grierson 1902:
26); MUNDA languages borrowing "Modifier precedes Modified"-
type ordering rule(s) from DRAVIDIAN languages (Pinnow 1960;
cf. also Lehmann 1973); some KWA languages such as NUPE,
YORUBA, EWE and IGBO borrowing "Possession precedes
Possessor"-type ordering rule(s) from BANTU languages

(Hyman 1975).[4] The borrowing of an intonation pattern into YID-
DISH is claimed by Weinreich (Weinreich 1966: 38).

In addition to some hypotheses that would universally exclude
from the class of borrowable properties some major rule types,
there are also some plausible hypotheses of another kind that also
turn out to be counter-to-fact. Some of these hypotheses would
make the borrowing of some property dependent on some structural
property of the borrowing language; others would make it dependent
on some non-structural properties of the two languages involved.
One a priori plausible hypothesis of the former kind pertains to
restricting the possibilities involved in borrowing sound-meaning
correspondences, in that it stipulates that if a language borrows a
particular phonetic expression for a particular meaning, this happens only if the language does not already have an expression of the
given meaning by the same means. Particular manifestations of
this principle may be, first of all, that a language borrows a monolexemic expression for a meaning only if it otherwise has only multilexemic or periphrastic, expression for it; and, second, that if
it borrows a new monolexemic expression for a meaning which already has a monolexemic expression in the language, the type of the
lexeme will be of a different kind: if a language already expresses
a particular meaning through a particular intonation pattern, it will
not borrow another intonation pattern from another language to express the same meaning (although it may borrow a morpheme or an
order pattern as a synonym for the indigenous intonation); if a language expresses a certain meaning through a particular temporal
order pattern of two constituents, it will not borrow a different
order pattern for the same constituents as an alternative expression
of that meaning (although it may borrow an intonation pattern or a
morpheme as alternative expressions); and if a language has a
particular lexical item to express a particular meaning, it will
not borrow another lexical item to alternatively express the very
same meaning (although it may borrow an intonation or order pattern as alternative expressions). The hypothesized principle
would find some intuitive appeal in the general assumptions that
borrowing takes place with the borrowing individuals having some
purpose in mind; and that a legitimate purpose for speakers of a
language is to obtain an alternative expression for a concept if and
only if this alternative expression is of a different type (where
"type" refers to monolexemic versus multilexemic expression and,

---

[4] For extensive descriptions of the geographic distribution of
various syntactic constituent ordering patterns in Africa, see Heine
1975, and in Africa, Europe, and Asia see Masica 1976: especially 13-39.

within monolexemic expressions, to morphemic versus precedential
versus intonational expressions).

There is some support for this hypothesis. In particular, in a
substantial number of cases borrowed morphemes, for instance,
provide expressions for meanings for which no monolexemic expression was available in the borrowing language before. Such
concepts usually include concepts introduced with the influx of the
culture of the source language. Thus, for example, Spicer points
out that in YAQUI "to all those items [newly introduced from SPAN-
ISH culture] which had no aboriginal equivalents SPANISH names
were applied; examples are sewing machine, clock, lamp, chimney,
fork, window, and chair" (Spicer 1943: 423-4). Furthermore, even
if objects of the same kind do have lexemic expressions in the borrowing language as the kind of object introduced from the source
culture, the borrowed lexemes, in a somewhat onomatopoetic way,
are often reserved to designate the foreign tokens of that object
type, with the native term either reserved for the native tokens or
to cover both. Thus, for example, in AMERICAN YIDDISH, the
form lójer, borrowed from ENGLISH lawyer, has the meaning 'a
lawyer in the U.S.' whereas the indigenous morpheme advokát
means 'a lawyer elsewhere but in the U.S.' or simply 'a lawyer'
(Weinreich 1966: 55). Similarly, the borrowed word dancing in
HUNGARIAN means 'dancing American style,' whereas the corresponding HUNGARIAN term tánc refers to any kind of dance. The
example of NAHUATL is especially interesting in this respect since
here newly introduced cultural objects were alternatively named
either by the borrowed name, or by the corresponding indigenous
name and the qualifier 'Spanish,' or, in some cases by the borrowed
name and the qualifier 'Spanish.' Thus, the concept 'garlic' had
these two synonymous expressions: caxtillan xonacatl "Spanish
onion" (where xonacatl is a native term for onion) and ajo (which
is a borrowed form from SPANISH). An example of the borrowed
form used in conjunction with the qualifier 'Spanish' is castilla vino
'Spanish wine' (Karttunen and Lockhart 1975: 91ff).

In spite of these examples that are consistent with the hypothesis,
there is also much evidence that amply bears out its lack of truth.
Languages do borrow sound-meaning correspondences even if the
indigenous language itself is able to provide a monolexemic expression for the same meaning which expression is of the same kind as
the one borrowed. All the relevant examples that I can cite show
that languages borrow morphemes which become synonyms to indigenous morphemes. Thus, for example, YAQUI has borrowed, in
addition to the great number of SPANISH lexemes for which there

were no monolexemic equivalents in YAQUI itself, also a number
of lexemes for which similar equivalents were available in the language. The most striking illustration of this is that even lexemes
for the members of the immediate family were borrowed, such as
mamá 'mother,' synonymous with YAQUI ?ae or máala: or papá
grande 'grandfather,' synonymous with YAQUI ?apa (Spicer 1943;
cf. also Johnson 1943). Similarly, YAQUI also borrowed subordinate
clause markers from SPANISH which were then used either in cooccurrence with or in replacement of indigenous morphemes of the
same function. For example, a subject complement clause may be
formed to alternatively include either the clause-final native morpheme -kai or the clause-initial borrowed morpheme ke (spelled
que in SPANISH); or both:

a. Tuisi tu?i hu hamut bwika-kai.
"very good this woman sing-that"

b. Tuisi tu?i ke hu hamut bwika.   'It is very good that
"very good that this woman sing"   this woman sings.'

c. Tuisi tu?i ke hu hamut bwika-kai.
"very good that this woman sing-that"

(compare SPANISH: Es muy bueno que esa mujer cante. "is very
good that this woman sings," 'It is very good that this woman sings.')
(Lindenfeld 1975).[5] A similar example of a language borrowing a
morpheme when it already has one expressing the same meaning
is NAHUATL which borrowed from SPANISH the plural morpheme
-s even though it had a plural morpheme of its own, -me. The
case is all the more similar to the YAQUI example since just as in
YAQUI the indigenous complementizer and its borrowed equivalent

_____

[5] A further plausible hypothetical restriction on lexical borrowing
would be that if a language does borrow an expression of the same
type for a meaning that is already available in the language, this
happens only if the language in fact borrows two (or, in general, more
than one) such expressions which do not overlap in meaning with each
other and which jointly exhaust the meaning of the indigenous lexeme.
Although some instances of borrowing can indeed be interpreted as
an attempt to replace an ambiguous (or vague) indigenous lexeme by
two more specific borrowed ones (such as the case of YAQUI borrowing SPANISH cuando 'when' and si 'if' to replace (or cooccur with)
the indigenous -o which covers both meanings; cf. Lindenfeld 1975),
many other instances of lexical borrowing, as the above examples in
the text indicate, cannot be so interpreted.

could occur either singly or jointly in the same sentence, in NA-
HUATL, too, the plural of some nouns (in particular, of SPANISH
loans) could be alternatively expressed either by suffixing -me or
by suffixing -s or by suffixing -sme (examples for the latter two
are españoles and españolesme both meaning 'Spaniard' and formed
from the singular español 'Spaniard') (Karttunen and Lockhart 1975:
49ff). For further examples of borrowed morphemes that are synonymous to indigenous morphemes, see loanwords in ATESO as
discussed in Scotton and Okeju 1973: especially 873.

Another hypothesis of the kind that attempts to make the borrowing of a particular structural property dependent on some structural
properties of the borrowing language and that is also refuted in spite
of its initial appeal would serve to restrict the borrowing of ordering
regularities. The hypothesis stipulates that the ordering of two syntactic constituents can be borrowed only if the phonetic form of at
least some members of each constituent class is also, or has also
been, borrowed. This principle would predict, for instance, that
if a language borrows an ordering regularity according to which the
descriptive adjective should precede its nominal head, this is possible only if the phonetic forms of at least some adjectives and some
nouns have also been borrowed from the same language. The intuitive rationale behind this hypothesis would be that a borrowed order
pattern is always extracted from the corresponding phonetically borrowed phrase. Although the hypothesis may be valid in some cases,
I know of two instances where it is not. One of these two cases is
the "adposition precedes its head" rule which YAQUI, a UTO-
AZTECAN language, is conjectured to have borrowed from SPAN-
ISH. YAQUI, prior to SPANISH influence, is said to have postposed
all of its adpositions. In present-day YAQUI, however, according
to Johnson (1943: 432), all adpositions apparently freely vary in their
preposed and postposed positions; the phrase 'for my father,' for
instance, has these two alternative expressions: ?in-ačai betči?ibo
"my-father for" and bétči?ibo ?in-ačai "for my-father." Since
nouns are known to have been borrowed from SPANISH into YAQUI,
this is a counterexample to the generalization only if it is indeed
true that the phonetic forms of no prepositions have been borrowed
from SPANISH into YAQUI. My assumption that this is so is not
based on anybody's explicit statement but simply on the fact that
none of the sources that I consulted (Spicer 1943, Johnson 1943,
Lindenfeld 1975) listed prepositions among the borrowed elements
in YAQUI. [6]

---

[6] Lindenfeld (1975) mentions that YAQUI borrowed the phonetic
form of the SPANISH proposition para (as parake/pake) in its

The other counterexample to the hypothesis that the ordering of only such syntactic constituent classes can be borrowed of which at least some members are, or have been, borrowed in their phonetic manifestation comes from KONKANI. According to Nadkarni (1975), KONKANI, an INDOEUROPEAN language of India, has borrowed a rule from the DRAVIDIAN languages according to which relative clauses of a particular type must immediately precede their heads. If our hypothesis were correct, KONKANI should also have borrowed entire relative clauses and head constituents in their phonetic manifestations from DRAVIDIAN. There is nothing in Nadkarni's account which would lead us to believe that this may be the case; to the extent that it is indeed not the case, the hypothesis is again proven to be false. It is very interesting, however, to note that the particular type of relative clause in KONKANI for which this borrowed order holds is nonetheless defined by the presence of some other structural properties that are also borrowed from DRAVIDIAN. Thus, even though it is not true that the constituent types whose ordering is borrowed from DRAVIDIAN (the relative clause and the head) have members that have DRAVIDIAN phoneticization in KONKANI, it is true that these constituents have some additional DRAVIDIAN properties. The facts, gleaned from Nadkarni's description, are the following.[7] KONKANI has two types of finite relative clauses from the point of view of the lexeme that is used as the relative pronoun in them. In one type, the relative pronoun is jo which has no other function in the language. In the other type, the relative pronoun is khanco which has the additional function of being the interrogative pronoun 'which.' Examples of the two types of relative clause are these:

a.   jo mhāntāro pepar vāccat$\left\{ \begin{array}{l} \text{āssa} \\ \text{āssa-ki} \end{array} \right\}$ to ḍakṭaru āssa

    "which old:man paper reading$\left\{ \begin{array}{l} \text{is} \\ \text{is-particle} \end{array} \right\}$that doctor is"

b.   khanco mhāntāro pepar vāccat$\left\{ \begin{array}{l} \text{āssa-ki} \\ \text{*āssa} \end{array} \right\}$ to ḍakṭaru āssa

    "which old:man paper reading$\left\{ \begin{array}{l} \text{is-particle} \\ \text{is} \end{array} \right\}$ that doctor is,"

both meaning 'The old man who is reading a newspaper is a doctor.' As these examples show, the two types differ not only in the choice

---

(ftnt. 6 cont.)
complementizer function. There is no evidence, however, that it is also used in YAQUI with nominal, rather than sentential, heads.

[7] In what follows, some of the statements and some of the example sentences are not based on explicit statements and examples in Nadkarni but have rather been inferred from what he says.

of the relative pronoun but also in the optional versus obligatory
absence of the particle ki at the end of the clause. The particle ki,
just as the form khanco, has double function in the language: just
as khanco is used both as a relative pronoun and also as an interrogative pronoun, ki is used both as a relative clause particle and
as an interrogative particle. The following two sentences illustrate
the interrogative use of khanco and -ki, respectively:

   c. khanco mhāntāro pepar vāccat $\begin{Bmatrix} \text{āssa} \\ *\text{āssa -ki} \end{Bmatrix}$
      "which old:man paper reading$\begin{Bmatrix} \text{is} \\ *\text{is -particle} \end{Bmatrix}$"
      'Which old man is reading the newspaper?'

   d. mhāntāro pepar vāccat āssa-ki
      "old:man paper reading is-particle"
      'Is the old man reading the newspaper?'

The rule concerning the optional versus obligatory absence of the
particle ki is that if the relative pronoun is the question pronoun
khanco, the question particle ki must cooccur with it in the relative
clause; and if the relative pronoun is the form jo, ki may or may
not cooccur with it. Of the two types of relative clause, Nadkarni
takes the first one to be the indigenous kind and the second, borrowed
from KANNADA. That the first kind is indeed indigenous is supported
by the fact that languages genetically related to KONKANI, such as
HINDI, know only this type. That the second one is borrowed from
KANNADA is supported by the fact that KANNADA only has the second kind of relative clause structure, as well as by the independently
supported contention that KANNADA has exerted structural influence on KONKANI. A HINDI sentence evidencing the existence of
the first structural type in HINDI, and a KANNADA sentence evidencing the existence of the second structural type in KANNADA
are these:

   e. HINDI:
      jo būṛhā akhbār paṛh rahā hai vo ḍākṭar hai
      "which man old paper reading is that doctor is"

   f. KANNADA:
      yāva mudukanu pēpar ōdutta iddān-ō avanu ḍākṭaranu iddāne
      "which old:man paper reading is-particle that doctor is"

(both meaning 'The old man who is reading the newspaper is a doctor.');
where HINDI jo is not also an interrogative pronoun but KANNADA
yāva is indeed also an interrogative pronoun and the KANNADA particle -o is also an interrogative particle, used, as -ki, in yes-no

questions. In addition to the presence of the interrogative pronoun and interrogative particle, there is one more shared property of the KANNADA relative clause structure and the second type in KON-KANI. This is that both of these, as opposed to the HINDI relative clause and the first, indigenous, KONKANI type, must in all of their occurrences immediately precede their head:

g. HINDI:
   vo ḍākṭar hai jo būrhā akhbār paṛh rahā hai
   "that doctor is which man old paper reading is"

h. KANNADA:
   *avanu ḍākṭaranu iddāne yāva mudukanu pēpar ōdutta iddan-ō
   "that doctor   is which   old:man paper reading is-particle"

i. KONKANI:
   to ḍākṭaru āssa jo mhāntāro pepar vāccat$\begin{Bmatrix} \text{āssa} \\ \text{āssa-ki} \end{Bmatrix}$
   "that doctor is which old:man paper reading$\begin{Bmatrix} \text{is"} \\ \text{is-particle"} \end{Bmatrix}$

j. KONKANI:
   *to ḍākṭaru āssa khanco mhāntāro pepar vāccat āssa-ki
   "that doctor is which old:man paper reading is-particle"

(all meaning 'The old man who is reading the newspaper is a doctor'). The order pattern borrowed from KANNADA -- the obligatory adjacence of relative clause and head -- thus holds only for those relative clauses that are constructed on the KANNADA pattern otherwise as well in that they include an interrogative pronoun for a relative pronoun, rather than a morpheme that has no interrogative pronominal function and in that they include an interrogative particle. Thus the borrowed ordering pattern does imply some other borrowed properties of the constituents to be ordered as well, even though these additional borrowed properties do not include, as our hypothesis would have had it, borrowed phoneticization.

As pointed out by Nadkarni, the KONKANI borrowings from KANNADA are interesting also in that they refute an additional otherwise plausible restriction on borrowings. This hypothesis belongs to the type where a restriction is proposed in terms of certain non-structural properties of the languages involved and it stipulates that nothing can be borrowed from a language which is not regarded to be prestigious by speakers of the borrowing language. According to Nadkarni, KANNADA has no prestige whatever in the eyes of KON-KANI speakers.

Nonetheless, there are some restrictive hypotheses on borrowing which are consistent with all evidence that I am familiar with.
Of the three possible basic types of constraints that were delimited
above -- constraints on borrowable structural properties that are
valid for all human languages; constraints that are stipulated for a
structurally defined subclass of languages; and constraints that are
stipulated for a non-structurally defined subclass of languages --
the sample of seven such unrefuted hypotheses will exemplify the
first (4., 6) and the second (1.-3., 5., 7.). In what follows, I will
state and exemplify them.

1. No non-lexical language property can be borrowed unless the
    borrowing language already includes borrowed lexical items
    from the same source language.

This statement excludes a language that has borrowed properties
from a source language which do not include lexical items. All cases
of borrowing that I know of exemplify this principle.[8]

2. No member of a constituent class whose members do not
    serve as domains of accentuation can be included in the class
    of properties borrowed from a particular source language
    unless some members of another constituent class are also
    so included which do serve as domains of accentuation and
    which properly include the same members of the former class.

This statement excludes a language where "bound morphemes" -
such as clitics, affixes and parts of compound stems -- are borrowed
but no free forms that they are proper parts of; and a language where
phonetic segments or features are borrowed but not accentuated lexemes that they are proper parts of. The principle is exemplified by
the suffix -ette in ENGLISH in words as kitchenette. The suffix
-ette is a borrowing from FRENCH; the condition stated above is
fulfilled by ENGLISH also having forms such as cigarette and sta-
tuette which are FRENCH borrowings in their entirety and which

---

[8]Charles Ferguson points out to me that intonation patterns may
be possible counterexamples: they do get borrowed, at least on the
level of idiolects, without lexical items having previously been taken
over such as in the speech of tourists visiting foreign-speaking countries which, according to him, often shows a transfer of the foreign
intonation pattern into native speech. I do not, however, know of
evidence to indicate that the borrowing of intonation may precede in
time the borrowing of lexical items in the context of language-to-
language borrowing as well.

property include the suffix -ette (Weinreich 1966: 31). The principle, in respect to various types of bound morphemes, has been suggested by Hermann Paul (for quote, see Kiparsky 1949: 501), Bloomfield (1933: 454), and Leslau (1945: 66). Possible counterexamples were suggested but not established in Kiparsky 1949 and Weinreich 1966 (31ff).

3. No lexical item that is not a noun can belong to the class of properties borrowed from a language unless this class also includes at least one noun.

This statement excludes a language where all lexical items that have been borrowed from a language are non-nouns. All instances of borrowing that I know of illustrate the principle since the majority of them involve a language having both nouns and non-nouns in the set of properties that it has borrowed from another language (such as GERMAN borrowings in HUNGARIAN) and one of them involves a language having borrowed only nouns from another (SPANISH loans in sixteenth-century NAHUATL ("...borrowed SPANISH vocabulary in NAHUATL is numerically dominated by nouns, which were practically the only loans during the 16th century..." — Karttunen and Lockhart 1975: 37)). For the possibly related phenomenon of a language always having a larger number of borrowed nouns than the number of borrowed items in any other lexeme class, see also Scotton and Okeju's account of loans in ATESO (1973: 883) and such general account of borrowing as Haugen 1950 and Deroy 1956 (67ff).

4. A lexical item whose meaning is verbal can never be included in the set of borrowed properties.

This statement excludes a language that has borrowed the symbolic association of a verbal form and a verbal meaning. The principle is exemplified both by languages that do not borrow phonetic forms of verbs at all and also by languages that do borrow phonetic forms of verbs; such as, for instance, ENGA, a New Guinea language. As pointed out by Lang (1971: 96-7), all ENGA loan items whose model is a verb are used in ENGA immediately followed by either of the two indigenous verbs lengé 'utter' and pingi 'hit.' Thus, for example, the ENGLISH verb lose is borrowed as lúsa lengé "lose utter," and the verb win is borrowed as winí (or winími) lengé "win utter." Since (I gather) the ENGA verbs lengé and pingi 'hit' are otherwise used in conjunction with nominal complements only and they are not used with verbal complements, the forms lúsa and winí/winími have to be considered as having been borrowed with a non-verbal — in particular, nominal -- meaning. For exemplification of the principle in some UTO-AZTECAN languages, compare

112   Edith A. Moravcsik

Spicer 1943 (concerning SPANISH verb forms borrowed into YAQUI)
and Karttunen and Lockhart 1975: 60ff (concerning SPANISH verb
forms borrowed into NAHUATL); for further exemplification from
other languages and for general discussion, see E. Moravcsik 1975.

    5. No inflectional affixes can belong to the set of properties
        borrowed from a language unless at least one derivational
        affix also belongs to the set.

This statement excludes a language that has borrowed inflectional
affixes from another one but not derivational ones. The validity of
the principle is exemplifiable either by languages that have only
borrowed derivational affixes from a language or by languages that
borrowed both derivational and inflectional ones. For an example
of the latter kind, see the SEMITIC languages of Ethiopia described
by Leslau (1945) which appear to have borrowed both derivational
affixes from the CUSHITIC languages, such as -ta '(abstract nom-
inalizer)' in TIGRIÑA and also inflectional affixes, such as a reduplication pattern to express nominal plurality in TIGRIÑA (e.g.
tämamen 'snakes,' tämän 'snake').

    6. A lexical item that is of the "grammatical" type (which type
        includes at least conjunctions and adpositions) cannot be
        included in the set of properties borrowed from a language
        unless the rule that determines its linear order with respect
        to its head is also so included.

This statement excludes a language which borrows the form and
the meaning of a preposition and uses it postposed, or which borrows
the form and meaning of a postposition and uses it preposed, or
which borrows a clause-initial conjunction and uses it in clause-
final position, or which borrows a clause-final conjunction and
orders it clause-initially.[9] A language supporting the principle

---

[9] The same may also hold for "bound" grammatical morphemes
such as suffixes, prefixes, and constituents of compounds. The prediction would be that there is no language that borrows the meaning
and form of a prefix and uses it as a suffix; or one that borrows the
meaning and form of a prefix and uses it as a prefix; or that borrows
the form and meaning of a compound constituent that precedes its
sister in the source language and uses it so as to follow its sister.
Convincing exemplification of this hypothesis would have to come
from cases where the ordering of the borrowed constituent would be
different in the source language than the ordering of the indigenous
synonymous counterpart; i.e. from a language, for instance, that
is exclusively suffixing and that borrows a prefix. I have, however,
no such examples.

is YAQUI which has borrowed the forms and meanings of SPANISH conjunctions and which uses these clause-initially as they would be used in SPANISH, even though the indigenous synonymous counterparts of the conjunctions are clause-final. Compare, for instance, the clause-initial order of ke 'that,' borrowed from SPANISH que, with the SPANISH clause-initial position of que and with the YAQUI clause-final position of the indigenous morpheme -tia:

a. aapo hunen hia ke hu hamut tutu?uli
    "he thus say that this woman pretty"

b. dice que esa mujer es linda
    "says that this woman is pretty"

c. aapo hunen hia hu-ka hamut-ta tutu?uli-tia
    "he thus say this-dependency:marker woman-dependency:marker pretty-that"

all meaning 'He says that this woman is pretty' (Lindenfeld 1975). Another example is HUNGARIAN. This language has no indigenous prepositions: all adpositions are postposed to their heads. In casual, joking speech, some GERMAN prepositions may be borrowed, such as ohne 'without.' When this happens, the GERMAN prepositions must be preposed, rather than postposed; even though the indigenous synonym of ohne, nélkül, is a postposition.

7. Given a particular language, and given a particular constituent class such that at least some members of that class are not inflected in that language, if the language has borrowed lexical items that belong to that constituent class, at least some of these must also be uninflected.

This statement excludes a language in which all borrowed members of a constituent class are inflected but not all indigenous members are. The validity of the principle is exemplified either by languages where all borrowed and indigenous members of a constituent class are uninflected, or by languages where both some borrowed and some indigenous members of a constituent class are uninflected. The latter type of exemplification is provided by RUSSIAN where both some indigenous nouns (such as abbreviations) and some borrowed nouns (such as kino 'movie theater') are uninflected; or by NAHUATL where both some native nouns and also some SPANISH-borrowed nouns occur without the so-called absolutive suffix (Karttunen and Lockhart 1975: 45ff) and where no borrowed adpositions, but all indigenous ones, were inflected according to some properties of their heads (Karttunen and Lockhart 1975: 76f).

2.2 The explanatory value of constraints on borrowing

Having established what the general nature of constraints on
borrowing is and having suggested that that are indeed some particular tokens of this statement schema that are empirically valid, I
will next turn to the demonstration of the usefulness of such statements, by showing that they can be used to explain facts about languages that linguists are required by their assumed goals to explain.

Phenomena that are in need of explanations are those that are
counter to one's expectations. The range of phenomena to be explained will thus be defined by what the initial expectations are.
The basic expectation of linguists concerning similarities and differences of linguistic utterances is that two linguistic utterances
will be similar in a particular way -- i.e. they will share property
P_1 -- if and only if they are also similar in some other way -- i.e.
if they also share some property P_2 which is distinct from P_1. The
conditioning, or "explanatory," property P_2, may in principle be
any structural or non-structural property of linguistic utterances.
P_2 may be, first of all, some structural property: given that the two
utterances that share P_1 also share a structural property P_2, and
given the observation that all pairs of utterances that share P_1 also
share P_2, the similarity between the two utterances with respect to
P_1 can be explained by the presence of P_2. Secondly, P_2 may be a
property not of the structures of the two utterances but of their
speakers. Thus, a shared property of two utterances can be explained by reference to the fact that they are spoken by members of
the same language community -- i.e. that they are utterances of the
same language -- or, if they are not used by members of the same
language community, by reference to the fact that the two distinct
language communities in which they are used are similar or related
in some ways. Since all language communities will always be similar to each other to the extent that they consist of people, some
similarities of linguistic utterances -- in particular, those that are
either present in or non-applicable to all linguistic utterances in all
languages — can be explained by reference to the humanness of inter-
locutors. Since some language communities will be more similar
to each other by the genetic relationships among their members,
some similarities of linguistic utterances -- in particular, those
that are present in utterances used by just those language communities that are so related — can be explained by reference to the
genetic relations of their users. The basic problem is, of course,
to establish just which structural similarities among utterances
are amenable to being explained by one, rather than by another,
additional similarity -- that is to say, just what are the structural

similarities that are entailed by some other structural similarities (or, in other words, what are the structural types of human languages), what are the structural similarities that are entailed by the utterances belonging to the same language, or to genetically related languages, or simply to the class of human languages. [10] Given these possible ways of explaining similarities among linguistic utterances, the expectation of a linguist is that sentences belonging to the same language will be more similar than utterances that belong to different languages; and that utterances that belong to different but genetically related languages will be more similar than utterances belonging to different languages that are not so related. It is because of such initial expectations that it is deviations, rather than similarities, among tautolingual utterances that a linguist will need to explain; that it is deviations, rather than similarities, among genetically related language stages that he will need to explain; but that it is the (non-universal) similarities, rather than differences, among genetically unrelated languages that he will want to account for. The significance of constraints on borrowing is just this: that it provides for a way for the linguist to explain some of three types of phenomena -- in particular, to explain

a. deviations among utterances of the same language
b. differences among genetically related languages
c. genetically unexplainable similarities among languages. [11]

In what follows, I will exemplify each of these three explanatory uses of borrowing constraints.

The example to illustrate how borrowing constraints are capable of being instrumental in explaining intralinguistic deviations comes

---

[10] For detailed discussions on alternative ways of explaining language similarities and on certain distinctive properties of those similarities that can be explained by one, but not the other, kind of explanation, see Greenberg 1953: especially 267ff. Compare also Masica 1976: especially 180-5.

[11] It is possible, in principle, that a language affects another one in a negative fashion, inducing elimination of those structural properties in the affected language that are present in the affecting one. In such a hypothetical instance, of which I know of no actual instance, constraints on what structural properties could be eliminated would serve to explain differences of the two languages, more than their similarities.

from ZOQUE, a ZOQUE-MIXE language of Mexico (Wonderly 1951).
In this language, there are certain near-exceptionless phonetic
segment sequence regularities within words. These include the
non-occurrence of an alveolar consonant t, d, c, s, or n immediately followed by a y; the non-occurrence of a y immediately followed by an alveolar consonant t, d, c, s, or n, and the non-
occurrence of any (voiced) nasal immediately followed by a voiceless
stop. These regularities are, however, only near-exceptional since
there is a small number of words that violate them. Thus, the first
constraint is violated by words such as tyenda 'store,' since here
a t is immediately followed by y; the second constraint is violated
by words such as r·eyna 'queen,' since here a y is immediately
followed by an n; and the third constraint is violated by words such
as kampo 'airstrip,' since here an m is immediately followed by a
voiceless stop. The question thus arises as to why a small set of
words that includes these examples deviate from all the rest of the
words in ZOQUE with respect to the segment sequences that occur
in them. Fortunately, there is an explanation in that all those words
that include otherwise non-occurring sequences share a common
property: they are all borrowed from SPANISH. Of course, the
fact itself that all such words are SPANISH loans does not yet provide for an explanation. If we were not able to assume any constraint on how the phonetic form of a model and the phonetic form
of the borrowed replica can differ from each other, then the reten-
tion and the elimination of these consonant clusters would be equally
consistent with the fact that these words are loans and thus the re-
tention, rather than elimination, of these clusters in all borrowed
words would not be explained by appealing to the borrowed status
of these words. (Although the fact that any one single borrowed
word includes such otherwise non-occurring clusters would be explained by reference to the fact that all borrowed words may include
such clusters in the language.) An explanation would be provided,
however, by a hypothetical (and, as it turns out, counter-to-fact)
constraint on borrowings which stipulates that a lexical item cannot
be borrowed from a member of the language class L_1 into a member
of the language class L_2 unless the borrowing includes the transfer
of the consonant clusters that are involved in the phonetic form of
the item.

    An example to illustrate how borrowing constraints can explain
some differences between genetically related language stages, consider the case of AMHARIC and HEBREW. These two languages
are genetically related in that they are both preceded in time by
common ancestor language and thus the basic expectation is that
they are very similar. Nonetheless, in most pragmatically neutral

main declarative sentence of AMHARIC, the verb is sentence-final
and in most such HEBREW sentences the verb is in some position
other than sentence-final. This difference could of course be explained by reference to laws of diachronic change -- i.e. by showing
that (assuming that one of the two orders was the order in the ancestor language) both the non-change of the ancestral pattern and
also the change in the direction evidenced are within the range of
what can happen in a language in the course of time. If, however,
it can be established that speakers of one or the other of the two
languages have been in contact with speakers of a third language
and that furthermore the assumption that there has been a borrowing of constituent order is consistent with known constraints of
borrowing, then there is also an alternative explanation. As it
happens, in this case there is evidence that one of the two languages,
AMHARIC, has been in contact with another language (some CUSHI-
TIC one), that that language had sentence-final verb position, and
that the assumption that this verb position was borrowed by AMHARIC
is consistent with what we know about constraints on borrowing. The
particular constraints that are relevant here is, first of all, the fact
that the borrowing of constituent order patterns is within the range
of properties that are metatheoretically characterized as borrowable;
and that constituent order borrowing is possible only if it has been
preceded by at least some lexical borrowing (a constraint which is
not contradicted by the AMHARIC evidence in that present-day AM-
HARIC includes both the sentence-final verb position, presumably
borrowed from CUSHITIC, and also some lexical borrowings from
CUSHITIC).

Finally, an example of how borrowing constraints can explain
unexpected (non-universal) similarities between languages that are
not known to be genetically related -- or, for that matter, similarities between genetically related languages which, however, fall
outside the domain of those similarities that are explainable by appeal to their genetic relatedness -- consider any of the countless
examples of lexical similarities among languages, such as the fact
that the term for 'thinking machine' in ENGLISH is computer and
in HUNGARIAN kompjúter. The question clearly arises as to why
these two (but not all other) languages that are not known to be
genetically related should share this particular meaning-sound
correspondence, in the midst of all their very pervasive structural
and lexical differences. An answer to this question offers itself by
recognizing that HUNGARIAN -- and especially its substyle related
to technology -- has been in contact with ENGLISH and has been
heavily influenced by it. Again, the explanation of course depends
on what constraints we may assume about borrowing. If it were

the case, for instance, that we wanted to account for the similarity
between the two verbs compute in ENGLISH and kompjútol in HUN-
GARIAN, and if it were further the case that there were no borrowed
nouns of ENGLISH in HUNGARIAN, the similarity between the meanings and forms of compute and kompjútol could not be explained in
terms of borrowing since, as noted above, there is a constraint that
no non-noun can be borrowed into a language from a language unless
some noun has already been borrowed into that language from the
same source. In the case of computer - kompjúter, however, the
hypothesis is the borrowing of a noun and thus the hypothesis is
consistent with our borrowing constraints and therefore capable of
providing an explanation for the shared meaning-sound correspondence in the two languages.

2.3 Constraints on borrowing as explananda

Even though constraints on borrowing, as we have just seen, can
serve to explain observations about similarities and differences
within and among languages, such constraints themselves are also
in need of explanations. The questions that have to be answered
are these: why is there borrowing at all between languages? and,
given that there is, why is it constrained -- that is, why does it
take place with respect to just those properties that constraints on
borrowing define as borrowable and why does it take place with
respect to just those structurally or non-structurally defined languages that constraints on borrowing define as possible source and
borrowing languages?[12] In other words, what has to be explained
is, first, that linguistic theory includes mention of the concept
"borrowing" at all; that linguistic metatheory incorporates constraints on borrowing; and that these constraints define borrowed
property types, source language types, and borrowing language

---

[12] These questions parallel, of course, the questions that have
to be asked about linguistic change in general -- i.e. why does change
occur at all? and if it does, why is it constrained the way it is, both
in terms of the structural language properties that participate in
change and also, possibly, by extralinguistic factors characterizing
those societal stages in which particular language changes occur.
The question: "why does borrowing occur at all?" is all the more
interesting since there are a number of two-language situation --
seemingly comparable to situations where borrowing do occur --
where no manifestations of language contact evolve. For a discussion of ATHABASCAN and TIBETAN, see Sapir 1949:196ff. For a
case where undesirable homonymy prevents the borrowing of a lexical item, see Weinreich 1966:55.

types (or P_x, L_1, and L_2 in our schema given above) in just the
way in which they do. Since, as it is generally assumed (compare
Deroy 1956, Masica 1976), the primary agent of contact-induced
language change is the bilingual — a person, that is, that knows
at least some of both the source language and the borrowing language — the more particular questions that arise are: under what
conditions does the bilingual start mixing properties of his two
languages and under what conditions do such mixed-in properties
become accepted by the total population of a language including the
non-bilingual members? The conditions here may in principle be
either related to the structures of the two languages in question or
to the capabilities and intentions of the speakers. Potentially relevant structural factors are qualitative differences — i.e. to what
extent are the two languages structurally similar in the first place
— and evaluative differences concerning such ill-understood notions
as ease and expressiveness. Potentially relevant non-structural
factors include the degree of proficiency and the number and status
of bilinguals in the language community; and the status of the two
languages within the community.[13]

In closing, I would like to point out that there is much evidence
to indicate that the question: what language properties can be borrowed? indeed cannot be answered without reference to a very
specific characterization of the borrowing situation in question —
i.e. of the source and borrowing languages involved. A very interesting piece of evidence supporting this contention is provided by
Dixon (1972: 331ff). He points out that it is customary in many AUS-
TRALIAN language communities to name people after names of
objects, such as the term for 'water' etc.; and that there is also a
rule that once a person who carries the name of an object dies, the
name cannot be applied to that object anymore but has to be replaced
by another one. Names thus required to replace the old ones are
generally borrowed from the language of some neighboring tribe.
As a result, neighboring languages often share a very high percentage (40-60%) of their vocabulary. Clearly, in a situation like this,[14]
if there are any constraints on the resulting borrowings, these will
be identical with the constraints (if any) on what things people can
be named after; and there is no reason to expect that these will in

---

[13] For some discussion of possible reasons of borrowing, see
Weinreich 1966: e.g. 56ff. and Winter 1973.

[14] For another instance in ATESO where the fact that a word is
near-homonymous with a taboo word apparently invites its being
replaced by a borrowed item, see Scotton and Okeju 1973: 886.

turn have anything to do with the constraints that determine what
can be borrowed between two languages such as ENGLISH and
RUSSIAN whose speakers simply culturally interact. The characterization and explanation of what can be borrowed from one
language into another is therefore a truly complex task that requires knowledge about the speakers of the two languages and their
relations.

3. Conclusions

   Studies in language contact were shown to constitute a necessary
part of the endeavor to explain why human beings communicate by
means of orally articulated sounds the way they actually do. The
nature of constraints on borrowing was explored by informally
characterizing the set of logically possible such constraints and
by proposing a small subset of these constraints as being empirically true. The explanatory value of constraints on borrowing
was illustrated by showing that they can be used to explain intra-
lingual heterogenieties and genetically unexplainable similarities
and differences among languages. The problem of how to explain
constraints on borrowing was briefly outlined.

BIBLIOGRAPHY

Bach, E. 1970. Is Amharic an SOV language? Journal of Ethiopian
   Studies, 8.1. 9-20.

Bloomfield, L. 1933. Language. New York, Chicago: Holt,
   Rinehart and Winston.

Deroy, L. 1956. L'emprunt linguistique. Paris.

Dixon, R.M.W. 1972. The Dyirbal language of North Queensland.
   Cambridge: Cambridge University Press.

Greenberg, J.H. 1953. Historical linguistics and unwritten lan-
   guagues. Anthropology today, ed. by Kroeber, 265-86. Chicago:
   University of Chicago Press.

Grierson, G.A. 1902. Notes on Āhom. Zeitschrift der deutschen
   morgenländischen Gesellschaft 56. 1-59.

Haugen, E. 1950. The analysis of linguistic borrowing. Language
   26. 210-31.

Heine, B. 1975. The study of word order in African languages. Proceedings of the sixth conference on African linguistics, ed. by R.K. Herbert. Working Papers in Linguistics 20. 161-83. (Ohio State University, Columbus, Ohio)

Hudson, G. 1972. Why Amharic is not a VSO language. Studies in African Linguistics 3.1. 127-65.

Hyman, L.M. 1975. On the change from SOV to SVO: Evidence from Niger-Congo. Word order and word order change, ed. by Ch. Li, 113-47. University of Texas Press.

Johnson, J.B. 1943. A clear case of linguistic acculturation. American Anthropologist 43. 429-34.

Karttunen, F. and J. Lockhart. 1975. Nahuatl in the middle years: language contact phenomena in texts of the colonial period. Manuscript.

Kiparsky, M.V. 1949. L'emploi artificial d'un préfixe étranger. Actes du sixième congrès international des linguistes, 501-4. Paris.

Lang, A. 1971. Nouns and classificatory verbs in Enga (New Guinea): a semantic study. Unpublished Ph.D. dissertation, Australian National University.

Lehmann, W.P. 1973. A structural principle of language and its implications. Language 49.1. 47-66.

Leslau, W. 1945. The influence of Cushitic on the Semitic languages of Ethiopia: A problem of substratum. Word 1. 59-82.

Lindenfeld, J. 1975. Spanish influence in Yaqui syntax. Manuscript.

Little, G.D. 1974. Syntactic evidence of language contact: Cushitic evidence in Amharic. Toward tomorrow's linguistics, ed. by R. W. Shuy and Ch.J.N. Bailey, 267-75. Georgetown University Press.

Masica, C.P. 1976. Defining a linguistic area: South Asia. Chicago and London: The University of Chicago Press.

Moravcsik, E.A. 1975. Borrowed verbs. Wiener Linguistische Gazette 8. 3-30.

Moravcsik, J.M.E. 1975. Understanding language. The Hague: Mouton.

Nadkarni, M.V. 1975. Bilingualism and syntactic change in Konkani. Language 51.3. 672-83.

Pinnow, H.-J. 1960. Über den Ursprung der voneinander abweichenden Struktur der Munda- und Khmer-Nikobar-Sprachen. Indoiranian Journal 4. 81-103.

Sanders, G.A. 1972. Equational grammar. The Hague: Mouton.

Sapir, E. 1949. Language: an introduction to the study of speech. New York: Harcourt, Brace and World, Inc.

Scotton, C.M. and J. Okeju. 1973. Neighbors and lexical borrowings. Language 49.4. 871-89.

Spicer, E.H. 1943. Linguistic aspects of Yaqui acculturation. American Anthropologist 45. 410-20.

Vogt, H. 1954. Contact of languages. Word 10. 365-74.

Weinreich, U. 1966. Languages in contact: findings and problems. The Hague: Mouton.

Winter, W. 1973. Areal linguistics: some general considerations. Current trends in linguistics, ed. by T. Sebeok, vol. 11, 135-47. The Hague: Mouton.

Wonderly, W.L. 1951. Zoque II: phonemes and morphophonemes. International Journal of American Linguistics 17.2. 105-23.

Language Samples

ALAN BELL

ABSTRACT

Typological comparison is a means of generalizing from a selected sample of languages. The validity of the generalizations depends in part upon sampling error, which is a function of sample validity. The concepts of sampling theory that are most appropriate to typological research are sketched, including the distinction between nonprobability and probability samples and their relative values. Examples of typological samples are presented and evaluated. Some means of obtaining better samples are discussed, including use of more sophisticated sampling methods, exploiting knowledge about the language characteristics under investigation, and discovering the general sources of bibliographic, areal and genetic bias in language samples. The relevance of the problem of generalizing from the world's languages to possible languages is clarified.

CONTENTS

1. Introduction

Typological comparison of languages requires that certain languages be chosen for comparison, or sampled. It is one of the
chain of steps from observation to generalization that profoundly
affects the validity of an investigation. Some researchers feel
that the problem is negligible; others are concerned about it, yet
do not see that much can be done to improve current practices.
A very few maintain that the sampling methods in today's typological research can and should be improved. Any one of these positions may be true for a given study or type of study. This paper
seeks to provide insight into how one can tell when one of them is
right and the others wrong.

Explanation and illustration of how principles of sampling apply
to the choice of languages for studies of language universals takes
up most of this paper. The principles derive from a highly developed statistical theory of sampling and the experience gained by
its application. While this experience comes from many fields,
the most extensive employment of sampling theory has been for
the purpose of choosing a sample of people for surveys of public
opinion, income, employment status, etc. The lessons learned
in a field so different from the study of language universals in
goals, resources, methods and data are nevertheless instructive.

Good sampling practice depends as much upon capitalizing upon
special characteristics of the objects to be studied as upon hewing
to sound sampling principles. This is the easiest part of the task
for the linguist and accordingly receives less attention here than
could profitably be given to it. Certain interesting special topics,
such as sampling for rare types and testing for the existence of
differences between languages, language groups or language types,
are not treated at all.

It is inevitable that as the study of language universals advances,
its practitioners become more adept, more difficult questions are
asked and standards of research quality rise. The reader should
keep this in mind when the samples of actual typological studies
are discussed. The point is not that previous sampling practices
are inadequate, but that we can do better, and for some types of
research must do better.

2. Basic Sampling Concepts

We shall require the following terms.

The universe is the class of objects which is the object of investigation. Examples: possible human languages; human beings; a pot of stew.

The frame is the means of access to the universe. Examples: languages described in the investigator's library; students in introductory psychology classes at the investigator's university; the portion of the stew within reach of a spoon.

The sample is the collection of objects that are observed. Examples: languages most familiar to the investigator; the first fifty students electing the investigator's study to satisfy one of their class requirements; a spoonful of stew taken from the front edge of the pot.[1]

Research on language universals, which is the main concern of this paper, deals with the universe of all possible human languages. This is not necessarily the case for all crosslanguage research. A study intended mainly for the guidance of second-language learning might take all the languages now spoken as its universe. The frames of typological studies are much more restricted either by the availability of adequate language descriptions or by the accessibility of speakers.

3. Error

There are three main sources of error which may weaken the validity of a typological study. The linguistic community is generally most sensitive to incorrect attribution of characteristics to languages or errors of observation. They are caused by incorrect or incomplete language descriptions, unresolved incomparability of descriptions, and mistakes of interpretation, coding and copying. If by choice or unavoidable circumstance the frame of the study is inappropriate for the universe that its results apply to, it is tarnished by the error of overgeneralization.

The third error is sampling error which concerns the relationship between the sample and the frame. There are two sorts.

---

[1] The terms universe, frame, sample are used by Deming (1968). Most standard statistical references (e.g. Blalock 1960, Cochran 1963, Sudman 1976) distinguish only "population" and "sample." The terms "target population" and "sampled population" (Mosteller 1968) can be taken as equivalents to universe and frame for our purposes.

Bias arises when objects with particular characteristics of importance to a study are more likely to be selected by its sampling procedure. A survey of employment status conducted by interviewing people at home during working hours will be distorted by bias. The astute buyer of strawberries does not expect the top layer to reveal the quality of the whole basket. The languages personally familiar to most linguists will not reveal a true picture of the role that pitch plays in language, how syntactic functions are marked, nor of many other characteristics. It is important to note that errors of bias cannot be remedied by increasing the size of the sample. Another sample of people at home will be just as biased as the first one. The only cure is to change the sampling procedure.

Random error,[2] on the other hand, is a measure of the variation of observations from one sample to another. The variation is generally less for larger samples.

4. Probability Sampling and Nonprobability Sampling

The term random sampling is familiar to most researchers, but its precise meaning is not always understood. A lottery ticket pulled out of a bowl by a blindfolded volunteer is not necessarily a random sample. If the tickets are not completely mixed, then some will be more likely than others to be chosen. Physical mixing is difficult to attain in practice, as the Selective Service so vividly demonstrated when it used the lottery drawing method to assign a callup order to birthdates. To qualify as random a sample must be chosen so that every possible sample from the frame has an equal chance of selection. For example, assume that a random sample of two is required from the Five Nations Iroquois languages. The frame is the set of CAYUGA (C), MOHAWK (M), ONONDAGA (O_1), ONEIDA (O_2) and SENECA (S). There are ten possible samples — CM, CO_1, CO_2, CS, MO_1, MO_2, MS, O_1O_2, O_1S and O_2S. Each must have one chance in ten of being chosen.

A random sample is a special kind of probability sample. The distinguishing characteristic of probability samples is that they are chosen so that whatever the chance of any possible sample's selection, it is known in advance. Since statistical sampling theory is based on this property, its results apply strictly only to probability samples (Section 8).

---

[2] Precision and random error are equivalent terms.

Nonprobability samples have been and continue to be widely used. Their main weakness is that it is very difficult to assess the amount of sampling error that they contribute to a study. On the other hand they generally require less effort to carry out than probability samples.

All the instances of samples given in Sec. 2 are a kind of non-probability sample called convenience or opportunity samples. The Literary Digest poll of 1936 in which 59% of some 3,000,000 respondents expressed their preference for Alf Landon is a famous example of the dangers of this sort of sample. (He received 41% of the vote.) It illustrates also that numbers cannot triumph over bias; current polling techniques are able to obtain results within a few percent with national samples of a few thousand.

Convenience samples are appropriate when very little is known very well. In exploratory studies the risk of sampling error may well be commensurate with other errors or with the expected level of validity. On the other hand, if the population is known to be homogeneous, one sample is as good as another. The experienced cook doesn't worry about what part of the stew he tastes from because he knows when it has cooked long enough for the seasoning to be well blended.

Quota samples strive for greater representativeness by partitioning the frame into categories and requiring that a certain number of objects be taken from each category. The categories might be regions, ages, education levels, occupations, religious affiliations, sex, etc. for an opinion survey. The sample can thus represent the frame closely for the pre-selected categories. This guarantees nothing about the sample's adequacy for other attributes, including, naturally, those being investigated. An unexpected bias in its quota samples was probably one reason for the startling misprediction of the Gallup Poll in the 1948 Truman-Dewey election. The Gallup organization severely restricted its quota sampling thereafter.

Other sorts of nonprobability samples may be called judgment samples. The selection of a judgment sample depends upon the investigator's expert knowledge of the subject matter. This he uses to obtain a sample that he deems representative. The criteria are at least in part unknown or unstated, for otherwise the sample would be some form of quota sample. One's judgment of the quality of such a sample rests essentially upon the investigator's reputation. Judgment samples are appropriate for surveys and for tests of hypotheses which depend crucially on extreme types. Their use

in other applications presumes that the risk of error they introduce
is worth taking.

5. Sampling in Cross Language Research

Current and past sampling practices in cross language research
provide many examples of the application of nonprobability sampling
methods. The examples that follow illustrate high and low quality
samples, large and small, and of varying degrees of suitability.
No cross language research has yet made use of probability sampling methods, to my knowledge.

5.1 Swedish as a target language

As part of a project investigating the structural properties of
Swedish that cause problems for learners of Swedish, Hammarberg
and Viberg 1975 conducted a pilot study of the errors made by learners of Swedish of different native languages.[3]

Universe: Contemporary languages spoken by Swedish immigrants.
Frame: Such languages with available speakers.
Size: 11.
Unit cost: High.
Method of selection: The sample is a judgment sample in which
 the main factors considered were number of immigrant
 speakers of the language and typological variety.
Documentation: The languages are specified.
Suitability: The sample is highly suitable. Including 9 of the 21
 languages with 1,000 or more speakers in Sweden, plus Per-
 sian and Japanese, it should provide an adequate guide for
 the project. The project's interest here is that it represents
 cross language research for which the proper universe is not
 existing or possible languages.

5.2 Voicing in initial stops

Lisker and Abramson 1964 documented the role of the onset time
of voicing relative to release of occlusion in initial stops. This
timing relation was chosen as the most promising single measure
to begin a study of the acoustic cues for the manner distinction of
stops.

---

[3] Material in this section is based on a seminar report by Björn
Hammarberg at the Linguistic Institute, July 23, 1976.

Universe: Possible human languages with one or more contrastive stop series.
Frame: Languages with available phonological descriptions and
with speakers available for laboratory recording.
Size: 11 languages.
Unit cost: High. Analysis of several hundred spectrograms
was required for each language.
Method of selection: An informal quota sample was apparently
used. Languages were selected from those with 2, 3 and 4
series of stops said to be distinguished by a variety of combinations of voicing, aspiration and articulatory force.
Documentation: Languages, descriptive sources and variety of
language recorded by speakers for instrumental analysis are
given.
Suitability: This is a paradigmatic example of the well-planned
and well-executed exploratory study. Its exploratory nature
is not used to excuse careless work; the sample, though of
low absolute quality, is highly suitable to the study's purpose
and an admirable balance in representing the validity of the
conclusions is struck. It is important to note that a sample
more representative of the world's languages would have been
extremely wasteful in this context. Its only contribution would
have been to raise the validity of the unforeseen result that
the distribution of boundaries along the voice onset time continuum is apparently nonrandom; but the diversity of the
sample was sufficient to render the result sufficiently cred-
ible that further investigation was spurred. It would have
been required in any case.

5.3 Causative structures

The syntax of the noun phrase arguments of causative structures
is the target of Comrie 1976. He is interested in structures where
the causative element and the embedded verb have fused, resulting
in a single surface structure clause. He characterizes the "paradigm case" of such causative constructions by a set of four generalizations which, though not exceptionless, are violated only rarely
and only in certain ways.

Universe: Possible human languages. The class of languages
without fused causative and embedded verbs, e.g. ENGLISH,
is however of no evidential value.
Frame: Languages with available adequate description or with
available informant as supplement.
Size: 17 (partial information is provided from nine others).

Unit cost: Medium to high. Sources are published grammars or grammatical analyses, supplemented for at least six languages by information from native speakers.

Method of selection: Apparently convenience sample; method is not stated.

Documentation: Languages are listed by genetic affiliation. Possible consequence of weaknesses in sample are fully discussed.

Suitability: This is another excellent model of an exploratory study. It is neither superficial nor does it pretend that its generalizations are definitive, and it provides most of the information needed to assess their validity. The sample, between medium and low quality, is adequate to demonstrate the variety of deviations from the "paradigm case" and is roughly commensurate with other sources of error. The sample quality does, however, threaten the validity of the major conclusion, "that the vast majority of languages differ from the paradigm case in only one or two respects," as well as the subgeneralizations. If additional effort had been possible, it would have been well spent in better protecting against bias (over half of the languages are European) and perhaps increasing the sample size.

5.4 Order of meaningful elements

The influential work of Greenberg 1963 states 45 generalizations about order of elements and morphological structure.

Universe: Possible human languages.

Frame: Languages with a reasonably adequate grammar.

Size: 30 (basic sample). Size of larger sample is not indicated explicitly, but probably over 200.

Unit cost: Medium.

Method of selection: "The sample [of 30] was selected largely for convenience." Bibliographic availability was thus a major factor. "...an attempt was made to obtain as wide a genetic and areal coverage as possible." The larger sample was presumably selected in much the same manner. Since the sample of 30 was chosen from at least part of the larger sample, it is likely that the characteristics of the languages under study themselves played some role in selection so that the sample should be regarded as having some of the qualities of a judgment sample.

Documentation: The languages of the basic sample are listed according to continental distribution. Sources are not given.

The larger sample can only be inferred from a classification listing many languages but referring also to groups such as "ROMANCE languages," "most MANDINGO and VOLTAIC languages," etc.

Suitability: The sample of medium quality is commensurate with other sources of error (misclassification, for instance) and the level of generalizations proposed (no serious claim is made to distinguish disfavored types from nonoccurring ones, nor degree of disfavor). The unspecific total sample and the many categories considered combine to make difficult any assessment of the relative strength of some of the generalizations applying to subcategories of languages.

5.5 Position of modal elements

Steele 1975 describes the pattern of sentential position of occurrence of modal elements and explains the pattern in terms of attraction to initial position and to the verb.

Universe: Possible human languages.

Frame: Languages with available adequate written description or for which native speakers were available. Only languages with grammatical modal elements occurring in a single position were pertinent to the study.

Size: 44.

Unit cost: Medium.

Method of selection: Although not stated in the article the selection method is a combination of quota and judgment methods. Eighty languages were examined in all. Some were discarded because their modal elements did not meet the study's requirements. From the rest 22 OV languages and 22 VO languages were selected (Steele, personal communication).

Documentation: Languages are listed by genetic affiliation, source are given and weaknesses of the sample are discussed.

Suitability: The sample is of medium quality, that is to say much better than used in most nonphonological studies. The effort to control bias is fully commensurate with the study's objectives. Its size, however, is not fully adequate for the study. The problem arises because one category of modals that is central to the study's conclusions occurs only 12 times in the sample, thus greatly reducing its precision. For a random sample of the same size the observed tendencies of positional occurrence of such modals could be expected about once out of five samples, assuming all positions equally favored.

5.6 Syllable structure

Bell 1971 studied the patterns of syllable margin length, using a probabilistic Markov chain model. The model provided an explicit state-process representation of syllable structure types and the historical processes shaping them.

Universe: Possible human languages.
Frame: Languages with phonological descriptions containing adequate phonotactic detail.
Size: 144 (134 after adjustment).
Unit cost: Medium.
Method of selection: Largely convenience, although a balanced representation was attempted from areas and genetic families, and some languages were included because they exemplified an unusual type of syllable structure. It was judged in retrospect that some families were overrepresented; accordingly, 10 languages were randomly deleted from them.
Documentation: Languages are listed by genetic family, sources are given and method of selection described.
Suitability: The quality of the sample is as high as any on phonology at the time that it was done. It is nevertheless one of the weakest points of the study. The problem is that it relies specifically on estimates of relative frequency of occurrence of a large number of language subtypes. While the methods used were not very sensitive to random error in the occurrence frequencies, the conclusions could be profoundly affected by bias. The nonprobability sample is thus not appropriate for the goals of the state-process portion of the study, sufficing only for the general observations about regularities of syllable structure.

5.7 Linguistic stress

The cross-linguistic study by Hyman 1977 of stress accent, based on one of the largest samples used for a typological study, is as much concerned with the function of stress accent and the mechanisms of stress accent change as with synchronic generalizations.

Universe: Possible human languages.
Frame: Languages with available statement of stress accent system.
Size: 444. Source for approximately 300 of these was published descriptions; for the remainder it was the brief abstracts provided by Ruhlen 1975.
Unit cost: Low.
Method of selection: Bibliographic convenience, although no explicit statement is given (Hyman, personal communication)
Documentation: The sample is listed according to major genetic or areal groups. Sources for each language are not given, but are presumably listed among references. Languages known only from the abstracts of Ruhlen 1975 are indicated. The possibility of bias in the sample is discussed.

Suitability: The sample is perfectly adequate for the survey of stress accentual phenomena that is the study's main purpose. It is larger than necessary, however, and some sampling effort might have been profitable devoted to further analysis. On the other hand the conclusions that deal with the relative frequency of occurrence of stress accent types should not be given undue credence because of the large sample size. A convenience sample is subject to unknown biases, and as the Literary Digest poll illustrates numbers are no protection against them.

5.8 The Stanford Phonology Archive

The sample of the Stanford Phonology Archive is of particular interest. It was chosen by a research group whose intimate experience with cross language phonological research is probably broader than any other's. Because the Archive is a general purpose tool and not directed to a single goal and because the cost of archiving a single language is high, the problem of sampling figures larger than in many other projects. The following description is based on Vihman 1974, the only published source. It may not reflect accurately subsequent versions of the Archive.

Universe: Possible languages or any subset thereof.
Frame: Languages whose phonology has been described in sufficient detail in published sources.
Size: 277.
Unit cost: High. Each language's phonological characteristics are coded in machine-retrievable form according to a uniform format. The coding then must be verified independently.
Method of selection: Combination of convenience, quota and judgment sampling. The sample was designed to contain a) the eleven languages of the world with the greatest number of speakers and b) equal numbers of languages from each of five continental areas (Americas, Europe, Asia, Africa, Oceania). Within each continent the initial selection was based upon the judgment of Joseph H. Greenberg. He used the following criteria. Within continental areas preference was given to languages belonging to internally diverse genetic families and to families extensive in area, number of languages and number of speakers. "Atypical" languages (i.e. those known to be strongly influenced by languages from other families) were avoided if there were suitable alternatives. There being no explicit bibliographical frame, the known quality of a language's description also played a role. Some

languages were added and deleted from this initial sample by
analysts, presumably on the basis of convenience. (Joseph
H. Greenberg and Don Sherman, personal communication.)
Documentation: The sample is listed, sources are given, distribution by family and continent is provided.
Suitability: The Archive sample, tailored appropriately to the
   purpose of a given investigation (e.g. deletion of some INDO-
   EUROPEAN languages to remove the bias introduced by the
   widely spoken world languages) is probably of equal or better
   quality than any used in current research. See Sec. 10.2 and
   10.3 for further discussion.

6. Sampling in Related Disciplines

   Anthropologists, sociologists, political scientists and psychologists conducting comparative research face problems that resemble
those of linguists in many respects. Their richly documented experience is worth our attention, although the dominant concerns
in sociology, political science and psychology have not required
the general universes and frames which pose the greatest problems
in linguistics. Sociologists and political scientists deal largely
with complex modern societies. Psychologists employ comparative
research most frequently to test whether a certain kind of human
behavior is culture-free or not, for which small samples of diver-
gent societies are usually adequate. For further information the
reader may refer to the useful surveys of Frijda and Jahoda 1966,
Frey 1970, and Armer and Grimshaw 1973.

   The experience of cross-cultural researchers in anthropology,
beginning with Murdock 1949, applies more directly to cross language research. It provides case studies for consideration (O'Leary
1969, 1973), many of whose samples are compared and discussed by
Tatje et al. 1970. Methodology of sampling societies, including the
relative benefits of nonprobability and probability sampling, is considered by Murdock 1966, Chaney and Revilla 1969, Driver and
Chaney 1970, Naroll 1970a, 1970b, and Rohner and Pelto 1970. Of
great value are three "standard samples": The Human Relations
Area Files (HRAF) Probability Sample (Naroll 1967), the Standard
Cross-Cultural Sample of Murdock 1968, Murdock and White 1969;
and a Standard Ethnographic Sample proposed by Naroll et al. 1970,
Naroll and Sipes 1973. They are, respectively, a stratified random
sample, a quota sample and a frame. Recurring themes in this
literature that linguists should be aware of are the focus on "primitive" societies, the extensive use of correlational analysis, often

with very large numbers of culture traits,[4] and a preoccupation
with statistical solutions to the problems of distinguishing functional
and diffusional origins of culture traits and trait occurrences.[5] Due
allowance for these should be made in transposing the results of
sampling societies or cultures to cross language problems. Since
documentation of languages will only partially overlap documentation of societies the standard samples themselves are unlikely to
be appropriate for linguistic topics. The careful grouping of societies into 200 areas of the world, which is the basis of the sample
of Murdock and White 1969 (Murdock 1967, 1968), on the other hand,
could possibly serve as the areal framework for quota or stratified
samples.

7. Appropriateness of Probability Samples

Linguists will find the advice of a statistician helpful in choosing
a sample design for their research, even if they have some acquaintance with statistical theory at the level of Blalock 1960, for example.
The investigator with relatively little statistical background can
profit from Mosteller 1968, who lucidly sets forth the general context of the sampling decisions faced by an investigator. Stuart 1968
is an informative source on nonprobability samples.

When one decides whether to use a probability sample or a nonprobability sample, the most important consideration is the trade-off
between the additional cost of a probability sample and the protection
it affords against bias.

The additional cost of a probability sample is largely the construction of an explicit frame. For studies of universal scope this
step also provides the greatest rewards, even if a nonprobability
sample is subsequently drawn from it. Its construction ensures that
the investigator becomes acquainted with the full range of language
data appropriate to his study and makes painfully clear whatever
effect constraints on access to language information have upon the

---

[4] Textor's 1967 20,000 correlations among over 500 culture
traits over 400 societies epitomizes this research style.

[5] "Since some of the relationships among cultural elements are
surely functional whereas others are not, statistics offers the only
dependable technique for segregating them and thus arriving at
scientifically valid generalizations" (Murdock and White 1969: 330).
The lengthy discussions of "Galton's problem" are also based on
this point of view. See Sec. 10.2 below.

investigation. The value of at least an initial attempt at frame
description for any investigator without some acquaintance with
all the world's language families and areas should be evident. The
work of Murdock and White 1969 and Naroll and Sipes 1973 mentioned
above exemplify the research needed to construct a general worldwide frame for a probability sample. [6]

In gauging the threat of bias the following factors may be some
guide: commensurability with other errors (don't squander a sure
foundation on a ramshackle house), tendency of investigators to
assume a benevolent universe (who packs the strawberry baskets,
philanthropists?), impossibility of ex post facto detection and cor-
rection of bias except by comparison with independent studies (Sec.
10.3), and strength of claims to be made (true pilot and survey
investigations can tolerate considerable bias, since results must
be confirmed by further studies in any case).

Random error is usually of less concern for most current linguistic work. Instead of relying heavily on statistical measures
of correlation, linguists tend to establish significance of cross
language generalizations by demonstrating their relevance to other
observations and generalizations, e.g. diachronic, acquisitional
or synchronic principles of language structure.

Note that probability samples do not necessarily have lower
random error than nonprobability samples. The former's advantage
is rather that they permit the use of statistical theory codified,
for example, in terms of significance tests, to estimate the extent
of the error from a single sample. For further discussion of random error see Sec. 9.2 on sample size.

8. Some Types of Probability Samples

The simplest probability sample is the random sample which we
discussed in Sec. 4. Many more sophisticated types of probability
sample exist. Of these, stratified samples and systematic samples
are the most appropriate for cross language research. [7]

---

[6] See especially the discussion following Naroll and Sipes 1973.

[7] Yamane 1967 is an elementary account of the principles of
sample design including particularly stratified and systematic samples; Deming 1968 and Sudman 1976 are helpful guides to the researcher at a more advanced level; Cochran 1963 is a standard
technical reference on sampling theory.

Stratified and systematic samples are most effective when the variation between objects in the frame is greater <u>within</u> certain classes than it is <u>between</u> them. This is what we expect for language areas and families. Languages spoken in the same area resemble each other more than languages from widely separated areas; languages with a recent common origin resemble each other more than languages with a remote common origin.

8.1 Stratified samples

A stratified sample is selected from a frame which has been partitioned into nonoverlapping categories or strata. Survey respondents might be stratified by age, income, education or some combination of these; languages might be stratified by continent, genetic affiliation, word order type, type of prosodic system or a combination of these. Then from each category a random selection of objects is chosen; the number is proportional to the size of the category or may be determined by other criteria.

The practical difficulties of drawing a stratified sample are constructing a frame, choosing appropriate categories for its partition and making random selection from them.

Useful exemplars of stratified frames for the cross language researcher are those of Murdock and White 1969 and of Naroll and Sipes 1973. For a worldwide sample the task is costly; it requires the listing of every language for which suitable information is available, which depends upon the resources at the researcher's disposition. Note that the problem could be greatly simplified by trivializing the frame, for instance, by limiting it to references in a personal library. This merely trades one weakness for another, namely inappropriateness of frame to universe. Nor is there any universally applicable definition of "suitable." An explicit, objective characterization of this quality of frame members may touch off violent disagreement, as illustrated in the discussion following Naroll and Sipes 1973, but it is no less desirable for that.

What are the appropriate strata categories? How many? The answers depend upon the structure of variation of the parameters under investigation, which are often poorly known in advance. In practice the investigator has a can't-lose situation. No stratification can make the sample worse than a random sample, nor is it greatly sensitive to the fine details of the partition. Thus, if genetic affiliation is used as a category, the researcher need not agonize about the justification of a particular classification. Similarly,

areal partitions less carefully constructed than Murdock's 1968
will probably still be effective.

Having partitioned his frame the investigator arrives at the
tedious part of his task — random selection from each stratum.
The use of random number tables is very strongly urged, for
methods of selection are notoriously fallible. The best-known table
of random numbers is Rand Corporation 1955; shorter tables may
be found in many texts on sampling. The investigator unfamiliar
with their use may find it helpful to beg a five-minute lesson from
a statistician colleague. The following example illustrates one
straightforward method.

Let us assume that the first two categories of our frame contain
8 and 13 languages, respectively, arranged in some known order
from which one each is to be chosen. We use the following random
digits:[8]

    09647   32348   56909   40951   00440   etc.

For the first category we will consider only digits 1 through 8 so
that each will have equal chance of selection. Accordingly, the
first digit, 0, is ignored; so is the second, 9. The third digit is 6;
the sixth language is chosen. For the second category we consider
two digits at a time for we require 13 possibilities. We decide to
use digit sequences 01 through 13, ignoring all others. Now the
next pair of digits is 47, which we ignore; we continue, discarding
in turn 32, 34, 85 and 69 until we come to 09; the ninth language
is chosen.

An alternative to establishing a stratified frame of languages is
random "fishing" from a list of world languages such as Voegelin
and Voegelin 1966 or Grimes 1974. For each stratum in turn random
selections are made until a language is caught which belongs to the
stratum and meets predetermined bibliographic and other criteria.
This is unlikely to be more efficient except for relatively small
samples from relatively few strata. Many other methods can be
devised; the essential point is that they all require 1) an explicit
frame, 2) explicit definition of the strata categories and 3) predetermined criteria of suitability of the languages as a sample

---

[8] The 20th line of digits in Sudman 1975. Where we start is not
significant; the same numbers should not be reused in a given
application, however.

member. The HRAF Probability Sample (Naroll 1967) is an example
of a stratified sample.

8.2 Systematic samples

   Like stratified samples systematic samples assure selection
distributed over chosen attributes of the frame, but achieve it in a
slightly different manner. In the simplest case the objects are
ordered along a given dimension, from 1 to K. Let us say that
the desired sample size is one-tenth the frame size. A number
from 1 to 10 is selected randomly, e.g. 4. Then the sample will
consist of the 4th, 14th, 24th, 34th, etc., members of the frame.
If the frame is ordered alphabetically, this is a convenient way to
obtain a sample essentially equivalent to a random sample.

   The importance of systematic sampling for cross language research is that it can provide implicit stratification under certain
circumstances. This occurs when the frame is constructed so that
adjacent objects tend to be more similar than more widely separated
ones. Languages arranged by geographical location or by some
measure of relative degree of historical relationship fit this description. Usually refinement of precision is not a major consideration in sampling languages, yet it is worth noting that under certain
circumstances a systematic sample is more precise than an equivalent stratified sample (Cochran 1963). Intuitively we can see this
as a result of the maximum distance between objects obtained in
a selectional sample compared to the randomly varying distances
(but the same on the average) between objects in a stratified sample.
For further discussion see Deming 1968 and the references cited
therein.

9. Some Considerations for Choice of Sample Method

   Finding the right sample for the right job depends foremost upon
the investigator's judgment of the importance of sampling error
after consideration of the study's purpose, the universe and frame
and other sources of error. His choice of method to obtain an
appropriate sample will then depend largely upon his knowledge or
assumptions about the language characteristics under study. Con-
versely, from the claimed generality of conclusions based upon a
given sample, the investigator's assumptions about the language
characteristics can be inferred. The obvious example is the one-
language sample combined with a claim of universality; a reasonable
inference is that the characteristic is assumed to have zero diversity across languages, though perhaps exhibiting diversity across

individuals, perhaps because it is assumed to be wholly determined by the psychophysical nature of man.

The investigator is always faced with the paradox that the optimum sample requires the very knowledge that he seeks. This situation, which is not unique to cross language studies, does not excuse one from the consequences of his sample. If we truly know nothing about the language characteristics to be studied, then the first order of business is to learn something. A pilot study is required, perhaps; or a sample can be drawn in two stages, the form of the second stage using information obtained from the first. This state of ignorance is rare, however.

9.1 Exploiting distribution of language characteristics

One of the most important things we know is provided by a diachronic view of language characteristics. In different degrees, in different ways, they tend to be retained as languages diverge through time and they tend to be acquired from other languages in contact. This is why closely related and/or closely situated languages will be more similar in most respects than more distant ones. It is thus entirely proper that a major consideration in most judgment samples of languages is the representation of the world's language families and areas (e.g. the samples of Greenberg, Bell, Steele, and the Phonological Archive in Sec. 5) and that the first criticism leveled at a sample is that its coverage is partial or lopsided (e.g. Comrie). The justification of this approach is not that the sample bears a close resemblance to the frame with respect to the salient characteristics of the family and area, but that a major source of sample variability and potential bias is controlled. A simple random sample takes no advantage of this distinctive trait of languages.

It is important to keep in mind that what counts for a given study is similarity among related languages with respect to the variables under investigation and that this can vary immensely. One reason for this, as Greenberg 1974: 60 points out, is that characteristics differ in their historical stability, which is necessarily reflected in their synchronic distribution. Compare the variable of vowel nasality with the variable of prosodic type (tonal vs. nontonal). About the same proportion of the world's languages have nasal vowels as have lexical tone, somewhere between 25 and 40 percent. The contrast in distribution is striking: tone languages are essentially highly concentrated in three areas, sub-Saharan Africa, Middle America, and Eastern Asia; but languages with nasal vowels are scattered all over the world and through most language families. A consequence for choice of sampling plan would be the degree of stratification. More than 20 areas would bring little additional benefit for the tonal variable; a much finer mesh would be desirable for nasality. Application of such principles to actual studies is complicated by the fact that they usually involve a number of different variables with widely varying distributions.

Area and family resemblances are not the only factors that can be exploited in this way. If the investigator has reason to suspect that the language characteristics that interest him are apt to be more diverse between major language types (such as prosodic type, word order type) than among them, then a stratification design is worth considering. On the other hand, in the absence of such supposition or special requirements of sample design, stratification over some variable just to ensure that the sample more closely replicates the frame has no merit.

9.2 Questions of sample size

There is rarely any easy way to know ahead of time how big a sample should be. Even the common method of using the same sample size as another investigator with a comparable problem is not of much use in cross language research, for opinions vary widely and there is not yet enough followup research to confirm the value of earlier studies. My own feeling is that most current studies do not use a large enough sample. This section will therefore limit itself to discussion of a few general principles that affect sample size.

One reason for a larger sample is greater precision of observation. If the observations are represented by the mean of some variable, then the precision of the observations increases proportionately with the square root of the number of observations. Put another way, to cut random error in half, you have to double the number of observations twice. High precision gets expensive fast.

Large samples are usually required for reasons beyond global precision. It is important to realize that the precision of observations does not depend upon the frame size, it depends upon the sample size. For example, if a sample of 3,000 is adequate for a national survey (with frame size, say, of 100,000,000) it is not the case that the same precision can be obtained for a statewide survey with a sample of 300 if the frame is only 10,000,000. A sample of 3,000 is still required. This means that a study which includes analysis of subtypes may require a larger overall sample to ensure that the subtype analysis is sufficiently precise. See the discussion of Steele's sample in Sec. 5.5 for an example.

The rarity of a language characteristic also affects the sample size needed for a given precision. The simplest example is the estimation of proportions. Let us say we wish to know what fraction of the world's languages have interdental fricatives and what fraction have lexical tone and that we require a sample that would not yield an estimate with an error of 20% more than five times out of 100. If we assume the true proportion of interdental fricatives is 10% and that of tonal languages is 40%, a larger sample will be required for the former:

	Assumed true proportion	Required sample size[9]
Interdental fricatives	10%	900
Tonal languages	40%	150

Inferences from nonoccurrence of languages belonging to a given type in the sample are similarly related to sample size. Consider, for example, the typology of basic word order of Greenberg 1963, which is based on the six possible orders of the elements S(ubject), O(bject), V(erb). If we observe no languages with O preceding S in a sample, what can we conclude? Such languages might be nonexistent or else just rare. A sample of languages obviously cannot establish that a language type is impossible. The investigator can ask, though, how large a sample is needed to make it likely that an example of the type will turn up if it does exist. Table 1 illustrates how the sample size depends upon the rarity of the type.

Table 1. Likelihood that a sample contains no instance of a language type

Rarity of type	1	5	Sample Size[10] 10	20	30	50	100	200	300	500
10%	.90	.59	.35	.12	.04	.005	.0003	--even less--		
1%	.99	.95	.90	.82	.74	.60	.36	.13	.05	.0006

If 10% of languages belong to the type, then 995 out of 1,000 samples of 50 languages will contain at least one such language. But if only one percent of languages belong to the type, then 400 out of 1,000 samples will contain such a language. A sample 10 times larger containing 500 languages would be needed to obtain the same level of confidence.

---

[9] Random samples are assumed to calculate the sample sizes.

[10] Based on a random sample.

There are therefore many reasons to disagree with the Murdock
and White 1969 dictum applied to languages that "a carefully drawn
sample of around 200 cases essentially exhausts the universe of
known and adequately described culture types." Larger or smaller
samples may "essentially exhaust" the information contained in the
diversity of the world's languages, depending on the typology and
purposes of the investigation.

How many languages should be chosen from each stratum in a
stratified sample? Proportional sampling, in which an equal fraction of languages from each stratum is selected, is a straightforward procedure. It is particularly appropriate when the universe is the world's existing languages. If the strata are not
equally homogeneous, some increase in sampling efficiency may
be achieved by weighting the samples according to strata variability. For cross language studies whose universe is possible
human languages which are implicitly or explicitly concerned with
the relation of the distribution of language characteristics to the
historical processes of language change and which employ stratification by language area or family, unweighted proportional sampling
is not as appropriate. See below for further discussion.

If sample variability is a major concern, the investigator should
preferably not rely on estimates of variation from a single sample.
Direct estimation from independent subsamples can be used for
both probability and nonprobability samples. More sophisticated
techniques using overlapping subsamples may also be applicable
(Mosteller 1968, Stuart 1968, Sudman 1976).

10. Post hoc Assessment of Language Samples

As a basic principle of accountability every study should state
its sampling plan. If nonprobability sampling is used, the sample
should be listed, for this is the only means that a reader has of
forming his own judgment of the sample's adequacy. Since the
soundest sampling plans are easily flawed by unforeseen circumstances or errors in execution and since the temptation to cut cor-
ners on sampling is great, the reader of a study is justified in
suspecting the worst when discussion of sampling is omitted.

Such documentation has a further cumulative importance. It
facilitates the post hoc assessment of language samples against
each other and against other bodies of data which will lead to better
means of control of sampling errors. Again the problem is not
unique to language sampling. The presence of significant bias had
to be demonstrated in survey sampling before methods to avoid it

were generally adopted. Even today nonresponses in survey samples always occur, which makes true probability samples unattainable in practice; but careful study of the nature of biases introduced by nonresponse allows surveys to protect against them.

There is one unproductive line of criticism that is common enough to warrant comment, namely the "how can you say that if you haven't studied IKI and IKIKI?" line. Granted that the investigator's choice of languages may have biased his results, it does no good to insist that he substitute the biases preferred by another linguist. This kind of criticism sometimes occurs because of a tradition of exemplification; for example, FINNISH, HUNGARIAN and TURKISH for vowel harmony. A study of vowel harmony that omitted these languages could legitimately be criticized for ignoring prior scholarship, but not simply for having included some languages rather than others. The omission of extreme types of languages is another cause for this sort of criticism. If omissions are symptomatic of general weakness in sample design, then it is another matter, and it suffices to point out the weakness and its effects.

10.1 Bibliographic bias

From today's vantage point the earlier biases that corresponded to the concentration of adequate descriptions in particular language families or groups are obvious. We need to know more about the present situation. The problem is acute for the study of such relatively poorly documented aspects of language as acquisition, discourse functions, intonation, text frequency of grammatical categories and even phonotactics. The direct comparison of characteristics of described languages against those of undescribed ones is naturally impossible. Since we do now have information about the undescribed languages of 1960 or some other previous year, it seems to me that a comparison of samples of "before" and "after" languages is worth considering.

10.2 Areal and genetic bias

A major source of a sample's bias is the areal and genetic distribution of its languages. We need more specific bases for assessing samples' adequacy than inclusion of languages from all "major families" or from all continents, criteria now commonly employed. Are AMERIND languages underrepresented or overrepresented? Is South East Asia underrepresented or overrepresented? Even at this general level the practice of past studies is the only available guide, a dim and flickering beacon at best.

The problem for studies aimed at general regularities of language, assumed to be systematically related to historical process, is an intriguing one. One principle, analogous to proportional sampling, is that more languages be sampled from more numerous areas or families. It is readily recognized that this is an imperfect guide, however, for intuitively some groups have more information to offer than others of the same size. We expect to learn more from the 200 or so AFROASIATIC languages than from the much more homogeneous BANTU languages, though they number over 300. Furthermore, the problem is complicated by the fact that language groups may be homogeneous in some respects but diverse in others; the great phonological similarity of AUSTRALIAN languages is an example (Wurm 1971: 724).

Anthropologists have devoted a great deal of attention to this issue, known to them as Galton's problem. Linguists will find the general arguments of this research more helpful than the specific details because the principle concerns relate to the statistical significance of correlation matrices. The critical summary of Strauss and Orans 1975 and the comments following it are highly recommended.

Here I take a somewhat different approach based on the concept of sampling unit. Let us ask first about the sampling units of a study of just existing languages.

The sampling units are clearly languages, just as the children in an elementary school are the units for a study concerning the children. But what if we wish information about the children's parents but have no access to them except through their children? The sampling units are the parents, though no information is obtained from them directly. The situation is not so clear-cut for research on language universals, but I think that a case can be made that such research can properly be conceived as sampling language changes, not languages themselves.[11] Notice that in sampling parents through the selection of children a random selection of children will yield a biased selection of parents because siblings will be accorded equal weight. From this point of view according BANTU languages less weight in a sample than AFRO-ASIATIC languages is not a marginal matter of increased sample efficiency but an attempt to avoid potentially serious biases.

---

[11] Suggested to me by Joseph Greenberg.

As a first step toward the attack of this problem a guide to genetic distribution is constructed below and applied to selected language samples.[12]

The yardstick is based upon estimated centuries of divergence. This is obtained from historical knowledge, when available, from glottochronological estimates and on informal published estimates of divergence such as Haas' comment that ALGONQUIAN and MUSKOGEAN show similar divergence to ROMANCE and GERMAN (1969). The weaknesses of such information are fully realized; in particular if the assumed genetic grouping is incorrect, the glotto-chronological estimates will not correspond to temporal divergence. Furthermore, in areas such as South America and New Guinea, so little information is available that I simply had to use my best guess. The relatively gross distinctions attempted here should not be much affected by such errors. What emerges is a general purpose index of the genetic diversity of the world's languages based on neither phonological nor grammatical structure.

Having arbitrarily selected 3,500 years divergence as a break-point, I determined the language groups separated by this amount for the world's genetic stocks. Where information was insufficient, as for New Guinea, I estimated the number of languages and language groups. Nothing hinges on the genetic assumptions about the listed stocks; I have chosen the largest groupings usually proposed for convenience here. For finer detail or for other purposes smaller groups could be used. The results appear in Table 2 (next page).

The average size of language groups separated by 3,500 or more years is about 9. The size ranges from one (BURUSHASKI, KET, etc.) to over 300 (BANTU). Thus we see that DRAVIDIAN is less diverse than average for its size, AFROASIATIC is close to average and NILO-SAHARAN is more than usually diverse.

This measure is applied to the comparison of five language samples in Table 3. Samples A, B, C all contain 30 languages. Sample A is a random sample selected from the list of languages in Voegelin and Voegelin 1966. Sample B, though not actually selected, represents a sample stratified by the 16 language stocks with selection proportional to the number of groups in each stock.

---

[12] No analysis of areal distribution will be attempted here. A useful starting point would be the culture areas of Murdock 1967, 1968.

Table 2.   Estimated number of languages and 3500-year
           groups in major linguistic stocks of the world

Linguistic stock	Estimated no. of languages	Estimated no. of groups separated by 3500 yrs. or more	
Dravidian	20		1
Eurasiatic	70		13
Indo-European	90		12
Nilo-Saharan	100		18
Niger-Kordofanian	900		44
Afroasiatic	200		23
Khoisan	20		5
Amerind	900	est.	150
Na-Dene	30		4
Austric	800	ca.	55
Indo-Pacific	700	est.	100
Australian	200	ca.	27
Sino-Tibetan	250	ca.	20
Ibero-Caucasian	35		4
Ket	1		1
Burushaski	1		1
TOTALS	ca. 4300		478

Sample C is the judgment sample of Greenberg 1963.   The larger
judgment samples of Bell 1971 and the Phonology Archive are D
and E respectively (see Table 3 next page).

The proportions at the bottom of the columns will help the reader
compare the samples with the 3500-year groups in the second column.   The clustering of BANTU and AUSTRONESIAN languages
in the random sample is not bias; however, one would want to check
results from such a sample to ensure that they were not explainable
by the chance concentration in those groups.

The judgment samples suggest that we still have not escaped our
European biases.   The obviously large number of AMERICAN IN-
DIAN languages in D and E is typical of many cross language
studies, perhaps because of their relatively easy access in the
pages of IJAL.   From the point of view of genetic divergence it
appears to be perfectly justified.   The great gap in the samples is
clearly in the INDO-PACIFIC languages.   There are relatively
few well-described languages in this group.   The information of
Table 3 suggests that more intensive use be made of what descriptions that are available.

Table 3. Comparison of five language samples. A = 30-language random sample; B = 30-language stratified sample; C = 30-language judgment sample (Greenberg 1963); D = 144-language judgment sample (Bell 1971); E = 277-language judgment sample (Phonology Archive).

Linguistic stock	No. of groups	No. of language in sample				
		A	B	C	D	E
Dravidian	1	0	0	1	4	5
Eurasiatic	13	0	1	3	13	26
Indo-European	12	1	1	6	12	27[c]
Nilo-Saharan	18	3	1	4	6	8
Niger-Kordofanian	44	8[a]	3	2	17	27[d]
Afroasiatic	23	0	1	2	9	17
Khoisan	5	0	0	0	1	3
Amerind	150	8	9	5	46	80
Na-Dene	4	0	1	0	1	5
Austric	55	8[b]	4	3	19	36
Indo-Pacific	100	1	6	0	3	12
Australian	27	0	2	1	6	8
Sino-Tibetan	20	1	1	1	6	15
Ibero-Caucasian	4	0	0	1	1	6
Ket	1	0	0	0	0	1
Burushaski	1	0	0	1	0	1
TOTALS	478	30 =1/15	30 =1/15	30 =1/15	144 =1/3	277 =1/2 of 478

[a] 7 Bantu

[b] 7 Austronesian

[c] 5 Romance, 4 Germanic

[d] 7 Bantu

□ = overrepresented; △ = underrepresented.

10.3 Other sources of bias

Analysis of typological characteristics of the languages of a
sample cannot usually add to the credibility of a study for the same
reason that quota sampling is insufficient to protect against bias.
Establishing that the sample is unbiased with respect to characteristics R, S, T guarantees nothing concerning X, Y, Z. When certain
characteristics are suspected to influence the variables of concern
significantly, however, it is of course prudent to control them or
check them for bias. Checking selected characteristics for bias
can also be helpful in evaluating general purpose samples, as
Sherman 1975 has done for the Phonology Archive. He compared
an incomplete version of the Archive sample of 106 languages with
the 570-language sample of Ruhlen 1975 with respect to characteristics of phonetic inventory such as occurrence of [ɸ], [f], [ɸ] and
[f], etc. In almost all cases there appeared no differences that
would not be expected by chance, which was interpreted as contributing to the validation of the Archive sample. In fact, although for
other reasons the Archive sample appears to be quite satisfactory
for its intended uses (5.8, 10.2), I believe that Sherman's results
are of limited help in assessing it for two instructive reasons.
First, size alone cannot affect bias. Although Ruhlen's sample is
large, it is asserted to have the same rationale as the Archive
sample, and Ruhlen drew it while working on the Archive project.
One might readily grant that "it would be improbable that both samples could be equally and identically biased" (13), yet a substantial
similarity of bias cannot be ruled out. The two samples are thus
inappropriate for the study of bias, although they could profitably
be used to investigate sampling variation.

Significantly more languages were found to possess voicing contrast in stops in the Ruhlen sample than in the Archive sample.
As it turns out,voicing contrast is rarer in the Americas than in
the rest of the world, and further, the areal distribution of the two
samples differed most in the Americas (Ruhlen 26%, Archive 36%).
This illustrates how a hidden bias in a sample, having no effect on
numerous variables and passing numerous tests based on them,
can still strike without warning on variables of apparently similar
nature.

11. From World's Languages to Possible Languages

Some readers will have found that the foregoing discussion does
not respond to their skeptical question, "What good can counting
languages do?" It is the relation between possible languages and

the world's languages, i.e. between the universe and the frame of most typological studies, that is their concern. If the frame is inappropriate, then care in choice of a sample is like waterproofing boots with a hole in the sole, for sample quality can only strengthen the links of inference between the sample and the frame.

Imagine that we could take a total sample -- all the languages in the world. The sampling problem is solved. We know all we can know about the frame. Obviously, not all is known about the universe. Claims about possible languages, just as with a smaller sample, rest upon assumptions about how well the world's languages resemble them.

If we ask, for example, what sounds can be used distinctively in human language, we could hardly expect to achieve a definitive closed inventory by their exhaustive enumeration in existing languages. What if, by historical accident, the people speaking the ancestral language of the KHOISAN family of Africa died out? It is plausible that today no click sounds would exist.[12]

Once admitting such possibilities, what is the justification for taking great care to include INDO-PACIFIC languages or any given group in a sample? They exist on earth only by the historical accident that the communities speaking their ancestral languages happened to survive. If they are omitted from the sample, this is equivalent to the nonsurvival of the communities; hence, a sample without them is as good as one with them. Reapplying this argument to further language groups leads to the conclusion that one sample is just as good as another, including samples of any single language. If all this is taken seriously, and I fear a few linguists have, perhaps, then typological comparison has little evidential value for the general properties of language. Haggling over inclusion or exclusion of particular languages in a sample is fruitless. What counts is the overall effect of the selection procedure. We can think of the world's languages as a special one-time sample, consider the historical processes as a selection procedure and inquire about their effect. One hypothesis is that language characteristics play no role in the historical processes that created the world's language communities. We should then have no qualms about our generalizations; the slight chance that we have been vouchsafed a freaky, misleading set of languages is an acceptable risk.

---

[12] This sort of scenario is depicted by Chomsky and Halle 1968.

The historical accident argument is only valid under the hypothesis that the historical processes and language characteristics
interact. How might this happen? Two ways have been suggested
that I know of. One is that there endure traces of the early state(s)
of language as it evolved into its present form. The other, suggested by Swadesh 1971, is that increased societal complexity is
linked with shifts in language characteristics. Such possibilities
deserve exploration; so far nothing suggests that such effects are
so significant to render invalid generalizations from observations
about the world's languages.

12. Conclusions

Some attention to the sample for a cross language study is always
needed. Whatever his conclusions the researcher should be account-
able for them. A discussion of the sampling method, preferably
including the sample itself, increases the value of any typological
study.

Low-cost, low-quality samples are preferred when a high risk
of sampling error is tolerable. An explicit consideration of the
universe and frame appropriate for the study's goals and of other
error sources helps assure that the risk is indeed tolerable. Con-
versely, if bibliographic or resource constraints essentially determine sample quality, the consequences for generality and validity
of the conclusions will be better understood.

When higher quality samples are necessary, the investigator
will profit by carefully considering principles of sampling theory
in conjunction with his knowledge of the subject matter and his
goals. There is much to be recommended in considering a probability sample even if its use is rejected; this makes clear what
risks are accepted and what costs are avoided; and partial use of
the procedures for drawing a probability sample, even a partial
survey of the available sources, will improve the quality of a
nonprobability sample. A point often overlooked is that a single
sample may not be suitable for a study with multiple purposes;
multiple samples, perhaps overlapping, are worth considering.

Since bias is usually the greatest threat to typological studies,
further work on the nature of bibliographic, areal, genetic and
other sources of bias would be an effective way to obtain a general
increase in sample quality.

Control of random error can sometimes be important, too. Here the use of subsamples for estimating variation, a rapidly developing topic in sampling theory, offers the greatest promise.

BIBLIOGRAPHY

Armer, Michael and A.D. Grimshaw (eds.) 1973. Comparative social research: methodological problems and strategies. New York: Wiley.

Bell, Alan. 1971. Some patterns of occurrence and formation of syllable structures. Working Papers on Language Universals 6. 23-137.

Blalock, Hubert M., Jr. 1960. Social statistics. New York: McGraw-Hill.

Chaney, Richard P. and Rogelio Ruiz Revilla. 1969. Sampling methods and interpretation of correlation: a comparative analysis of seven cross-cultural samples. American Anthropologist 71. 597-633.

Chomsky, Noam and Morris Halle. 1968. The sound pattern of English. New York: Harper.

Cochran, William G. 1963. Sampling techniques. New York: Wiley (second edition).

Comrie, Bernard. 1976. The syntax of causative constructions: cross-language similarities and divergences. Syntax and semantics, vol. 6. The grammar of causative constructions, ed. by M. Shibatani, 261-312. New York: Academic Press.

Deming, W. Edward. 1968. Sample surveys. I: The field. International Encyclopedia of Social Sciences. New York: MacMillan - Free Press.

Driver, Harold E. and Richard P. Chaney. 1970. Cross-cultural sampling and Galton's problem. Naroll and Cohen 1970: 990-1003.

Frey, Frederick W. 1970. Cross-cultural survey research in political science. The methodology of comparative research, ed. by Robert T. Holt and J.E. Turner, 173-294. New York: Free Press.

Frijda, N. and G. Jahoda. 1966. On the scope and methods of cross-cultural research. International Journal of Psychology 1. 110-27.

Greenberg, J.H. 1963. Some universals of grammar with particular reference to the order of meaningful elements. Universals of language, ed. by J.H. Greenberg, 73-133. Cambridge: M.I.T. Press (second edition).

_____. 1974. Language typology: a historical and analytic overview. The Hague: Mouton.

Grimes, Joseph E. 1974. Word lists and languages. Ithaca: Dept. of Modern Languages and Linguistics, Cornell University.

Haas, Mary. 1969. The prehistory of languages. The Hague - Paris: Mouton.

Hammarberg, Björn and Åke Viberg. 1975. Plåtshallartvånget, ett syntaktiskt problem i svenskan för invandrare. SSM Report 2. Stockholm: University of Stockholm, Institute of Linguistics.

Hyman, Larry. 1977. On the nature of linguistic stress. Studies on stress and accent, ed. by L. Hyman. 37-82. Los Angeles: University of Southern California.

Lisker, Leigh and Arthur Abramson. 1964. A cross-language study of voicing in initial stops: acoustical measurements. Word 20. 384-422.

Mosteller, Frederick. 1968. Nonsampling errors. International Encyclopedia of the Social Sciences. New York: MacMillan- Free Press.

Murdock, G.P. 1949. Social structure. New York: Macmillan.

_____. 1966. Cross-cultural sampling. Ethnology 5. 97-114.

_____. 1967. Ethnographic atlas: a summary. Ethnology 6. 109-236.

_____. 1968. World sampling provinces. Ethnology 7. 305-26.

_____ and Douglas R. White. 1969. Standard cross-cultural sample. Ethnology 8. 329-69.

Naroll, Raoul. 1967. The proposed HRAF probability sample. Behavior Science Notes 2. 70-80.

_____. 1970a. Chaney and Ruiz Revilla: a comment. American Anthropologist 72. 1451-53.

_____. 1970b. Cross-cultural sampling. Naroll and Cohen 1970, 889-926.

_____ and Ronald Cohen (eds.) 1970. A handbook of method in cultural anthropology. New York: Natural History Press.

_____ and R.C. Sipes. 1973. A standard ethnographic sample: second edition. Current Anthropology 14. 111-40.

_____ et al. 1970. Standard ethnographic sample. Current Anthropology 11. 235-48.

O'Leary, Timothy J. 1971. Bibliography of cross-cultural studies: Supplement I. Behavior Science Notes 6. 191-203.

_____. 1969. A preliminary bibliography of cross-cultural studies. Behavior Science Notes 4. 95-115.

_____. 1973. Bibliography of cross-cultural studies: Supplement II. Behavior Science Notes 8. 123-34.

Rand Corporation. 1955. A million random digits with 100,000 normal deviates. Glencoe, Ill.: Free Press.

Rohner, Ronald P. and Pertti J. Pelto. 1970. Sampling methods: Chaney and Ruiz Revilla, Comment 2. American Anthropologist 72. 1453-56.

Ruhlen, Merritt. 1975. A guide to the languages of the world. Stanford.

Sherman, Don. 1975. Stop and fricative systems: a discussion of paradigmatic gaps and the question of language sampling. Working Papers on Language Universals 17. 1-31.

Steele, Susan. 1975. On some factors that affect and effect word order. Word order and word order change, ed. by C.N. Li, 197-268. Austin: University of Texas Press.

Strauss, David J. and Martin Orans. 1975. Mighty sifts: a
   critical appraisal of solutions to Galton's problem and a partial
   solution. Current Anthropology 16. 573-94.

Stuart, Alan. 1968. Sample surveys. II: Nonprobability sampling.
   International Encyclopedia of the social sciences. New York:
   MacMillan-Free Press.

Sudman, Seymour. 1976. Applied sampling. New York: Academic
   Press.

Swadesh, Morris. 1971. The origin and diversification of language.
   Chicago: Aldine.

Tatje, Terrance A., Raoul Naroll and Robert B. Textor. 1970.
   The methodological findings of the cross-cultural summary.
   Naroll and Cohen 1970, 649-75.

Textor, Robert B. 1967. A cross-cultural summary. New
   Haven: HRAP Press.

Vihman, Marilyn M. 1974. Excerpts from the Phonology Archive
   Coding Manual. Working Papers on Language Universals 15.
   141-53.

Voegelin, C.F. and F.M. Voegelin. 1966. Index to languages of
   the world. Anthropological Linguistics 8.6.7.

Wurm, Stephen A. 1971. Classifications of Australian languages,
   including Tasmania. Current trends in linguistics, vol. 8, ed.
   by T.A. Sebeok, 721-78. The Hague - Paris: Mouton.

Yamane, Taro. 1967. Elementary sampling theory. Englewood
   Cliffs: Prentice Hall.

Universals and Linguistic Explanation

HANS-HEINRICH LIEB

ABSTRACT

After a brief discussion of the generative treatment of universals
and explanation (Section 1), the author characterizes in Sec. 2 the
results that have been obtained in the philosophy of science with
respect to concepts of explanation, and the attempts to apply such
concepts in linguistics. Linguistic applications are confronted with
the problem of how abstract entities (such as properties of languages)
may be related to facts about actual speech. This problem is studied
in Sec. 3 for language universals, in particular for 'communication
universals' and 'system-related universals.' Sec. 4 suggests examples of linguistic explanations and analyzes the rôle that is assumed
in such explanations by universals of the two types. Basic, intermediate, and general linguistic explanations are distinguished, and a
conception of basic linguistic facts is proposed that requires a reversal of generative conceptions of explanation. Finally, the results of
this paper are summarized as guidelines for possible explications
of "linguistic explanation" (Sec. 5).

CONTENTS

1. Introduction

1.1 The connection between universals and linguistic explanation

It has been recognized by a number of linguists that universality research is intimately connected with the search for explanations in linguistics. This position is generally taken in generative grammar, where a special conception has been developed for interrelating the two types of research. Even before universals became a topic in generative grammar, universals were linked to linguistic explanation in the programmatic Memorandum Concerning Language Universals by Greenberg, Osgood and Jenkins (1966, esp. Sec. 7).[1] In my recent attempt to solve inherent problems of the concept of language universal, I also assume an essential link between universality research and linguistic explanation (Lieb 1975, esp. Sec. III).

Informally, the rôle of language universals in linguistic explanations can be described as follows (Lieb 1975: 498):

Any grammar of a language (at least any non-algorithmic grammar) can be considered as a theory of that language. Trivially, the grammar will contain a theorem of the form: x is a language. Let F be any property that is attributed to x by a theorem of the grammar. Assuming a theory of language with a theorem that attributes F to all languages, we may say that the theorem of the grammar is given a general linguistic explanation by the theorem of the theory of language (it follows from the latter and from the theorem stating that x is a language).

Taking a traditional position on language universals we may say that F is a language universal (in case the theorem of the theory of language is 'true'). Assume that x is indeed a language. We may then say that the fact that F is a language universal 'explains' the fact that x has property F.

This is not yet the complete picture: the fact that F is a language universal may again be 'explained'; such an explanation induces, so to speak, a 'deeper' explanation of the fact that x has property F (Lieb 1975: 498f):

Suppose a theorem of a grammar is given a general linguistic explanation by a theorem of a theory of language. That theorem might in turn be explained by theorems of other theories,

---

[1]The Memorandum dates back to 1959, cf. Greenberg 1966: v.

e.g. might receive a semiotic explanation. Then it seems
reasonable to say that the theorem of the grammar has been
given the same explanation. In this way, theorems of a grammar may ultimately be explained, via a theory of language, by
theorems of non-linguistic theories.

There may also be theorems of a theory of language that claim
certain properties as universal and are completely derivable from
other theorems of the same theory. Greenberg et al. distinguish
the two cases as 'external' vs. 'internal deductions' (1966: xxvi --
an 'external deduction' involves 'non-linguistic predicates').

Universals are, so to speak, both explanatory and explainable,
and their explanatory usefulness partly depends on their explainability.

For a more precise formulation, the concept of language universal must be explicated, and the concept of explanation has to be
further clarified with special reference to linguistics. The first
task is tackled in Lieb 1975, and I shall rely on its results. A
major part of the present paper will be devoted to the second task.
I shall not come up with a definite solution; but a thorough discussion of problems of explanation is indispensable for our immediate
purpose, which is a better understanding of certain aspects of language universals.

General concepts of explanation have always figured large as a
topic in the philosophy of science. In Sec. 2 I first characterize
the 'state of the art' in that discipline with respect to questions of
explanation (Sec. 2.1, 2.2), and then outline the rôle played in
linguistics by concepts of explanation taken from the philosophy
of science (Sec. 2.3). In Sec. 3 I shall deal with different types
of language universals and study the question how universals can
be related to speech; such a relation is required because of the
explanatory function of language universals. In Sec. 4 the concept
of linguistic explanation is clarified though not formally explicated.
Sample explanations centering around a semantic example are suggested, and the rôle of universals in these explanations is analyzed.

Contrary to what may be expected, I do not intend to dwell much
on the concepts of linguistic explanation and language universal as
developed in generative grammar. Enough has been written on the
first concept, and I do not think much of the second. The following
subsection is meant as a basis for relating the main topics of my
paper to generative conceptions.

1.2 Generative views

Generative grammarians have implicitly or explicitly stressed the explanatory rôle of universals:

> We are looking for explanations of the facts of individual languages, embodied in grammars, and we are looking for explanations for these explanations, a general theory of language (Bach 1974: 156).

As I understand this, Bach is claiming that the rules of a grammar explain facts of an individual language, and the 'general theory of language' explains the rules.[2]

Chomsky's assumption of an "innate schema (the general definition of "grammar") that gradually becomes more explicit and differentiated as the child learns the language" (1965: 27) implies that language universals are explainable, or partly so, by the 'innate schema.' More recent work in the generative camp has assumed that Chomsky's 'innate schema' is not sufficient; cf. Bever 1974: 199:

> I have described an interactionist program of linguistic description. It assumes that acceptability facts and universals in language involve a variety of systems of linguistic knowledge and skill.

In describing the general rôle of language universals in linguistic explanations, I tacitly assumed that a theorem of a grammar has the form of a statement; a theorem of a theory of language is on languages, not grammars; a language universal is a property of languages, not grammars, and does not depend on grammars; and explanation is based on deductive relationships between theorems of the same or of different theories. May all these assumptions simply be carried over to generative grammar? They may not. Hence, in characterizing the generative views, I only established an analogy between my account of 'universals and explanation' in Sec. 1.1 and the way in which the generative grammarian describes the relation between universals (in his sense) and explanation.

In the previously quoted passage Bach goes on to remark: "Linguistics necessarily involves theories and metatheories." This betrays the classical approach of the generative grammarian to the theory of language: basically, a theory of language is a theory of grammars, hence, a metatheory (each grammar is to be a theory

---

[2] Similarly, Sanders 1974: 2.

in its own right).[3] I have been arguing against this approach for
years;[4] the extent to which it has been uncritically accepted is
sometimes stunning.[5]

The generative approach to the theory of language has led to a
misconception of language universals (cf. Lieb 1975: Sec. 1.4).
The generative conception of grammars (as algorithms for gener-
ating formal objects) makes it difficult to actually use grammars
in a context of explanation (cf. Lieb 1974: 100). Possibly, these
problems can be solved, but this is not the place to attempt a solution. In the present paper, I shall apply myself to more fundamental matters, leaving it to others to decide how my results may
be put to use in the context of generative grammar. In particular,
I am not going to add to the voluminous discussion on 'explanatory
adequacy,' 'explanatory theories' etc.

As a frame of reference for my later discussion, I first characterize concepts of explanation as found in the philosophy of science
(in a broad sense in which it does not restrict itself to the natural
sciences). These concepts will be found wanting in various respects. Still, they embody important points of view that should
not be neglected in linguistics. It will be shown, though, that current attempts to apply these concepts in linguistics have been unsuccessful.

2. 'Explanation' in the Philosophy of Science

    2.1 The 'Covering Law Model'

    'Explanation' has always been a central topic in the philosophy
of science, especially under the influence of 'logical empiricism.'[6]

---

[3] Cf. Bach 1974: 157: "A. What is the class of grammars $\underline{G}$ from
which the acquirer of a human language selects the grammar for
his/her language?" -- "An answer to $\underline{A}$ would be exactly an answer
to the question: what is human language?" The generative approach
has a weaker variant where a theory of language is not identified
with, but derivative on, a theory of grammars.

[4] Lieb 1968a: Sec. 1; 1970: Sec. 1.7 and Chs. 10f; 1974: Sec. 1 and
4.4; 1975: Sec. 1.4; for a brief statement, cf. 1976e.

[5] Cf. Dougherty 1974 or Sanders (1974: 17) who accepts it "as,
perhaps, even conceptually necessary."

[6] The philosophy of science should not be equated with logical
empiricism. By "science" I mean not just the natural sciences,

Until very recently, linguists simply failed to take notice of this fact. Generative grammarians, in particular, have been quite satisfied to mull over Chomsky's notion of the 'explanatory,' which does not seem to owe much to non-linguistic discussions on 'explanation.'[7] Now it may well be that proposals made in the philosophy of science are not very relevant for linguistics, but this cannot be decided by simply ignoring them.

For linguists who read GERMAN (as they should) there is no excuse for being unfamiliar with the philosophers' views on explanation; thirty years of discussion are minutely represented and critically evaluated in Stegmüller 1969. Here are some of the basic points that evolve from Stegmüller's presentation:[8]

1. a. Most efforts are devoted to developing concepts of explanation that would be applicable in the natural sciences.

   b. All concepts (a) are 'non-pragmatic': researchers who do the explaining are not considered.[9]

   c. At least with respect to the natural sciences, a three-fold distinction is made:
      i.   'Explanation of facts' vs. 'explanation of laws.'
      ii. 'Deductive' vs. 'inductive explanation.'
      iii. 'Nomological' vs. 'probabilistic explanation.'

   d. Discussion is concerned almost exclusively with 'explanation of facts.'

(ftnt. 6 cont.)
but also the social sciences and the humanities. "Philosophy of science," in this sense, also covers developments in, say, 'hermeneutic philosophy.'

[7] The generativist's attitude is well documented by the linguistic contributions to Cohen 1974 which, after all, contains the papers from a symposium on 'explaining linguistic phenomena.' Only the Introduction by Sanders betrays any knowledge of the concept of explanation that for decades prevailed in the philosophy of science.

[8] For simplicity's sake I shall take Stegmüller as my principal source.

[9] In discussions on 'explanation' vs. 'prediction,' time is taken into account (cf. Stegmüller 1969: Ch. II). This leads to an indirect consideration of the researcher.

e. Especially in the case of deductive-nomological explanation of facts, discussion is dominated by a conception
whose best-known form -- usually called the 'Covering
Law Model of Scientific Explanation' -- is essentially due
to C.G. Hempel.

Let us briefly characterize the Covering Law Model for the case
of deductive-nomological explanation of facts.[10] According to the
Covering Law Model, any scientific explanation of this type is an
argument of the following form: It consists of two parts, the explanans and the explanandum. The explanandum is, roughly, a
sentence E that describes an event whose occurrence is to be
explained. The explanans consists of n sentences A_1, .., A_n and
m sentences L_1, .., L_m such that A_i is a non-general sentence
that is (or formulates) an antecedent condition for the event described by E: A_i specifies a state of affairs prior to, or simul-
taneous with, the occurrence of E. L_j is (or formulates) a general
(non-probabilistic) law; L_j therefore has the form of a 'universally
quantified' sentence. The explication is adequate (or correct) only
if E is a logical consequence of $\{A_1, .., A_n, L_1, .., L_n\}$, and
certain other conditions are satisfied.[11] The occurrence of non-
probabilistic laws makes the explanation 'nomological'; the logical
consequence relation between explanandum and explanans makes
it 'deductive.'

In the case of explanation of laws, the basic idea for the Covering
Law Model consists in taking a law as the explanandum and allowing
for an explanans without any A_i.

In the case of inductive-probabilistic explanation (which is always
explanation of facts), the basic idea for the Covering Law Model
consists in allowing probabilistic laws among the L_j and specifying
an appropriate relation -- different from logical consequence -- to
connect the explanandum with the explanans.

Stegmüller's presentation concentrates on concepts (1.a), in particular on deductive-nomological explanation of facts. On several
hundred pages, Stegmüller discusses the problems that arise in

---

[10] Cf. Stegmüller 1969: Ch. I, Sec. 2. Notice that "fact" in "explanation of facts" refers to 'individual' facts; in a wider sense of
"fact," a fact is stated also by a law.

[11] Cf. Stegmüller 1969: Ch. I, Sec. 2e.

connection with the Covering Law Model of deductive-nomological explanation of facts, and reconstructs the attempted solutions.[12] Explanation of laws is dealt with only briefly (1969: Ch. I, Sec. 3). Stegmüller's discussion of probabilistic explanation is restricted to the inductive case, and is quite inconclusive (1969: Ch. IX). More recently, Stegmüller has devoted a special volume to the foundations of probability theory (1973b), in which more definite conclusions are reached with respect to probabilistic explanation (Sec. IV).

Stegmüller's results may be summarized as follows:

2. a. 'Explanation of laws' is a concept that is ill-understood.

   b. 'Inductive-probabilistic explanation' (of facts), as understood in the literature, should not be called "explanation" at all; furthermore, there does not seem to be any acceptable explication of "inductive-probabilistic explanation."[13]

   c. All attempts to formally explicate the concept of 'deductive-nomological explication of facts' on the basis of the Covering Law Model have failed; there are strong reasons to believe that any such attempt must fail.

The first part of 2.c is demonstrated in Stegmüller 1969: Ch. X. He attributes the general failure to neglect of a basic distinction (due to Hempel): there are two types of why-questions in science, 'explanation-seeking' questions asking for explanations (by which we ask for the 'causes' for some phenomenon) and epistemic or 'reason-seeking' why-questions by which we ask for reasons (why the phenomenon was to be expected). Any adequate explanation also provides reasons, but a case of scientific justification (Begründung) may not be an explanation. According to Stegmüller the attempts in 2.c, while intended as explications of "explanation," were really attempts to explicate a more general concept of justification (1969: 760f).

The second part of 2.c is argued in Stegmüller 1969: 768ff. The upshot of the argument (credited to Stegmüller's student Ulrich Blau) is, briefly, that only 'pragmatic' concepts of scientific explanation

---

[12] Cf. in particular 1969: Ch. X, "Die Explikationsversuche des deduktiv-nomologischen Erklärungsbegriffs für präzise Modell-sprachen."

[13] Cf. Stegmüller 1973b: 350-357.

can be adequate: the entire approach in the philosophy of science
is basically mistaken by adopting 1.b.[14]

2.c is, however, not a completely negative result. Explications
as described in 2.c, although they fail with respect to 'explanation,'
may still be important steps towards a precise concept of 'justification'; and attempts may now be made to explicate the concept of
'explanation' as a pragmatic one.[15]

From a cursory check of subsequent literature, it appears that
there has been no significant progress in connection with 2.c.[16]
As to 2.a, there has been potential progress in the following sense.
In Sneed 1971, a new analysis of physical theories is proposed that
seems to avoid certain problems of the 'received conception of
theories' as developed by Carnap and others, problems that have
proved troublesome in connection with 'explanation of laws' (cf.
Stegmüller 1969: 93-96). Sneed also makes some progress on another point that is essential to explicating "explanation of laws":
the problem of interrelating different theories. Sneed's work has
been taken up by Stegmüller (1973a). This new approach to physical
theories has not yet been applied to questions of explanation.

At this point, the linguist may finally come up with his perfectly
legitimate question: what does all this mean to me as a linguist?

---

[14] In 1973b: 295, Stegmüller emphasizes the importance of Blau's
argument: "Was anscheinend von vielen Lesern jenes Buches [sc.
1969] übersehen wurde, ist die Tatsache, daß damit die Versuche,
den deduktiv-nomologischen Erklärungsbegriff durch die Angaben
hinreichender und notwendiger semantischer und syntaktischer
Bedingungen für die erklärenden Argumentformen zu präzisieren,
anscheinend zu einem tödlichen Ende geführt worden sind."

[15] This is well put by Stegmüller himself (1973b: 296): "Die Kon-
sequenz, die man im deduktiv-nomologischen Fall daraus zu ziehen
hat, ist jedoch nicht, daß die vorliegenden Explikationsversuche
uninteressant und wertlos sind. Vielmehr müssen wir, auf eine
etwas vereinfachte Formel gebracht, zwei Schlüsse ziehen: erstens
daß in keinem dieser Explikationsversuche ein adäquater Erklärungsbegriff zu präzisieren versucht wurde, sondern ein wesentlich all-
gemeinerer Begründungsbegriff; zweitens daß es unmöglich sein
dürfte, adäquate Erklärungsbegriffe ohne Heranziehung pragmatische
Gesichtspunkte zu präzisieren."

[16] Cf. also Stegmüller 1975: 105f.

After all, 2. may be rather sad for the philosophy of the natural sciences, but linguistics is not a natural science. True enough, the logical empiricists had hoped that their concepts of explanation would cover scientific explanation in any discipline (Hempel's original proposal for a 'Covering Law Model' was made for historical studies) but -- so the linguist might continue -- such hopes were ill-founded to begin with. Concepts of causal explanation are (at best) irrelevant to the humanities and the social sciences to which linguistics belongs.

Such views, traditional in hermeneutic philosophy, have received new support by von Wright's analysis of 'explanation and understanding' (1971). I shall discuss von Wright's views in some detail because he offers the best formulation yet of a traditional challenge to the idea of a unified concept of scientific explanation.

2.2 Explanation of actions

It has always been realized that there are at least two different types of answers to explanation-seeking why-questions. As reasons, we may indicate either causes or purposes ("he did it in order to..."). The customary labels are 'causal explanation' vs. 'teleological explanation.' The Covering Law Model was meant for causal explanation to the extent that it was meant for nomological-deductive explanation of facts. Logical empiricists generally upheld the view that any teleological explanation could be reformulated as a causal one, perhaps allowing for causal explanations in probabilistic terms. A detailed and able analysis of teleological explanations in causal terms is given by Stegmüller (1969: Ch. VIII, cf. also Ch. VI).

Of the various types of teleological explanation, there is only one that poses real problems for causal reformulation: teleological explanation of intentional human actions (Stegmüller's "echte materiale teleologische Erklärung"). Attempts to explain intentional human actions in terms of the Covering Law Model usually take the following form:[17]

3. a. A intends to bring about p.

   b. A considers that he cannot bring about p unless he does a.

   c. Whenever somebody intends to bring about p and considers

---

[17] The actual formulation would have to contain a number of refinements, cf. Stegmüller 1969: 536ff.

that he cannot bring about p unless he does a, he will
(necessarily or very likely) set himself to do a.

    d. A sets himself to do a.[18]

"A", "p", and "a" may be understood as free variables ranging over
persons, states of affairs, and actions, respectively. 3. is a schema
for explanations that yields a Covering Law Model explanation when
the variables are replaced by constants. In this case, 3.a and 3.b
formulate the antecedent conditions, 3.c formulates a law (determi-
nistic or probabilistic), and 3.d becomes the explanandum. 3.a and
3.b indicate causes for the state of affairs in 3.d, and 3.c establishes
a law-like connection between aims and beliefs on the one hand and
actions on the other. In brief, actions have (psychological) causes,
on this account.

Like other philosophers, von Wright rejects a causal explanation
of actions. His own proposal amounts to accepting 3. without 3.c,
i.e. without the formulation of an empirical law. He introduces
what he calls a practical syllogism, an inference schema whose
final formulation is given as follows (1971:107):

    4. a. "From now on A intends to bring about p at time t."

       b. "From now on A considers that, unless he does a no later
          than at time t', he cannot bring about p at time t."

       c. "Therefore, no later than when he thinks time t' has ar-
          rived, A sets himself to do a, unless he forgets about the
          time or is prevented."

Von Wright's views on explanation can be summarized as follows:

    5. a. Causal explanation of facts is essential to the natural
          sciences. [19]

---

[18] Formulations a, b and d are adopted from von Wright 1971:
96. 3.c is an adaptation of Stegmüller 1969:535,(d), to von Wright's
formulations.

[19] Von Wright offers his own analysis for the concept of causal
explanation (Ch. II); this analysis is non-standard and cannot here
be discussed any further.

b. Teleological explanation of actions is essential to the humanities and the social sciences; causal explanation of facts that cannot be reduced to actions plays only a subsidiary rôle.

c. Teleological explanation of actions cannot be reduced to causal explanation of facts.

d. The practical syllogism provides a schema for teleological explanation of actions.

Obviously, it is only 5.c and 5.d that indicate serious disagreement with the proponents of 3. As von Wright presents his case, the force of 5.c entirely depends on 5.d. Let us therefore consider the practical syllogism and its alleged irreducibility to 3.

The key problem in 4. is the interpretation of "therefore" in 4.c: what kind of relation justifies the transition from the 'premises' to the 'conclusion' of the argument? Von Wright investigates in great detail whether the transition involves 'logical necessity,' i. e. whether the conclusion is a logical consequence of the premises. The result is negative (despite a somewhat misleading formulation -- 1971: 117). It is, therefore, completely unclear how anything can be explained by means of von Wright's practical syllogism as it stands.

We may still try to improve the syllogism so as to make it logically valid. Such an attempt has been made by Tuomela (1974). Stegmüller has demonstrated that Tuomela's proposal amounts to re-introducing an empirical law in agreement with 3.c (Stegmüller 1975: 116-119). At present, we can only draw the following conclusion: either the practical syllogism is logically invalid, hence, not a schema for explanation in any clear sense (which is contrary to 5.d); or teleological explanation of actions can be reduced to causal explanation as envisaged by the logical empiricist (which is contrary to 5.c).[20]

We may still decide to accept the first part of the alternative. In this case, we would attempt an explication of "explanation" that

---

[20] Note that in the second case 2.c would immediately apply to von Wright's schema, unless von Wright's proposal for causal explanation solves the previously unsolved problems.

does not require the logical validity of the practical syllogism and
still retains essential features of von Wright's approach:

> Als Rechtfertigung für die Suche nach einer solchen anders-
> artigen Deutung könnte man z.B. anführen, daß Aussagen von
> der Gestalt (C_e)[as in 3.c, H.L.] vorläufig fast ausschließlich
> als Projekte existieren und wir daher noch nicht einmal sagen
> können, ob es sich dabei nicht bloß um Wunschträume von
> Psychologen und Verhaltensforschern handelt. (Stegmüller
> 1975: 119f.)

Such an attempt is made by Stegmüller (1975: 119-122). The practical
syllogism, while logically invalid, may still be understood as a
means to gain 'an intentional understanding of an action' or 'intentional depth analysis,' which might also be called an 'explanation'
of the action. In this case, 5.d can be accepted, and 5.c is true
for a trivial reason: "explanation" has been re-introduced in a new
sense. Moreover, 5. loses all interest for those who would insist
on the need -- other than practical -- for a special 'humanistic' concept of explanation, for the following reason. 5.b has to be supplemented by a thesis of compatibility:

5.b' [= 5.b, adding:] Whenever a teleological explanation of an
      action can be given, then a causal explanation of the same
      action is, in principle, also possible.[21]

Stegmüller's re-interpretation retains an essential feature of
von Wright's analysis: 'explanation' is linked to 'understanding.'
Von Wright correctly points out that in history and in the social
sciences 'higher-order acts of understanding' are frequently involved (1971: 133f). Understanding the 'meaning' of, say, a demonstration, cannot necessarily be reduced to the intentions of the
individual demonstrator. Stegmüller introduces a generalized concept of explanation along Wrightean lines that takes such factors
into account (1975: 138). There is, then, a basic difference between

---

21 Cf. the corresponding formulation in Stegmüller 1975: 121.
"Teleological explanation" is to be understood in the newly introduced sense, and "causal explanation" along the lines of 3., duly
improved to account for 2.c. "In principle" allows for great practical difficulties. 5.b' may seem in agreement with von Wright's
own position (1971: Ch. III, Secs. 9f; cf. p. 129). Von Wright is,
however, not concerned with causal explanation of actions in the
sense of 3.

explanation in the natural sciences and in the social sciences, but
for the same trivial reason as before: "Die letzte Wurzel für diesen
Unterschied bildet aber die triviale Tatsache, daß der Ausdruck
'erklären' äquivok ist" (135).

Understanding actions often involves knowledge of 'rules' or
'norms.' Like other philosophers (e.g. Searle 1969), von Wright
distinguishes

> between norms which regulate ... conduct and rules which
> define various social practices and institutions .... Norms
> of the first kind tell us that certain things ought to or may be
> done. Norms of the second kind tell us how certain acts are
> performed. (151)

He calls them primary and secondary norms (rules), respectively.
Only primary rules play a part in explaining actions:

> Secondary rules, as far as I can see, play no characteristic
> or important role in the explanation of behavior. This is so
> because they are not mechanisms for making people do things.
> But they are of fundamental importance to understanding be-
> havior.... (152)

Lately, the concept of norm or rule has acquired some importance
in philosophical and linguistic discussion of natural languages. It
is generally recognized that 'language norms' must be secondary
ones. If von Wright's observation is correct, we must be careful
in explaining 'linguistic' behavior by reference to language norms.

The problems of 'explanation' have not been solved in the philosophy of science. Even so, the level of understanding that has been
reached should also be the level from which the linguist starts when
he tries to clarify 'explanation' for linguistics.

2.3 Linguistic applications

I know of only one explicit attempt to apply the Covering Law
Model for nomological-deductive explanation of facts in linguistics:
Wang 1972. Wang proposes a method for mechanically correlating
an axiomatic theory with a generative grammar such that the theory
is 'equivalent' to the grammar; in particular, phrase structure
rules of the grammar are made to correspond to universal implications in the theory. Wang now constructs 'explanations' of the following type: the universal implications that correspond to phrase

structure rules are taken as formulations of laws; sentences that assign lexical items to lexical categories are taken as formulations of antecedent conditions; and sentences that assign a sequence of lexical items to the category Sentence are taken as explananda.

Let us, for the moment, accept the Covering Law Model. Wang's proposal would still be a misapplication of the Model in the following sense: the explanandum would not be about a spatio-temporal object or event (a sentence, as opposed to an utterance, is an abstract entity).[22] For this very reason, an 'explanation' as proposed by Wang could never be called a causal one, in any non-metaphorical sense of "causal." Although the Covering Law Model can be generalized by dropping the requirement of a spatio-temporal object or event, such a generalization is contrary to the spirit in which the Model was developed.

It may also be objected that the universal implications corresponding to phrase structure rules are not formulations of laws. This would be a weak argument for two reasons: a) so far, there does not exist a satisfactory explication of "law" even for the natural sciences;[23] b) it is certainly not laws of nature that are formulated by the universal implications. In the humanities, however, we may have to admit laws of a different type, and Wang's universal implications might still formulate such laws.

Wang's proposal is an attempt to indirectly apply the Covering Law Model to generative grammars.[24] Chomsky's own account of various types of 'adequacy,' if carefully reconstructed, should involve both 'explanation of facts' and 'explanation of laws' understood

---

[22]It is, of course, not the object or event that is explained by an 'explanation of facts' but some 'fact' or, rather, 'state of affairs' involving the object or event. Cf. Stegmüller 1969: Ch. IV for a detailed analysis.

[23] This presents a major problem for the Covering Law Model; for details, cf. Stegmüller 1969: Ch. V.

[24] It is directly applied to the correlated axiomatic theories. There is a persistent tendency in generative grammar to consider the differences between 'grammars' and 'theories,' 'rules' and 'laws' as merely terminological; the applicability of the Covering Law Model may thus naively be taken for granted (e.g. by Sanders 1974: 17). For the two known methods of understanding generative grammars as theories, cf. Lieb 1974: Secs. 1.5f.

along the lines of the Covering Law Model. The emphasis would
be on 'explanation of laws,' which is directly relevant to 'explanatory adequacy.'

Recently, it has been claimed that such an account of explanation
is necessarily inadequate in the field of generative grammar. According to Itkonen (1974), generative grammarians are wrong in
their basic beliefs about their field. Linguistics -- at least if narrowed down to generative grammar -- is not an empirical science;
this is basically due to the subject matter of linguistics, the 'intuitive atheoretical knowledge' of speakers; in particular 'empiricist'
concepts such as 'explanation' (under the Covering Law Model),
'prediction' and 'confirmation' literally do not apply to generative
grammars (Itkonen 1974: Ch. VII). Itkonen correctly points out
that an 'explanation' as suggested by Wang differs from a Covering
Law Model explanation of facts by not involving any spatio-temporal
object or event in the explanandum.[25] Unfortunately, Itkonen's
involved discussion (Ch. VII) is quite empty.

The generative grammarian might simply argue as follows: Of
course there cannot be any prediction or confirmation if the predicted or confirming fact consists in a certain sentence (as opposed
to utterance) being correct or incorrect; similarly, for explanations.
However, the inapplicability of a concept is not shown by misapply-
ing it. What is to be explained or predicted by a generative grammar
is not the correctness (grammaticality) of sentences but certain facts
about the acceptability of utterances, and it is such facts that may
be used for confirmation.[26]

Itkonen also questions the possibility of using a 'universal theory
of language' for explanatory purposes in grammars (1974: Ch. VII,
Sec. 4). Since he subscribes to the generativist view of such a theory,
which I find unacceptable (cf. above, Sec. 1.2), I leave it to the generativist to defend himself.

---

[25] Itkonen does not mention Wang's work. Some of Itkonen's criticism no longer applies if Wang's approach is adopted, but the main
point remains valid.

[26] True enough, the generative grammarian would have to admit
to much confusion about 'grammaticality' vs. 'acceptability' and
'sentence' vs. 'utterance.' (For the second distinction in generative
grammar, cf. Lieb 1968b: Sec. 3). Also, I would reject the proposed
solution for independent reasons if "acceptability" is understood as
"normality"; see Sec. 9 below.

Itkonen attempts a complete re-interpretation of generative grammar based on the following idea. To the extent that linguistics is concerned with 'describing languages,' it is concerned with 'conceptual analysis,' with 'explication of concepts' (Ch. IX): "we describe a language L by analyzing the concept 'correct sentence in L' "(267); a grammar is "a formalization of intuitive atheoretical knowledge" (229). Itkonen is trying to lift generative grammar from its positivistic pedestal (as he sees it) and put it on a hermeneutic basis. Linguistics, at least of the generative brand, is not an empirical science but akin to logic and mathematics. Whatever the status of generative grammar, the arguments for the non-empirical nature of linguistics are totally unconvincing (cf. my demonstration in Lieb 1976c: Sec. 4, which is based on Itkonen 1974, a summary of his essential theses).

Understandably, Itkonen adopts von Wright's concept of explanation (1974: Ch. XI, "Explanation of linguistic actions"). Itkonen uses von Wright's practical syllogism for explaining utterance acts, extending his conceptual analysis to include the concept of 'correct speech act in L' (300f). Whatever the merits of this attempt, it inherits all the problems connected with the practical syllogism. In particular, Itkonen is wrong in believing that he has gained anything in his anti-positivist campaign (cf. above, Sec. 2.2).[27]

The concept of rule figures large in Itkonen's discussion. Similar concern with rules sometimes leads to the following position. Explanation in linguistics is totally different from explanation in the natural sciences because it consists in answers to how-questions, not why-questions (although answers to the latter may result from answers to the former):

Saying something to someone (understood as producing sounds with a meaning) is an institutional action; the production of the sound is a brute action. The system of rules (grammar) that transforms the brute action into an institutional action is a device by means of which we can explain, not why someone performed the institutional act (not why he said what he did), but

---

[27]Itkonen has the legitimate concern of pointing out essential differences between the humanities and the natural sciences. Unfortunately, his arguments often seem confused, and he tends to carry his views to the extreme where few may agree with them.

how one performs the institutional act by or in performing such brute acts.[28]

It was already pointed out by von Wright that secondary rules ('constitutive rules' in the sense of Searle) do not directly provide answers to why-questions. On the other hand, it is quite arbitrary to exclude why-questions from studies of linguistic behavior.[29]

On the basis of our previous discussion, we may formulate the following guidelines for any explication of "linguistic explanation":

6. Any explication of "explanation" for linguistics should meet the following requirements:

   a. It is not taken for granted that any explication of "explanation" offered by the philosophy of science (in the broad sense) is acceptable for linguistics; in particular, the general inadequacy of the Covering Law Model and the problematic nature of the Practical Syllogism are fully recognized.

   b. The positive results obtained in the philosophy of science are fully taken into account; in particular: i) it is recognized that the Covering Law Model may provide a basis for an adequate concept not of explanation but of scientific justification; ii) it is recognized that several types of explicata may be needed, some of which may not be relevant for, or even applicable to, the natural sciences.

   c. A threefold distinction is (or can be) made that is analogous to 1.c: 'explanation of facts' vs. 'explanation of laws,' 'deductive' vs. 'inductive,' and 'nomological' vs. 'probabilistic' explanation.

As to c, little was said that would justify the reconstruction of the

---

[28] Dretske 1974: 32f. Cf. also Clark and Haviland 1974: 119f. On the basis of Chomsky 1959, Itkonen (1974: 294f) attributes a similar view to Chomsky.

[29] This is also emphasized by Itkonen (1974: 295f). Interestingly enough, Dretske (1974) modifies his position in a postscript to his paper.

last two distinctions; the need for it is, however, fairly obvious.[30]
The first distinction is especially relevant in relation to universals.

It is apparent from Sec. 1.1 that something like 'explanation of
laws' is involved when universals are being explained. This may
also be the case when we consider the explanatory function of universals with respect to grammars; according to some generativists,
however, we would here be confronted with 'explanation of facts'
(cf. Sec. 1.2). Such questions can be decided only if the concept
of linguistic explanation is formally explicated; hence, they will
not be decided in the present paper.

The concept of linguistic explanation will be further clarified in
Sec. 4, and the rôle of universals in explanations analyzed. There
is, however, a problem that should be dealt with beforehand: Wang's
attempt to apply the Covering Law Model in linguistics failed because
the proposed explanations did not establish a relation to actual speech
events. Language universals -- properties of entire languages --
are highly abstract. An explanation that essentially relies on universals may be expected to fail for the same reason as the explanations proposed by Wang, unless we know how to relate language
universals to speech events. Sec. 3 will be devoted to language
universals and discuss their relatability to speech.

3. Language Universals and Speech

3.1 Types of language universals

In Lieb 1975 I studied two current conceptions of universals,
the 'Naïve View' and the 'Semantic View.' According to the former,
language universals are exactly those properties that are 'shared
by all languages'; according to the latter, they are exactly those
properties that are 'necessarily shared by all languages,' where
"necessarily" may be understood as: "because of the meaning of
the term 'language'." Both views were found wanting, and a third
one was proposed, the 'Pragmatic View': "A property F is universal in language relative to a person during a certain time, if that
person during that time requires that F should be attributed to all
languages by any theory of language" (Lieb 1975: 494). This view
was formally explicated and shown to meet the requirements that

---

[30] Note, however, that probabilistic linguistic explanations
should not be introduced at all if the notion of probabilistic explanation does not make sense; cf. 2.b.

the other views failed to meet. I shall here presuppose the Pragmatic View without further comment. In using "(is) universal in
language"or (is a) language universal" I shall frequently omit the
essential relativization to a researcher and a period of time; those
who still find nothing wrong with the Naïve View may in these cases
understand my formulations in the sense they prefer.

On the basis of current discussion in linguistics, the following
types of universals may be distinguished (which may partly overlap):[31]

7. a. Properties that are connected with the so-called system
       of a language (e.g. grammatical properties in a traditional
       sense).

   b. Properties that are connected with systematic conditions
       of natural language communication even if those conditions
       cannot be reduced to the system of a language.

   c. Properties that are connected with the development or
       decline of languages, or with the internal variability of
       languages both from a synchronic and a diachronic point
       of view (properties concerning the temporal or dialectal,
       sociolectal etc. organization of languages).

   d. Properties that are connected with the ways in which a
       language or communication in a language is related to
       non-linguistic actions or to thinking, or to having certain
       intentions, emotions, etc.

   e. Properties that are connected with the relations between
       a language and a society in which it is used.

   f. Properties that are connected with ontogenetic language
       development (both in the case of primary and non-primary
       language learning); in particular, properties concerning
       the physiological and psychological foundations for master-
       ing a language.

   g. Properties that are connected with phylogenetic language
       development.

---

[31] The following list is additive. Each type is recognized somewhere in present-day linguistics, but I do not know any linguist who
explicitly recognizes all of them (except myself — Lieb 1976d: Sec. 1. 3).

h. Properties that are connected with the ways in which
natural languages compare with other objects -- human
or otherwise -- in the domain of semiotic.

In the present paper I shall concentrate on 7.b and, to a lesser
extent, 7.a. Universals as in 7.a will be called type 1 language
universals or system-related universals; universals as in 7.b are
type 2 language universals or communication universals. They
will be further discussed in Secs. 3.2 and 3.3. As a preliminary
step, I characterize my conception of natural languages and their
systems in a deliberately informal way.

On my conception, no natural language is a system; it has systems, but is not itself a system.

I assume that a speaker's total share of a natural language can
be decomposed into 'homogeneous parts.' Any such part is a 'means
of communication,' and only in its entirety can it be assigned to a
variety of the language. Such parts are called idiolects. Though
'homogeneous,' an idiolect as a rule belongs to a number of varieties simultaneously (say, to a certain dialect, sociolect, etc.). An
idiolect must not be confused with a speaker's total share of a language, which is, rather, a set of idiolects.

Any idiolect is a set of abstract texts. Each text is a pair of a
phonetic (or graphic) form and a meaning. The form is abstract
as compared to concrete utterances which are objects or events in
space-time.

A natural language is construed as a set of idiolects. As natural
languages I allow only complete historical languages through time
(ENGLISH) and certain periods of such languages (MIDDLE ENG-
LISH). A variety of a language is understood as a subset of a language. Natural languages and their varieties may be called linguistic
complexes.

Obviously neither a linguistic complex nor an idiolect is a system
on this conception. Systems are introduced as follows.

It is assumed that any idiolect has a system (at least one) that
determines precisely which texts belong to the idiolect. Systems
of idiolects form the basis for systems for linguistic complexes
in the following way. Any linguistic complex is a set of idiolects.
Each idiolect has a system. Hence, for any linguistic complex
there is a non-empty set of idiolect systems: the set of systems

of idiolects that are elements of the linguistic complex. A system
for the complex is construed as an 'abstraction from' the set of
systems of idiolects that belong to the complex.[32]

For clarifying "abstraction" I shall rely on the concept of shared
property. A system for a linguistic complex is a construct based
on properties that are shared by the systems of all idiolects in the
complex; or, with "common structure of" instead of "construct
based on properties that are shared by": a system for a linguistic
complex is a common structure of the systems of all idiolects in
the complex. (The converse does not hold.)[33]

The phrase "construct based on" has to be explicated. For
simplicity's sake we choose the most elementary explication, using "set." Thus, a system for a linguistic complex is a set of
properties that are shared by the systems of all idiolects of the
complex.

Consider a simple example: all systems of ENGLISH idiolects
(so far) have the property of containing both verbs and nouns. They
also have the property of having verbs that belong to different form
classes. Both properties could be considered for inclusion in a
system for ENGLISH. Both properties could also appear in a system for GERMAN, but not necessarily in systems for all languages.

Obviously, there may be several systems for a single linguistic
complex. In particular, we may obtain systems of different degrees
of abstraction, depending on the nature of the properties involved.
Existence of such systems allows us to break the Saussurean bond
between 'the systematic' and 'the synchronic.'[34]

Given this conception of language systems, system-related universals are more easily related to speech.

---

[32] So far we have been characterizing some of the underlying
ideas of the comprehensive axiomatic theory presented in Lieb
1970. In that theory systems of idiolects and systems for linguistic
complexes are taken as entities of the same type. This assumption
will here be given up.

[33] Adopting such a concept of abstraction, we modify the conception in Lieb 1970: Chs. 13f. Cf. Lieb 1976a: Sec. 6.3 for justification.

[34] Lieb 1970: Part C develops this idea in a precise form. (It is
not yet clear to me which changes in my 1970 theory are required
by the new concept of 'system for.')

3.2 System-related universals and normal utterances

We may characterize the most elementary type of system-related universals directly in terms of properties of idiolect systems. Any universal property of languages that consists in having a system that contains a certain property is a type 1 language universal (the properties in the system are properties of idiolect systems). Type 1 language universals of this kind correspond to the simplest kind of 'language universals' as usually envisaged in universality research.

For a more precise formulation, we first introduce the following variables:

8. Variables:
   a. "$\underline{C}$", "$\underline{C}_1$", ... for any set of abstract texts.
   b. "$\underline{D}$", "$\underline{D}_1$", ... for any set of entities $\underline{C}$.
   c. "$\underline{S}$", "$\underline{S}_1$", ... for any system of entities $\underline{C}$.
   d. "$\underline{\varphi}$", "$\underline{\varphi}_1$", ... for any property of systems $\underline{S}$.
   e. "$\underline{\sigma}$", "$\underline{\sigma}_1$", ... for any set of properties $\underline{\varphi}$.
   f. "$\underline{\delta}$", "$\underline{\delta}_1$", ... for any property of entities $\underline{D}$.[35]

We now formulate the following assumption:

9. Assumption. Suppose that:
   a. $\underline{\delta}$ is a language universal.
   b. For some $\underline{\varphi}$, $\underline{\delta}$ = the property of being a $\underline{D}$ such that $\underline{\varphi}$ is an element of some system $\underline{\sigma}$ for $\underline{D}$.
   Then $\underline{\delta}$ is a type 1 language universal.[36]

For example, let $\underline{\varphi}$ = the property of being an $\underline{S}$ such that $\underline{S}$ contains both nouns and verbs. Let $\underline{\delta}$ = the property of being a $\underline{D}$ such that $\underline{\varphi}$ is an element of some system $\underline{\sigma}$ for $\underline{D}$. (It follows

---

[35] Variables a. and b. are used in agreement with Lieb 1970, 1974 and 1976a, variables c. and e. in agreement with Lieb 1976a. The precise logical status of the variables depends on the formal framework that is assumed; cf. Lieb 1976a for partial development of such a framework.

[36] Assuming the Pragmatic View of language universals, both "language universal" and "type 1 language universal" should be supplemented by the same two variables for a researcher and a time interval.

from our previous assumptions on systems-for that φ is a property
of each system $\underline{S}$ of each element $\underline{C}$ of $\underline{D}$.) Suppose that $\underline{\delta}$ is indeed
a language universal. Then by assumption 9. the following property
is a type 1 (or system-related) language universal. The property
of being a $\underline{D}$ such that: the property of being an $\underline{S}$ such that $\underline{S}$ contains both nouns and verbs is an element of some system $\underline{\sigma}$ for $\underline{D}$.
This formally exemplifies our basic idea for directly reducing sys-
tem-related universals to properties of systems of idiolects. We
may assume that at least an indirect reduction is possible for all
types of system-related universals; in case of an indirect reduction,
9.b has a more complicated form. [37]

Reduction to properties of idiolect systems is important for the
following reason. Given certain additional assumptions, we are
able to relate type 1 language universals to speech events, more
specifically to necessary conditions for 'normal utterances.' I
shall indicate in an informal way how such a relation is established. [38]

A few comments on the concept of normal utterance are needed.
"Normal utterance" may be construed as a name of a relation involving the following entities: a sound-event or graphic object, a
speaker, a text, one or more structures of the text (a phonetic structure, a syntactic structure, etc.), an idiolect system. The term
does not have to be introduced by a definition that is based on a
concept of utterance and specifies conditions for 'normal' utterances; it may not be defined at all. Use of "normal" should, however, be justified by the content of the concept. In particular, a
normal utterance should satisfy the conditions that are 'imposed

---

[37] Take, for example, so-called implicational universals. For
reducing such universals, we replace 9.b by 9.b': "There is a φ
and φ_1 such that $\underline{\delta}$ is the property of being a $\underline{D}$ such that, if φ is
an element of some system $\underline{\sigma}$ for $\underline{D}$, then φ_1 is an element of some
system $\underline{\sigma}$ for $\underline{D}$." (For a possible example, take φ as the property
of having nouns and φ_1 as the property of having verbs.) 9'. is ob-
tained from 9. by exchanging 9.b for 9.b'.

[38] The rest of Sec. 6 is not essential to understanding subsequent
parts of the present paper. I am going to propose a solution to a
basic problem presented by system-related language universals:
the problem of relating them to speech. My solution establishes
only a general relation. As I shall show below (Sec. 10), reduction
to idiolect systems also provides for relations of a more specific
type when communication universals are available.

by the idiolect system.' This is to be understood in the sense of
the following assumptions.

For any system S of any idiolect C there is a set of properties
of texts[39] such that the set is determined by S and any text belongs
to C, if and only if it has each of the properties. Any property in
a set determined in this way may be called a structural property
relative to S and C. Structural properties may be exemplified by
the following property of texts: the form of the text (understood as
a sequence of sets of sound-events: [æ] [t]...) begins with a set
of sound-events which all satisfy a certain disjunction of phonetic
conditions (are either [æ]-sounds or... or ...). For the structural
properties relative to S and C we assume that each represents a
necessary condition for normal utterances of the texts of C, in the
following sense. Consider a structural property, and a text in C,
a sound-event and a person such that the sound-event is a normal
utterance by that person of the text. Then sound-event, speaker,
or both satisfy a condition that is represented by the structural
property. Take, for instance, a structural property like the one
considered above. Given a normal utterance, the sound-event
begins with a part that satisfies the disjunction of phonetic conditions (is an [æ]-sound, or..., or...). This necessary condition
for normal utterances is represented, in an intuitively obvious
sense of "represent," by the structural property of texts.[40]

Certain properties φ of systems S are 'structurally necessary'
in the following sense. Let S be a system of C. φ is structurally
necessary for C and S, if there is a property of texts such that a)
the property is a structural property relative to C and S; and b) for
all C and S, if the property is a structural property relative to C
and S, then S has φ. For instance, the property of having a phonetic subsystem is structurally necessary for C and S, if there are
structural properties relative to C and S that are phonetic properties.

We previously assumed that a system σ for a set D of idiolects
is a set of properties that are shared by all systems of the idiolects.
We now strengthen this assumption by requiring properties that are
structurally necessary: for any system σ for D, element φ of σ,
element C of D, and system S of D, φ is structurally necessary
for C and S.

---

[39] Technically, relations-in-intension if texts are construed as
ordered pairs.

[40] The assumptions in the last paragraph are presented in a more
explicit way in Lieb 1976d: Secs. 3.1f.

In connection with 9. this establishes a direct link between
system-related universals and necessary conditions for normal
utterances.

3.3 Communication universals and normal utterances

Type 2 universals may be connected with conditions for normal
utterances in a specific way which may be characteristic of type 2
universals in general. For the following discussion the concept of
normal utterance has to be made more precise.

In the previous section I considered normal utterances of texts
(pairs of a phonetic or graphic form and a meaning). In this section I shall introduce a concept of normal utterance that refers to
syntactic units instead of texts. The two concepts are largely
analogous; later discussion (Sec. 4) will be made easier, if we can
speak of normal utterances of syntactic units.[41]

The term "normal utterance" will be construed as a name of a
six-place relation involving the following entities: a sound-event
or graphic (or other) object, a person, a syntactic unit (a noun
phrase, a sentence, etc.) of an idiolect system, a morpho-syntactic
structure of the unit (construed as an ordered pair), and an idiolect
system. Thus, we have expressions of the following form: something (a sound-event) is a normal utterance by somebody of (a syntactic unit) and (a morpho-syntactic structure of the unit) in (an
idiolect system). "Normal utterance" in this sense is introduced
in Lieb 1976a: 76, where the syntactic (and morphological) notions
are understood in roughly the following way.[42]

Assume an idiolect system, say, a system of a MODERN ENGLISH
idiolect. Any syntactic unit of the system is to be a sequence of
'phoneme' sequences, say, $\{[1, /ðe/], [2, /θi:f/]\}$.[43] A syntactic
structure of a syntactic unit is a triple consisting of a constituent
structure, the 'marking structure' of the unit relative to the

---

[41] Eventually, the two concepts will have to be related.

[42] For an outline of the presupposed morpho-syntactic framework, cf. Lieb 1976a: Secs. 2.1f; for a detailed version of the general
syntactic theory, cf. Lieb 1976d.

[43] We assume an interpretation of "sequence" by which a sequence
is a (many-one) relation between the first n positive integers and
given objects.

constituent structure, and an intonation structure (relative to the
constituent structure). The constituent structure, hence the syntactic structure as a whole, can legitimately be called a 'surface structure.' Given a constituent structure for a syntactic unit, we have
constituents of the unit, i.e. certain subsets such as {[1, /ʒe/]},
{[2, /θi:f/]}, and {[1, /ʒe/], [2, /θi:f/]} in the previous example
(the unit is a constituent of itself).

The phoneme sequences in a syntactic unit are, as a rule, phonological word forms. With each form we may associate one or more
morphological structures. By a morphological value assignment
for a syntactic unit, we understand a function that assigns to each
one-element constituent of the unit a morphological structure that
can be associated with the phonological word form in the constituent.
(Details are not important in the present context.) A morpho-syntactic structure of a syntactic unit is a pair consisting of a morphological value assignment and a syntactic structure (this is not a
definition).

A few words of explanation are needed concerning sound-events
(graphic objects) and speakers. They are events or objects in
space-time. Let us identify a spatio-temporal object or event
with the region in space-time it occupies in the course of its existence. We then need only one type of variables for speakers, sound-
events and graphic objects.

Generally, the following variables are used in connection with
'normal utterances':

10. Variables: [44]
    a. "V", "V_1", ... for any region in space-time.
    b. "f", "f_1", ... for any relation between positive integers
       and 'phoneme' sequences. [45]
    c. "v", "v_1", ... for any relation of the type exemplified
       by morphological value assignments. [46]
    d. "s", "s_1", ... for any triple of the type exemplified by
       syntactic structures.

---

[44] All variables are used in agreement with Lieb 1976a and 1976d.

[45] Variables b. can be used, in particular, for syntactic units
and their constituents.

[46] Variables c. and d. remain partly unspecified.

Our concept of normal utterance has the following form:

11. "$\underline{V}$ is a normal utterance by $\underline{V}_1$ of $\underline{f}$ and $[\underline{v}, \underline{s}]$ in $\underline{S}$ ",
      symbolically: "$NU\underline{VV}_1\,\underline{fvsS}$ ".

We shall assume that $NU\underline{VV}_1\underline{fvsS}$ implies that $\underline{S}$ is an idiolect system, $\underline{f}$ a syntactic unit of $\underline{S}$, and $[\underline{v}, \underline{s}]$ a morpho-syntactic structure
of $\underline{f}$ in $\underline{S}$.

Assumptions of this kind restrict the interpretations of "normal
utterance." Our previous remarks on introducing a concept of
normal utterance for texts carry over to 11. The term may be un-
defined; in particular, it does not have to be defined on the basis
of a previously given concept of utterance. Again, use of "normal"
as part of the term should be justified by appropriate assumptions
on normal utterances.[47]

Given the concept of utterance as in 11., we are able to characterize an important subtype of type 2 universals (communication
universals).

Consider a property of sets of idiolects of the following kind.
There is a relation between entities $\underline{V}$, $\underline{V}_1$, $\underline{f}$, $\underline{v}$, $\underline{s}$ and $\underline{S}$ such that
the property consists in being a set of idiolects which satisfies the
following condition: for any system $\underline{S}$ of any idiolect $\underline{C}$ in the set
and for all $\underline{V}$, $\underline{V}_1$, $\underline{f}$, $\underline{v}$ and $\underline{s}$, if $\underline{V}$ is a normal utterance by $\underline{V}_1$ of
$\underline{f}$ and $[\underline{v}, \underline{s}]$ in $\underline{S}$, then the relation holds between $\underline{V}$, $\underline{V}_1$, $\underline{f}$, $\underline{v}$, $\underline{s}$ and $\underline{S}$.
Assume that this property of sets of idiolects has been established
as a language universal. In this case we shall take the property as
a type 2 language universal (communication universal). The following assumption characterizes the universals of this kind:

---

[47] In this respect Searle's 'normal input and output conditions'
are important for both concepts (Searle 1969: 57): "the large and
indefinite range of conditions under which any kind of serious and
literal linguistic communication is possible." Searle covers both
hearer and speaker conditions ('input' — 'output'): "Together they
include such things as that the speaker and hearer both know how
to speak the language; both are conscious of what they are doing;
they have no physical impediments to communication...; and they
are not acting in a play or telling jokes, etc." (l.c). Although
there is no variable for the hearer in 11., input conditions can be
introduced by universal implications of the form: "for all $\underline{V}_2$, if $\underline{V}$
is addressed by $\underline{V}_1$ to $\underline{V}_2$, then ...."

12. <u>Assumption</u>. Suppose that:
    a. δ is a language universal;
    b. there is a ϱ [48] such that $\underline{\delta}$ = the property of being a $\underline{D}$
       such that, for all systems $\underline{S}$ of elements $\underline{C}$ of $\underline{D}$ and all
       $\underline{V}, \underline{V}_1, \underline{f}, \underline{v}$ and $\underline{s}$, if $\underline{V}$ is a normal utterance by $\underline{V}_1$ of
       $\underline{f}$ and $[\underline{v}, \underline{s}]$ in $\underline{S}$, then $\underline{\varrho VV_1 fvsS}$.
    Then $\underline{\delta}$ is a type 2 language universal. [49]

In Sec. 4 we shall use a communication universal of this kind
to exemplify the explanatory function of language universals. This
will be done by analyzing its role in a chain of explanations that
involve the meanings of a syntactic constituent. The most important one of these explanations uses both the meanings and the communication universal. Thus, we use a semantic example for the
functioning of universals in explanations. We concentrate on the
explanatory function of universals rather than on their explainability.

As a preliminary step the presupposed concept of meaning is
characterized; its salient feature — meanings are to represent
conditions of use — is emphasized by consideration of a concrete
speech situation (Sec. 4.1). This situation provides a reference
point for basic linguistic explanations (Sec. 4.2) which in turn may
be connected with general linguistic explanations (Sec. 4.3).

4. Universals and Linguistic Explanation: A Semantic Example

4.1 Syntactic meanings

In this section I shall characterize my conception of syntactic
meanings, i.e. meanings of syntactic constituents. I shall do so
in some detail because my conception is both unfamiliar and essential to the rest of the present paper. [50]

A 'complete syntactic meaning' of a syntactic constituent (hence,
of a unit) is construed as a relation between sound-events or graphic

---

[48] "ϱ" stands for any relation between entities $\underline{V}, \underline{V}_1, \underline{f}, \underline{v}, \underline{s}$ and $\underline{S}$.

[49] Assuming the Pragmatic View, both "language universal" and
"type 2 language universal" must again be supplemented by the same
two variables for a researcher and a time interval.

[50] For a more thorough exposition, cf. Lieb 1976a: Sec. 4, and
with some improvements, Lieb to appear: Sec. 3.

objects $\underline{V}$ and persons $\underline{V}_1$, in agreement with the following basic idea (Lieb to appear: Sec. 3.1):

13. Assume a constituent of a syntactic unit such that the constituent has 'complete syntactic meanings.'

     a. Each complete syntactic meaning is a relation-in-intension[51] between objects or events $\underline{V}$ and persons $\underline{V}_1$ that consists in $\underline{V}_1$ producing $\underline{V}$ and making certain references by means of $\underline{V}$, making certain presuppositions in producing $\underline{V}$, and the like.

     b. For any $\underline{V}$ and $\underline{V}_1$ such that $\underline{V}$ is a normal utterance by $\underline{V}_1$ of the syntactic unit, $\underline{V}$ and $\underline{V}_1$ are related by one of the complete syntactic meanings of the constituent.

The basic idea in 13. represents a 'meaning as use' conception in a precise sense. 13.a indicates the ontological status of complete syntactic meanings; they are construed as entities that can be directly related to speech. 13.b establishes such a relation by making a requirement that can be restated as: the complete syntactic meanings of a syntactic constituent jointly represent a necessary condition for normal utterances of the unit in which the constituent is contained.

Consider the following example (also adapted from Lieb to appear: Sec. 3. 3):

14. Jones is charged with stealing Smith's wallet. At one point during the court trial, Smith says, with a meaningful look at Jones: "Send the thief to jail."

Consider the occurrence of the thief in the sentence that has been uttered. Linguistically, the following entities are involved:

15. a. S: a system of an English idiolect.[52]

    b. f = send the thief to jail: a syntactic unit of S.

---

[51] Relations-in-intension are to relations-in-extension (sets of ordered n-tuples) as properties are to 'simple' sets.

[52] "S" is a constant. Generally, the non-italicized forms of variables are used as constants (relative to a given context).

15. c. [v, s]: a certain morpho-syntactic structure of f in S such that the intonation structure in s represents a 'normal declarative intonation.'

   d. $f_1 = \{[2,\ \underline{the}],\ [3,\ \underline{thief}]\}$: a constituent of f relative to s that is a 'definite singular noun occurrence' relative to f and s.[53]

   e. $f_2 = \{[3,\ \underline{thief}]\}$: another constituent of f relative to s.

   f. 'thief': a certain concept which is a 'morpho-phonological' meaning of $\underline{thief}$ (relative to $v(f_2)$ and S, where $v(f)_2 =$ the morphological structure of $\underline{thief}$ assigned to f_2 by v).[54]

   g. V: the sound-event produced by Smith in 14.

   h. V_1 = Smith: a person with an idiolect of which S is a system.

Assume that V is a normal utterance by V_1 of f and [v, s] in S. There is a certain part of V that corresponds to $f_1 = \{[2,\ \underline{the}],\ [3,\ \underline{thief}]\}$. In producing that part, Smith is <u>referring to</u> exactly one object, Jones. This object satisfies two conditions. a) At this moment, Smith is willing to apply the concept 'thief' to the object; technically, the object is in the reference basis for $\{[3,\ \underline{thief}]\}$ relative to $\underline{V}$, $\underline{V}_1$, and 'thief'.[55] b) Smith is <u>indicating</u> the object by means of a pointing gesture (looking). Moreover, Smith <u>pre-supposes</u> that the concept 'thief' does apply to the object he is re-ferring to; he presupposes that Jones is in the <u>extension</u> of 'thief' (is indeed a thief).

In producing the sound-event (V), Smith (V_1) is making the above references and presuppositions. Consider the relation between any $\underline{V}$ and $\underline{V}_1$ that consists in $\underline{V}_1$ making exactly these references and presuppositions:

---

[53] f_1 is characterized by the syntactic structure s in a certain way.

[54] "thief" is the orthographic name of the phoneme sequence /θiːf/; the raised dots in "'thief'" indicate the name of a concept. (For concepts as morpho-phonological meanings, cf. Lieb to appear: Sec. 2). There is, of course, only a single morphological structure that can be assigned to f_2 by any $\underline{v}$.

[55] Cf. Lieb to appear (30), for the concept of reference basis.

16. The relation (-in-intension) between any $\underline{V}$ and $\underline{V}_1$ such that:

  a. There is exactly one $\underline{z}$[56] such that $\underline{V}_1$ is referring by f_1 in $\underline{V}$ to $\underline{z}$.

  b. For all $\underline{z}$, if $\underline{V}_1$ is referring by f_1 in $\underline{V}$ to $\underline{z}$, then $\underline{z}$ is in the reference basis for f_2 relative to $\underline{V}$, $\underline{V}_1$ and 'thief', and $\underline{V}_1$ is indicating $\underline{z}$ at f_1 in $\underline{V}$ (by a pointing gesture).

  c. $\underline{V}_1$ presupposes that, for all $\underline{z}$, if $\underline{V}_1$ is referring by f_1 in $\underline{V}$ to $\underline{z}$, then $\underline{z}$ is in the extension of 'thief'.

On our previous assumptions, relation 16. holds between Smith and the sound-event V. In agreement with 13.a, we take 16. as one of the complete syntactic meanings of $f_1 = \{[2, \underline{the}], [3, \underline{thief}]\}$.

The concept of complete syntactic meaning will be relativized to a syntactic unit, a morpho-syntactic structure, and an idiolect system (cf. (15.a) to (15.c)). A relation is a complete syntactic meaning of a constituent relative to a unit, structure, and idiolect system. Using the following variables:

17. Variables. "$\underline{u}$", "$\underline{u}_1$", . . . for any relation-in-intension between arbitrary $\underline{V}$ and $\underline{V}_1$.

-- we have a concept of the following form:

18. "$\underline{u}$ is a complete syntactic meaning of f_1 relative to $\underline{f}$, $[\underline{v}, \underline{s}]$, and $\underline{S}$"; symbolically: "cs-mg($\underline{f}, \underline{v}, \underline{s}, \underline{S})\underline{u}f_1$".[57]

A syntactic constituent may have several complete syntactic meanings, or none. Let us assume that S is a 'normal Modern English idiolect,' 'thief' is the only meaning of thief, and 15.b to 15.c hold. Then, by the analysis given in Lieb to appear: Sec. 3,

---

[56] "$\underline{z}$" stands for entities that it is possible to refer to; for details, cf. Lieb to appear (11f).

[57] "cs-mg" denotes a function that assigns to a given $\underline{f}$, $\underline{v}$, $\underline{s}$ and $\underline{S}$ the set of pairs $[\underline{u}, f_1]$ such that $\underline{u}$ 'is a meaning of f_1' (satisfies, with respect to f_1, conditions as specified in 13.a). We assume: if cs-mg($\underline{f}, \underline{v}, \underline{s}, \underline{S})\underline{u}f_1$, then $\underline{S}$ is an idiolect system, $\underline{f}$ a syntactic unit of $\underline{S}$, and f_1 a constituent of $\underline{f}$ relative to $\underline{s}$.

there are four complete syntactic meanings of $f_1 = \{[2, \underline{the}], [3, \underline{thief}]\}$, to be denoted by "$u_1$" to "$u_4$," where $u_1 = 16$.

    19. The complete syntactic meanings of f_1 relative to f, [v, s] and $S = \{u_1, \ldots, u_4\}$.[58]

In view of 13.b, we now assume:

    20. For all $\underline{V}$ and $\underline{V}_1$, if $\underline{V}$ is a normal utterance by $\underline{V}_1$ of f and [v, s] in $\overline{S}$, then $u_1 \underline{V}\underline{V}_1$ or $u_2 \underline{V}\underline{V}_1$ or $u_3 \underline{V}\underline{V}_1$ or $u_4 \underline{V}\underline{V}_1$.

That is, it is a necessary condition for normal utterances of f and [v, s] in S that sound-event and speaker are related by one or more of the relations that are complete syntactic meanings of the constituent $f_1 = \{[2, \underline{the}], [3, \underline{thief}]\}$; one of these relations is 16., and the others are of the same kind.

In the next two sections, it will be shown how 20. is used in 'basic linguistic explanations' (Sec. 4.2) and is itself given a 'general linguistic explanation' by means of a communication universal (Sec. 4.3).

4.2 Basic linguistic explanations and basic linguistic facts

The situation in 14. might have the following continuation:

    21. Smith, still looking at Jones, shakes his fist at him.

We may ask: why does Smith shake his fist at Jones? An explanation of the following kind may be offered:

    22. a. Explanandum: the fact that 21.[59]

---

[58] Each meaning is of the same type as u_1, but only u_1 allows for a pointing gesture.

[59] In using "explanandum" and "explanans," I do not wish to imply anything about the character of the explanation, in particular I do not, by using these terms, subscribe to the Covering Law Model. The phrase "the fact that" usually implies the truth of the subordinate clause; I will use it more loosely.

b. Incomplete explanans: u_1VV_1, i.e. the immediately
preceding speech-event (V) and Smith (V_1) are related
by 16. [60]

It is not important how exactly this explanation is completed and
how it is formally construed, as long as the fact that V and V_1 are
related by u_1 figures in the explanans.

Assume that 20. holds and that V is indeed a normal utterance
by V_1 of f and [v, s] in S. We may then provide the following
explanation for the fact that u_1VV_1:

23. a. Explanandum: the fact that u_1VV_1.

    b. Explanans:
      i. V is a normal utterance by V_1 of f and [v, s] in S.
      ii. For all $\underline{V}$ and $\underline{V}_1$, if $\underline{V}$ is a normal utterance by $\underline{V}_1$
        of f and $\overline{[v, s]}$ in S, then $u_1\underline{VV}_1$ or $u_2\underline{VV}_1$ or $u_3\underline{VV}_1$
        or $u_4\underline{VV}_1$.
      iii. There is a $\underline{z}$ such that $\underline{V}$ is indicating $\underline{z}$ at f_1 in V_1
        (by a pointing gesture). [61]

23. can be reconstructed as a **deductive argument**: from b.i and
b.ii, we conclude that u_1VV_1 or u_2VV_1 or u_3VV_1 or u_4VV_1. Neither
u_2 nor u_3 nor u_4 allow for a pointing gesture (footnote 58); hence,
neither u_2VV_1 nor u_3VV_1 nor u_4VV_1, by b.iii. Therefore, u_1VV_1.

The explanans in 23.b has a characteristic form: it combines
i) the fact that something is a normal utterance by somebody of a
unit and structure in a certain idiolect; ii) a general fact about all
utterances and speakers of that unit and structure in the idiolect;

---

[60] Cf. 16. Immediately before shaking his fist Smith may be
assumed to believe that the one he is referring to (Jones) is a thief
(cf. 16.c). We might complete the explanans in roughly the following way: there is no reason to believe that Smith has changed his
beliefs in the meantime. Quite likely, Smith is mad at anybody of
whom he believes that he is — in the present context — a thief.
Smith wants to express his anger, and shaking one's fist at a person may serve such a purpose.

[61] Smith is giving Jones a meaningful look in producing that part
of the utterance which corresponds to $f_1 = \{[2, \underline{the}], [3, \underline{thief}]\}$, cf. 14.

and iii) a 'pertinent contextual fact.' This combination is typical
of a great number of explanations that arise in connection with
speech events. Explanation 23. is an example of a basic linguistic
explanation: an explanation whose explanans has the form 23.b —
possibly without the contextual fact — and whose general fact
satisfies certain additional requirements.[62]

Note that the suggested definition of "basic linguistic explanation"
presupposes a concept of explanation; thus, the problems connected
with explanations in general remain to be solved.

Given a definition of "basic linguistic explanation," we have a
natural way to introduce basic linguistic facts. A basic linguistic
fact is a non-general fact of a type that is required for the explanans
of any basic linguistic explanation — i.e. basic linguistic facts are
exactly those which consist in something being a normal utterance
by somebody of some unit and structure in a certain idiolect system.

On this conception of basic linguistic explanations and facts, it
appears that generative grammar has been fundamentally mistaken
in its attempts to apply the concept of 'explanation of facts' to linguistics. Characteristically, generative grammarians take the
'correctness' of a sentence, or, possibly, the 'acceptability' (normalcy) of an utterance, as the fact to be explained (see above, Sec.
2.3). This is true even for their critics (in particular, Itkonen

---

[62]Suppose there is exactly one speaker for S, who is six feet
tall. Then, for any normal utterance $\underline{V}$ by any $\underline{V}_1$ of f and $[v, s]$
in S, $\underline{V}$ is produced by $\underline{V}_1$ and $\underline{V}_1$ is six feet tall. This should
hardly be allowed as a general fact in a basic linguistic explanation.
Specifying the additional requirements on the general fact is a non-
trivial task. It is here that we might suggest bringing in the
'conventionality' of normal utterances. 23.b points in a different
direction, though. The general fact in 23.b.ii is clearly 'system-
related' (the u_i are meanings of f_1 in the system S), which is not
true of the spurious general fact we introduced. We are here
confronted with a problem that is analogous to the problem of 'laws'
(cf. above, ftnt. 23). A solution does not seem to consist in some
general standard for evaluating the 'law-like' character of general
facts, but in developing specifically linguistic criteria for the general facts to be allowed. In particular, if a general fact about a
specific idiolect system can be given a 'general linguistic explanation,' it may be used in a basic linguistic explanation. As we shall
see, 23.b.ii can be justified in this way.

1974: Ch. VII). Considering sentences -- abstract objects -- is a
mistake for independent reasons (see Sec. 2.3). The truly fundamental mistake, however, consists in the following error. What
should have been used as a basic linguistic fact in a linguistic
explanation -- that a given sound-event is a normal utterance -- was
mistaken for the fact to be explained. Reversing the relationship
immediately dissolves all problems that are not general problems
of explanation.[63]

Linguistically, the general fact in a basic linguistic explanation
is still highly specific (narrowed down to a specific syntactic unit,
structure, and idiolect system). Usually it will be the 'consequence'
of other facts of a less specific nature. In this connection, communication universals assume an explanatory rôle.

4.3 General linguistic explanations and language universals

4.3.1 Example: communication universals Going back to situation 14. we assume 15. and 19., but no longer 20., the general fact
used in the explanans of the basic linguistic explanation (23.). For
this fact we now construct an explanation that uses a type 2 language
universal (communication universal).

Consider the property defined as follows:

24. Definition. δ = the property of being a D such that, for any
    system S of any element C of D and all V, V_1, f, v and s,
    the following is true: if V is a normal utterance by V_1 of
    f and $[v, s]$ in S, then, for any f_1 such that there is a com-
    plete syntactic meaning of f_1 relative to f, $[v, s]$ and S,

---

[63] Assume we distinguish between the normalcy of a speech
event and its acceptability. Then the acceptability of a speech
event that is a normal utterance can be partly explained by the
very fact that it is a normal utterance. The generative grammarian might be understood as indirectly aiming at such an explanation.
He uses his grammar to derive a 'sentence' of which the speech
event is an utterance, thus giving a partial demonstration that the
speech event is a normal utterance. (Note that this is a demonstration, not an 'explanation' of the normalcy of the speech event.)
However, generative grammar does not seem to have an independent
concept of normal utterance. In any case, it would be arbitrary to
restrict basic linguistic explanations to explanations of acceptability
facts.

there is a complete syntactic meaning $\underline{u}$ of $\underline{f}_1$ relative to $\underline{f}$, $[\underline{v}, \underline{s}]$ and $\underline{S}$ that holds between $\underline{V}$ and $\underline{V}_1$.[64]

Assume that:

25. <u>Assumption</u>. δ is a general property of languages (i.e. for any language $\underline{D}$, $\underline{D}$ has δ).

25. is used in the following explanation for 20.:

26. a. <u>Explanandum</u>: For all $\underline{V}$ and $\underline{V}_1$, if $\underline{V}$ is a normal utterance by $\underline{V}_1$ of f and $[v, s]$ in S, then $u_1\underline{VV}_1$ or $u_2\underline{VV}_1$ or $u_3\underline{VV}_1$ or $u_4\underline{VV}_1$. (20. = 23.b.ii)

   b. <u>Explanans</u>:
      i.   The complete syntactic meanings of f_1 relative to f, $[v, s]$ and $S = \{u_1, \ldots, u_4\}$. (19.)
      ii. S is a system of an element of ENGLISH. (15.a)
      iii. ENGLISH is a language.
      iv. δ is a general property of languages. (25.)

Again, 26. can be construed as a <u>deductive argument</u>: By iii. and iv., ENGLISH has δ. Hence, by ii. and definition 24.: for all $\underline{V}$, $\underline{V}_1$, $\underline{f}$, $\underline{v}$ and $\underline{s}$, if $\underline{V}$ is a normal utterance by $\underline{V}_1$ of $\underline{f}$ and $[\underline{v}, \underline{s}]$ in S, then, for any $\underline{f}_1$ such that there is a c.s.m. of $\underline{f}_1$ relative to $\underline{f}$, $[\underline{v}, \underline{s}]$ and S, there is a c.s.m. $\underline{u}$ of $\underline{f}$ relative to $\underline{f}$, $[\underline{v}, \underline{s}]$ and $\underline{S}$ that holds between $\underline{V}$ and $\underline{V}_1$. By i. there is a c.s.m. of f_1 relative to f, $[v, s]$ and S. Hence for all $\underline{V}$ and $\underline{V}_1$, if $\underline{V}$ is a normal utterance by $\underline{V}_1$ of f and $[v, s]$ in S, then there is a c.s.m. $\underline{u}$ of $\underline{f}_1$ relative to $\underline{f}$, $[\underline{v}, s]$ and S that holds between $\underline{V}$ and $\underline{V}_1$. Hence 26.a by i. Q.E.D.

Now suppose that δ is a language universal, i.e. on the Pragmatic View of language universals:

27. <u>Assumption</u>. δ is a language universal for (a certain researcher) R during (a certain time interval) t.

---

[64] More informally, we consider the property of being a set of idiolects such that: for any normal utterance based on a corresponding idiolect system, if we have a constituent with a syntactic meaning the speech event and the speaker are related by one of the relations that are syntactic meanings of the constituent. Formally: $\delta = (\lambda \underline{D})$ $((\underline{S})(\underline{C})(\underline{DC} \,\&\, \text{Syst}\underline{SC} \supset (\underline{V})(\underline{V}_1)(\underline{f})(\underline{v})(\underline{s})(\text{NU}\underline{VV}_1\text{fvs}\underline{S} \supset (\underline{f}_1)((\exists \underline{u})\text{cs-mg}(\underline{f}, \underline{v}, \underline{s}, \underline{S})$ $\underline{uf}_1 \supset (\exists \underline{u})(\text{cs-mg}(\underline{f}, \underline{v}, \underline{s}, \underline{S})\underline{uf}_1 \,\&\, \underline{uVV}_1))))$.

Then, by 11.,

28. δ is a type 2 language universal (communication universal)
     for R during t.

We may then say that in 26. the explanandum is partially explained
by a general property of languages that is a language universal for
R during t. (δ may be assumed as a language universal for any
researcher at any time but this need not generally be the case.)

Obviously, 26. should be taken as a linguistic explanation: it is
only 'linguistic facts' that are used in the explanans. The explanans
26.b again has a characteristic structure: i. states a fact concerning a particular idiolect system and certain entities in the system;
ii. assigns this system to an idiolect from a particular set of idiolects; iii. guarantees that this set is a language. Finally, iv. attributes a certain property of sets of idiolects to all languages.
Any explanation of this kind may be called a general linguistic
explanation. If, moreover, the general property of languages is
a language universal for (an arbitrary researcher) R during (an
arbitrary interval) t, the explanation is an (Rt-) universal explanation. Different subtypes of general and universal explanations
are easily defined by referring to the type of general property involved.

Not all general linguistic explanations are of exactly this form.
There may be a complication by reliance on several general properties of languages or several facts about the idiolect system, but
this is taken care of by constructing 'complex' properties or facts.
There should, however, be a type of general (and universal) linguistic explanation whose explanans involves (at position i.) not a
fact about a particular idiolect system, but about a certain language
or language variety and its systems. [65] I leave it undecided which
changes in the form of 26. are required to accommodate such explanations. [66]

---

[65] See above, Sec. 1.1.

[66] In addition to basic and general (universal) linguistic explanations, we may assume intermediate linguistic explanations as a
third fundamental type of deductive linguistic explanations. They
differ from general explanations by involving at position iv. not a
general fact about all languages, but about certain languages only.

The fact that δ is a general (universal) property of languages
partially explains the fact 26.a about normal utterances of f and
[v, s] in S. This does not, however, exhaust the explanatory function of δ in our examples. The fact 26.a partially explains the
fact 23.a concerning a relation between a speech event and Smith.
This fact is the explanandum of a basic linguistic explanation, using
a basic linguistic fact, and is used in 22. to partially explain the
non-linguistic fact that Smith shook his fist at Jones; explanation 2.
is at best <u>partly</u> linguistic. Assuming that partial explanation
is a transitive relation, we have three different facts that are
partially explained by the fact that δ is a general (universal) property of languages; one of them is connected with a specific speech
event, and one consists in the occurrence of a non-linguistic
action.

There is, so to speak, a chain of explanations that connects a
general fact about languages with a singular fact about an actual
speech event and with a non-linguistic action. This chain may be
extended in the opposite direction. The general fact about languages
-- say, that δ is a general property of languages -- may be taken as
the explanandum of another deductive explanation. For obvious reasons, this explanation must use general facts in the explanans. If
these facts are at least partly 'linguistic' in nature, the explanation
should be considered as a <u>general linguistic explanation</u> of a third
type. Given an explanation of the first two types, the explanans
involves a fact about a specific idiolect system or language; this
does not hold for an explanation of the third type. We here have a
formal analogon to 'explanation of facts' vs. 'explanation of laws.'

Any linguistic explanation (whether basic, intermediate, or general) may adduce non-linguistic facts in the explanans. If, for
instance, it adduces psychological facts, it is both a linguistic and
a psychological explanation. Thus, we may have partly non-linguistic explanations of general facts about languages. Such explanations may be connected with entirely non-linguistic ones via
explanations of non-linguistic facts in the explanantia.

In the last two paragraphs I have given a few hints as to how the
'explainability' of universals may be reconstructed. I shall not here
pursue the matter any further.

The explanatory function of universals was clarified by constructing an explanation in which a type 2 universal was used. What is
usually considered are type 1 universals.

4.3.2 <u>System-related universals</u> I shall briefly show how type 1 universals can acquire an explanatory function concerning facts about speech events.

In 26. an idiolect-specific fact is used in the explanans: the complete syntactic meanings of f_1 relative to f, [v, s] and S = $\{u_1, \ldots, u_4\}$ (26.b.i). This is certainly not an irreducible fact. $f_1 = \{[2, \underline{the}], [3, \underline{thief}]\}$ is a non-simple constituent whose meanings are obtained according to a general 'rule' for obtaining meanings of any 'definite singular noun occurrence,' given concepts like 'thief' as morpho-phonological meanings. Actually, we may formulate a 'rule' that covers most, if not all, MODERN ENGLISH and MODERN GERMAN idiolects. [67]

Let φ be the property of having 'definite singular nouns' (i.e. syntactic units that consist of a definite article and a noun, are marked as singular, and possibly satisfy certain additional conditions). Let φ_1 be the property of being a system such that the meanings of all definite singular noun occurrences are obtained by the above general 'rule.' Let δ_1 be the property of being a <u>D</u> such that, if φ is an element of some system $\underline{\sigma}$ for <u>D</u>, then φ_1 is an element of some system $\underline{\sigma}$ for <u>D</u>.

Now assume that δ_1 is a general property of languages. We may then construct a general linguistic explanation for 26.b.i whose explanans is exactly like the explanans of 26. after "δ" has been replaced by "δ_1", and 26.b.i by something like "f_1 is a definite singular noun occurrence relative to f and s in S, and 'thief' is the only morpho-phonological meaning of <u>thief</u> relative to $v(f_2)$ and S." If δ_1 is universal for researcher <u>R</u> during <u>t</u>, the explanation is a (<u>Rt-</u>) universal explanation. [68]

The explanandum of this explanation is a fact about an idiolect system and entities of the system; it is not a fact about a speech event. However, it is used in the explanans of 26. to explain a fact that is used in the explanans of 23. to explain a fact about an individual speech event. Thus, the fact that δ_1 is a general property of languages partially explains a fact about an individual speech event.

---

[67] Cf. (66) in Lieb 1976a: 57, for GERMAN. (The formulation of (66) should be modified in view of (39) in Lieb to appear: Sec. 3.4.)

[68] See above, Sec. 3.2, ftnt. 37.

A relation to speech events is established only because a property intervenes (δ in 26.) that, if taken as universal, is a communication universal. It is an essential function of type 2 universals
to make type 1 universals 'applicable' in the partial explanation of
speech event facts.

5. Conclusion

Our discussion of linguistic explanations has been exploratory
rather than definitive. Some important questions were not even
mentioned. In particular, in formulating linguistic explanations,
we are always confronted with the following problem: where do we
get the sentences that are used for stating the facts in the explanans?

This question is especially pertinent in the case of general linguistic explanations. Consider, for instance, 26. Obviously, the
four sentences in 26.b are quite different in nature. We may suggest the following sources for the four sentences: i. and ii. should
be assigned to a grammar of a certain ENGLISH idiolect; iii. to
a grammar of ENGLISH (where it would appear trivially); and iv.
to a theory of language. [69]

This leaves us with the following problem: how may idiolect
grammars, grammars of language and theories of language be
related in such a way that we can construct deductive arguments
involving sentences from all of them? The difficulty is compounded
by the fact that we may also need sentences from non-linguistic
theories, such as psychological or sociological ones.

In Lieb 1976a I have shown in detail how this problem is solved
by the formal conception of theory integration developed in Lieb
1974: Sec. 3.4. Roughly, the more general theories are made
available in the more specific ones; in particular, a general linguistic explanation like 26. can be formulated within an idiolect
grammar. [70]

---

[69] Note that the universality assumption 27. does not directly
figure in 26. It would not belong to a theory of language but to some
application of a theory of linguistics — we do not speak about linguistics in a theory of language. (Cf. Lieb 1975: Sec. 5.)

[70] Actually, the basic idea for explanations like 26. was first outlined in Lieb 1976a: 78f (see also 1976b: Sec. 2.5). It certainly needed
expansion.

Many questions about linguistic explanations and their formulation remain open. We have not yet achieved an explication of
"linguistic explanation" and we were deliberately non-committal
with respect to the general problems of explanation that may be
expected to turn up in linguistics, too. We carefully paid attention
to the negative results in 5., adopting 6. as a guiding principle.
We did not even commit ourselves as to the ontological status of
explanations (although a fashion of speaking was favored by which
an explanation is a construct of 'facts' rather than a linguistic
entity). Still, the following result may be formulated:

29. In explicating "linguistic explanation" it is reasonable to
aim at explicata by which some or all linguistic explanations
are of the following kind:

   a. They are deductive.

   b. They are non-causal.

   c. They are linguistic because of specific conditions satisfied by the explanantia.

   d. They allow for a rough classification into basic, intermediate and general linguistic explanations by properties
   of the explanantia.

   e. They allow for a rough classification, based on properties
   of both the explananda and the explanantia, that is analogous
   to the distinction between 'explanations of facts' and 'explanation of laws.'

   f. They allow for chains of explanations that end in a basic
   linguistic explanation or an explanation of a non-linguistic
   action such that any non-basic explanation may be the
   beginning of such a chain.

   g. They allow for chains of explanations that begin in an
   entirely non-linguistic explanation such that any linguistic explanation occurs in such a chain.

   h. They accept the fact that something is a normal utterance
   as a basic linguistic fact (not to be explained linguistically).

Given a non-probabilistic language universal, we may characterize its explainability and explanatory function by constructing typical
chains of explanations. Different types of language universals may

play different rôles in such chains, and language universals of one
type may depend on universals of another for the existence of chains
that end in a basic linguistic explanation.

BIBLIOGRAPHY

Bach, E. 1974. Explanatory inadequacy. Explaining linguistic
    phenomena, ed. by D. Cohen, 153-171.

Bever, T.G. 1974. The ascent of the specious or, there's a lot
    we don't know about mirrors. Explaining linguistic phenomena,
    ed. by D. Cohen, 173-200.

Chomsky, N. 1959. Review of Verbal Behavior, by G.F. Skinner.
    Language 35. 26-58.

_____. 1965. Aspects of the theory of syntax. Cambridge, Mass.:
    M.I.T. Press.

Clark, H.H. and S.E. Haviland. 1974. Psychological processes as
    linguistic explanation. Explaining linguistic phenomena, ed. by
    D. Cohen, 91-124.

Cohen, D. (ed.) 1974. Explaining linguistic phenomena. Washing-
    ton: Hemisphere. Papers presented at a symposium held at
    the University of Wisconsin-Milwaukee, May 4-5, 1973.

Dougherty, R.C. 1974. What explanation is and isn't. Explaining
    linguistic phenomena, ed. by D. Cohen, 125-151.

Dretske, F.I. 1974. Explanation in linguistics. Explaining lin-
    guistic phenomena, ed. by D. Cohen, 21-41.

Greenberg, J.H. (ed.) 1966. Universals of language. (Report of
    a conference held at Dobbs Ferry, New York, April 13-15, 1961.)
    2nd ed. Cambridge, Mass.: M.I.T. Press. (2nd printing 1968;
    1st ed. 1963).

_____, C.E. Osgood and J.J. Jenkins. 1966. Memorandum
    concerning language universals. Universals of language, ed. by
    J.H. Greenberg, xv-xxvii.

Hutchinson, L.G. 1974. Grammar as theory. Explaining linguistic
    phenomena, ed. by D. Cohen, 43-73.

Itkonen, E. 1974. Linguistics and metascience. Studia Philosophica Turkuensia Fasc. II. Turku: Societas Philosophica et Phaeno-menologica Finlandiae.

Lieb, H. 1968a. Communication complexes and their stages. Janua Linguarum, ser. min. 71. The Hague: Mouton.

———. 1968b. Zur Kritik von N. Chomskys Theorie der Ebenen. Lingua 19. 341-385.

———. 1970. Sprachstadium und Sprachsystem, Umrisse einer Sprachtheorie. Stuttgart: Kohlhammer.

———. 1974. Grammars as theories: the case for axiomatic grammar (Part I). Theoretical Linguistics 1. 39-115.

———. 1975. Universals of language: quandaries and prospects. Foundations of Language 12. 471-511.

———. 1976a. Grammars as theories: the case for axiomatic grammar (Part II). Theoretical Linguistics 3. 1-98.

———. 1976b. Zum Verhältnis von Sprachtheorien, Grammatik-theorien und Grammatiken. Wissenschaftstheorie der Linguistik, ed. by D. Wunderlich, 200-214.

———. 1976c. Rekonstruktive Wissenschaftstheorie und empi-rische Wissenschaft: Kommentare zu Kanngießer, Ballmer und Itkonen. Wissenschaftstheorie der Linguistik, ed. by D. Wunder-lich, 183-199.

———. 1976d. Vorlesungen zur Sprachtheorie: Syntax, Seman-tik, Morphologie. Wintersemester 1975/76, Einleitung, Allge-meine Orientierung, Teil I: Syntax. Berlin: Freie Universität, Fachbereich 16, mimeographed. (Cf. Lieb in prep., below.)

———. 1976e. Reasons for abandoning generative grammar. Language Sciences 39. 21-22.

———. (to appear) Principles of semantics. Syntax and Seman-tics 10: Selections from the Third Groningen Round Table, ed. by F. Heny and H. Schnelle. New York: Academic Press.

———. (in prep.) Syntax, Semantik, Morphologie — eine Grund-legung. Berlin: de Gruyter (to be published in 1978).

Sanders, G.A. 1974. Introduction. Explaining linguistic phenomena, ed. by D. Cohen, 1-20.

Searle, J.R. 1969. Speech acts, an essay in the philosophy of language. Cambridge: Cambridge University Press.

Sneed, J.D. 1971. The logical structure of mathematical physics. Dordrecht: Reidel.

Stegmüller, W. 1969. Probleme und Resultate der Wissenschafts-theorie und analytischen Philosophie, vol. I: Wissenschaftliche Erklärung und Begründung. Berlin: Springer.

_____. 1973a. Probleme und Resultate der Wissenschaftstheorie und analytischen Philosophie, vol. II: Theorie und Erfahrung. Zweiter Halbband: Theorienstrukturen und Theoriendynamik. Berlin: Springer.

_____. 1973b. Probleme und Resultate der Wissenschaftstheorie und analytischen Philosophie, vol. IV: Personelle und statistische Wahrscheinlichkeit. Berlin: Springer.

_____. 1975. Hauptströmungen der Gegenwartsphilosophie, eine kritische Einführung, vol. II. Kröners Taschenausgabe 309. Stuttgart: Kröner.

Tuomela, R. 1974. Human action and its explanation. Helsinki.

Wang, J.T. 1972. Wissenschaftliche Erklärung und generative Grammatik. Linguistik 1971, Referate des 6. linguistischen Kolloquiums, August 11-14, Kopenhagen, ed. by K. Hyldgaard-Jensen, 50-66. Frankfurt am Main: Athenäum.

Wright, G.H. von. 1971. Explanation and understanding. London: Routledge and Paul.

Wunderlich, D. (ed.) 1976. Wissenschaftstheorie der Linguistik. Athenäum Taschenbücher Sprachwissenschaft. Kronberg: Athenäum.

Talking to Children:
A Search for Universals

CHARLES A. FERGUSON

ABSTRACT

Of the many ways to search for language universals, this paper chooses to study the relations between structure and use in a genetically and areally diverse sample of the world's languages, taking as its topic the special characteristics of speech addressed to young children. It identifies prosodic characteristics such as high pitch and exaggerated intonation contours, syntactic characteristics such as short sentences and limited grammatical relations, lexical characteristics such as 'baby talk' words and the use of hypocoristics, and discourse features such as frequency of tag questions and shifts in pronoun use. The register appropriate for young children is extended to other uses, shows variation in degree of 'babyishness,' and shows surprising lexical conservatism over time. It is concluded that in every speech community people modify their speech in talking to young children, and that the modifications have an innate basis but are largely conventionalized and serve important functions. Some 'universals' about this register are then extrapolated to register in general.

A slightly different version of this paper was presented in a symposium on Language Universals and Variation at Ohio State University, May 1977.

CONTENTS

1. Baby Talk Registers

1. 1 'Baby talk,' the special way we sometimes talk to infants,
seems an unlikely phenomenon to investigate if we want to find
universals of human language, i.e. things that hold for language
in general as opposed to characteristics of particular languages
at particular times. We generally feel apologetic or embarrassed
if caught engaging in unmistakable baby talk, and we certainly do
not like to give it serious attention, except perhaps to warn parents
against its use to children because it might deflect or retard their
language development.

There are, however, many ways to search for language universals, and marginal phenomena in language may sometimes be just
as revealing as the central topics of syntax and phonology. One
way to search for universals, surprisingly enough, is to study one
language in great depth. This was the path of the Indian grammarians and philosophers of language, who for centuries concentrated
their attention on SANSKRIT and discovered much about how human
language works. It has also been the preferred path of transformational grammarians, who have spent more effort on ENGLISH than
on all the other languages of the world combined and have greatly
extended our knowledge of human language. Another way is to work
with a handful of languages that are strikingly different from one
another or have some special position among the languages of the
world. This was the route followed by Helwig in the seventeenth
century when he wrote his universal grammar on the basis of the
characteristics of LATIN, GREEK, HEBREW and ARAMAIC --
the principal language of Western civilization plus the three languages of the sacred scriptures (Helvicus 1619). A recent example
of this approach is Vihman's search for universal principles of
consonant harmony in child language acquisition, although her
choice of six languages was dictated by the fact that these languages were the only ones for which full data from at least two
children were available (Vihman, vol. II of this book). Another
approach is to select a sizable sample of the world's languages,
at least 25 or so, representing different language families and
different parts of the world, in the hope that the sample will give
a good approximation to the nature and extent of interlingual variation on the phenomenon being investigated. This is the approach
familiar to us from Greenberg's well-known paper on basic word
order (Greenberg 1966a) and a number of more recent studies in
the same tradition, such as Steele's paper on word-order variation

(Steele, vol. IV of this book), which utilize data from a large number of languages.[1]

   1.2 The search for universals can focus just on matters of linguistic structure. What kinds of vowel systems do the world's languages have, and what principles explain their typological constraints (Crothers, vol. II of this book)? What kinds of interrogative systems are there, and why (Ultan, vol. IV of this book)? How do pronoun systems work in general (Ingram, vol. III of this book)? Or, the search for language universals can focus on uses of language. Do all languages have ways to show deference, to teach, to express affection? If so, are there universal principles about the occasions of these uses, the way they are acquired, and the way they vary in salience from one speech community to another? Or even, the search for universals can focus on the relation between structure and use. For example, are there universals about the relation between the showing of deference and the shape of pronoun systems (Brown and Gilman 1960)? Does teaching in all speech communities make use of questions of certain syntactic shapes to which the questioner already knows the answer (cf. Sinclair and Coulthard 1975)? Before deciding on any of these or other ways to search for language universals, let us better identify the phenomenon to be investigated: the way adults or older children modify their normal speech when addressing very young children.

   1.3 In spite of our embarrassment with the topic of baby talk, it is a promising field of study. In the first place, baby talk is very widespread. People who ridicule its use and deny using it themselves may find that they use it in talking to a pet animal or in making fun of someone else, and even people who avoid most of the extreme lexical and phonological characteristics of baby talk still modify their speech extensively in talking to very young children. It is easy to tell which of two tape recordings was addressed to an infant and which to an adult, entirely apart from the subject matter of the conversation. Second, analysis of the way people generally talk to young children is relevant to the larger question

---

[1] Linguists have not yet resolved the question of how to select a suitable sample of languages (cf. Bell, this volume). For research on phonological universals, the 200-language sample of the Stanford Phonology Archive (Vihman 1977) is now available and has been used for several studies in this book, but there is no comparable archived sample for other aspects of language.

of how children acquire their mother tongue. If the language addressed to children is markedly different from ordinary adult-to-
adult conversation, it seems plausible that this difference might
help or hinder the child in its language development, and our folk
beliefs take a definite position on this question. Finally, the study
of talk to children should bear on general questions of how language
varies. If the variation is not random, but has recognizable regularities — as it clearly does or one could not recognize baby talk —
it may be part of the speakers' linguistic competence that merits
inclusion in our grammars and theories of language.

Psychologists, linguists, anthropologists and others have studied talk addressed to children from various perspectives and for
various purposes.[2] Recent literature includes reports of psycholinguistic experiments about language acquisition, elicited accounts
exploring marginal systems in language, and participant observation of child socialization in different cultures. Our purpose here
is the search for language universals, using published studies from
a selected sample of the world's languages, and focused on the relation between structure and use. The 27 languages included in the
sample are (SYRIAN) ARABIC, (NEO-)ARAMAIC, BENGALI, BER-
BER, COCOPA, COMANCHE, DUTCH, (AMERICAN) ENGLISH,
GERMAN, GILYAK, GREEK, HIDATSA, HUNGARIAN, JAPANESE,
(HAVYAKA) KANNADA, KIPSIGIS, LATVIAN, LUO, MALTESE,
MARATHI, POMO, (BRAZILIAN) PORTUGUESE, ROMANIAN,
SAMOAN, SERBO-CROATIAN, SPANISH and TZELTAL (see
Appendix). The sample is high in INDO-EUROPEAN (ten languages)
and low in AFRICAN and OCEANIC languages, but we are limited
by the published sources. Most of the studies used as sources are
devoted primarily to an investigation of baby talk lexicon and have
only brief comments on other aspects. Studies that treat a full
range of topics are available only for ENGLISH and DUTCH. The
question of language universals in baby talk has been mentioned by
a succession of authors, including Jakobson (1960), Ferguson (1964,
1977b), Kelkar (1964), Drachmann (1973), and Ervin-Tripp (1977).
Of these, Ferguson (1977b) identifies about 30 'widespread characteristics' of baby talk structure and use. Snow (1977) identifies over
30 'dependent variables' in experimental studies of ENGLISH and
DUTCH talk to children. About a third of these two lists overlap.
Rūķe-Draviņa, in an article written after hearing the Ferguson

---

[2]For general reviews of the literature, see Farwell 1975 and
Slobin 1975. Snow and Ferguson 1977 contains new studies, reviews,
commentary, and Andersen's annotated bibliography.

and Snow papers, addresses the question of universals directly
(Rūķe-Draviņa 1976). She expresses caution about the universality
of the various characteristics that have been noticed, but submits
six probable universals: high pitch (Ammenton), reduplication,
hypocorism, names of body parts and events closely connected
with the young child, onomatopoeia and pronoun shift. In the
present paper, five of these, together with 17 other characteristics of talk addressed to young children, are examined across languages in the search for universals.

2. Characteristics of Talk to Children

  2.1 The most notable characteristics of speech addressed to
young children are prosodic. In accounts of baby talk in which intonation is mentioned, the authors comment on the overall higher
pitch and/or exaggerated intonation contours used.[3] Also, people
tend to speak more slowly, with exaggerated care in enunciation,
and to have fewer dysfluencies in their sentences and longer pauses
between them. There is, in short, a 'tone of voice' appropriate
for talking to young children that is surprisingly similar in every
speech community where observations have been made. For ENG-
LISH there are even careful measurements under controlled conditions that supply data on fundamental pitch, intonation contour, and
extra vowel length (Garnica 1977a, b). I think it is reasonable to
assume -- until we have direct counterevidence -- that this baby
talk tone of voice is a universal of human language behavior. But
where does it come from and what does it do? In the first place,
the overall high pitch may be imitative of what the infant produces.
Babies' early vocalizations, and indeed children's vocalizations
for a number of years, average much higher than normal adult
pitch, in part because of the size and shape of their vocal tracts.
Second, it corresponds to the perceptual sensitivities of the child.
Infants even a few days after birth can discriminate pitch differences, and they pay more attention to high pitches than to low ones,

---

[3] In several studies of speech addressed to young children in
AMERICAN-INDIAN speech communities, and authors have asserted
that the use of overall high pitch is not as noticeable as in AMERI-
CAN ENGLISH talk to young children, being limited chiefly to occasions of mimicking the child. Harkness 1975 also maintains that
in a Guatemalan Indian community the most typical style of talking
to children is in a rapid monotone, with willingness to repeat as
often as the child asks for it. All these studies are fragmentary,
however, and the question clearly needs further research.

so that the adults' use of higher pitch may serve the functions of
getting the child's attention and marking particular stretches of
speech by adults as being directed to the child, in distinction to all
the lower-pitched adult-to-adult talk. In the third place, the baby
talk tone may serve to give hints to the child about the grammatical
structure of the utterances. Boundaries are more clearly marked,
distracting false starts and interruptions are reduced, and intonation contours and extra vowel length highlight positions of primary
stress in the adult language. For discussion, see Sachs 1977.

All these sources and functions that seem reasonable to assume
for baby talk tone are also found in other modifications made in our
speech to young children. The modifications tend to reflect the
child's vocal behavior, they get the child's attention and coopera-
tion in verbal interaction, they mark the adult's speech as child-
directed, and they clarify the linguistic structure of the speech to
help in comprehension and in the acquisition of control of the language.

Although the prosodic modifications in talking to children are
important, they have not been as interesting to linguists as the
grammatical modifications. Most of the psycholinguistic investigation of the nature of mothers' speech to children that was undertaken during the late 60's and early 70's focused on syntax. This
was natural because linguistics during that period focused on syntax,
and exciting claims were being made that language development was
largely innate and took place almost independently of the language
input to the child. Linguists pointed to the fragmentary, often non-
grammatical nature of talk and emphasized the miraculous accom-
plishment of the child as somehow inducing from this mass of
difficult data the correct grammar of the language. Accordingly,
it was with considerable glee that psycholinguistic researchers in
study after study, with mothers and non-mothers, children present
and children absent, younger children and older children, male
and female adults, male and female children, and other variables,
demonstrated that the speech addressed to young children has shorter
sentences, fewer subordinate clauses, fewer grammatical relations,
and more repetitions than normal adult-to-adult speech. It also
often omits inflectional endings, function words, and the verb 'to
be.' It has, as we noted under prosody, fewer dysfluencies. As
Snow said in her 1972 paper, it is almost as if the adult were constructing a set of lessons for the child that would afford maximum
help in acquiring the grammar. Some researchers tried to see in
these grammatical modifications some general simplifying processes at work. Presumably, the parents were unconsciously untangling

the syntactic complexities of their normal speech in ways that reflected the linguists' notions of the derivational history of the sentences and were producing sentences closer to the 'deep structure' that some felt the child's use of language begins with. Alas, it has turned out that baby talk simplifications are as much concerned with surface brevity and semantic cohesion as with transformational simplicity. The miracle of the acquisition of syntax remains, but one argument of the nativists has been weakened; the language input to children is modified in ways that seem tailored to the needs of the child in verbal interaction and must somehow be relevant to the process of language acquisition. For full discussion of syntactic modification and its effects, see Newport et al. 1977; Snow 1977 reviews both prosodic and syntactic characteristics.

There are also lexical modifications in talk to children. Every speech community seems to have a small lexicon of words used primarily with young children.[4] Four aspects of this special lexicon are worth noting as universals of a sort. The words fall into certain semantic areas, they include greater use of hypocoristic affixes, they are used more freely in different word class functions than the normal adult lexicon, and they tend to be phonologically simplified. Typical semantic areas in baby talk lexicon are body parts and functions, kin terms, food, animals, and infant games (e.g. peekaboo, pattycake). Although all these areas are usually represented in a baby talk lexicon, the exact items included may be very variable, especially in food terms, which may be as limited as one word for 'food' in general or as elaborate as the more than a dozen names for different foods in BERBER nursery language. Here we will check for the presence of a) at least one name for a body part and one kin term, and b) at least one word for a game. The use of diminutives and hypocoristic formations seems universal, although the nature and extent vary from the -ie on ENGLISH nouns to the rich variety of diminutive formations in LATVIAN used with nouns, adjectives and verbs. The use of baby talk words in constructions of different word classes, reminiscent of the holophrastic utterances and early syntax of child language, is attested for several languages; here we will look specifically for the use of compound verbs made with general purpose auxiliaries (e.g. go bye-bye, faire dodo).

---

[4] Even Stross, who claims that there was little or no use of lexical or phonological features of a baby talk register in the village he studied, notes that two of the mothers "used three or four special words" (Stross 1972: 6-7 and footnote 2).

Phonological simplification includes a tendency toward simple canonical forms (e.g. CVCV) and the omission of more complex, difficult, 'marked' sounds or their replacement by less marked substitutes (e.g. stops for fricatives, singletons for consonant clusters, semivowels for liquids). Also typical are consonant and vowel harmonies of the kind often found in child language, reduplication being an extreme example. Here we will check only for cluster reduction, liquid substitution, and reduplication. A characteristic will be counted as present if at least one incontrovertible example of it is attested. Since the phonological simplifications found in the special baby talk lexicon may be productive outside it, i.e. may be applied to adult words in new baby talk formations, these processes may be regarded as a set of phonological modifications characterizing baby talk material rather than merely a characteristic of the special lexicon. A full discussion of lexical and phonological modifications appears in Ferguson 1977b.

Finally, some of the modifications are not grammatical in traditional senses of the word; they may be called discourse features. Examples: the high percentage of questions, frequent use of tags (o.k.?, hm?), the here-and-now semantics and high semantic continuity between pairs of utterances, and striking shifts in pronoun use (especially in alternatives for you). Every study that mentions pronoun use notes that first and second person pronouns are often replaced by third person nouns; several also note the use of first plural for second singular. Savić 1974 is an example of detailed treatment of the kinds of questions used by adults in interaction with young children; Wills 1977 is a similarly detailed study of pronoun shift in talk to children.

The primary occasion of use of baby talk register is in addressing young children, and that occasion of use serves as the defining frame for the study of its structural characteristics. Like other registers, however, it may be extended to secondary uses, as when the register appropriate for legal documents and technical exchanges in the courtroom is used elsewhere to poke fun at lawyers or to give an authoritative flavor to the proceedings. Baby talk, or selected features of it, may be used to suggest the speech of children. Also, it may be used in talking to pets, in coaxing other people (or even objects) to behave the way the speaker wants, in calling attention to someone's childishness, and in talk between lovers. Some of these extensions are undoubtedly widespread or even universal, but there is considerable cross-cultural variation. At times, only a limited set of baby talk features appear in a context that does not seem to be an extension of the register as a whole, and exploration of this phenomenon leads to the identification of structural-functional components that are combined in various ways to constitute different registers (cf. Brown 1977, Ferguson 1977b). These extended uses and related registers are generally mentioned incidentally or not at all in descriptions of talk to children, but here we will check the sample languages on three secondary uses: suggesting or reporting child speech, talking to animals, and use in adult intimate interaction such as between lovers.

The characteristics of talk to children co-occur regularly enough and are so interrelated that they constitute a register, but there is so much variation in the degree to which they occur and the relative incidence of different characteristics, that a range of intraregister variability must also be recognized.[5] The most striking -- and apparently universal -- variability is in what can be called 'degree of babyishness.' Changes in the degree of babyishness may reflect the age of the addressee, the nature of the situation, the speaker's estimate of the linguistic abilities of the child, the strength of the affective bond between the interactants, and so on. This variability has been investigated experimentally (e.g. Newport 1976, Cross 1977) and is discussed in several register descriptions (cf. Ferguson 1977b).

2.2 The discussion so far has been synchronic, although with some allusions to the diachrony of child language development. Greenberg's state-and-process model of language (Greenberg 1966 b) requires investigation of diachronic processes that lead to synchronic states, and the transmission (and change) of baby talk registers deserves comment. The only aspect of talk to children which has been considered diachronically is the lexicon, and it has been shown that core items of the baby talk lexicon tend to persist for long periods of time (e.g. 2000 years for LATIN-SPANISH pappa 'food').

Lexical items are, however, subject to areal diffusion, perhaps spreading with patterns of child rearing across linguistic communities.

---

[5]Variability across social classes in talking to children has been studied experimentally for ENGLISH (Holzman 1974) and DUTCH (Snow et al. 1976). Familial and individual variation in baby talk is considerable, presumably because of the nature of the interactions for which it is appropriate, but linguists generally pay little attention to individual linguistic profiles (but cf. Ferguson 1975 and Fillmore and Wang, forthcoming), and this variation will not be considered here for lack of data.

The important points here are two: a) the phonetic shapes and semantic areas tend to be universal, but the actual lexical items, i.e. the phonetic-semantic pairings, are specific to particular languages or speech communities; b) some lexical items undergo sound changes with the rest of the language, whereas others remain marginal and are not so affected. Sample evidence for a): ENGLISH (go) night-night, sleepy-bye; FRENCH (faire) dodo; LATVIAN aiju žūžū, čučēt; JAPANESE nenne (suru); ARABIC ninnī. Sample evidence for b): SYRIAN ARABIC nkəɣ 'baby's first word' is nčəɣ in those dialect areas in which the change k→č has taken place; the word for 'hurt, sore' is wawa in Middle Eastern languages that have w in their phonemic inventory, but vava in those that have v but not w. Other elements of baby talk have not been traced historically, but it would be interesting to know, for example, the history of such phenomena as ENGLISH baby talk constructions with go and FRENCH ones with faire; the omission of the copula in ENGLISH, ROMANIAN and other baby talk, patterns of inflection reduction in particular languages, and the like. Discussion of baby talk diachrony appears in Bynon 1968, Crawford 1970, Ferguson 1964 and Oswalt 1976.

2.3 The accompanying chart presents the facts of presence (+) and absence (−) of the putative universals in the baby talk registers of the 27 sample languages. If the source gives no indication of presence or absence, the box is left open on the chart. The evidence is confirmatory as far as it goes, but the gaps in the data are numerous. Examining these different descriptions of baby talk for comparable data is frustrating, much in the way language universals research is frustrating for grammatical phenomena. The authors of the various studies simply do not provide answers to the questions the researcher wants to ask. In spite of the gaps, however, the chart is informative, and the lack of minuses suggests that many of the gaps would be filled with plusses if the authors were asked specifically about them. In this way the chart as it now stands could serve as a minimum checklist of things to be looked for when a language researcher attempts to describe the baby talk register in a speech community, and indeed the preparation of such checklists is one of the useful by-products of universals research. (See chart next page.)

3. Summary and Conclusions

3.1 In every human society people modify their normal speech in talking to very young children. The modifications are prosodic (e.g. higher pitch), grammatical (e.g. shorter sentences), lexical (e.g. special baby words), phonological (e.g. reduplication), and

	Ar	Am	Bg	Br	Cc	Cm	Du	En	Ge	Gi	Gr	Hi	Hu	Ja	Ka	Ki	La	Lu	Ml	Mr	Pm	Pr	Ro	Sa	Se	Sp	Tz
PROSODY																											
1. High pitch	+						+	+									+	+	+	+		+			+	+	
2. Exaggerated contours							+	+								+	+	+	+	+		+		+	+	+	+
3. Slow rate							+	+	+	+	+	(+)														+	+
SYNTAX																											
4. Short sentences							+	+	+							+								+		+	
5. Parataxis							+	+																+			
6. Telegraphic style			+				+	+						+							+						
7. Repetition							+	+			+		+				+	+	+	+		+		+	+	+	+
LEXICON																											
8. Kin terms and body parts	+	+	+	+	+	+	+	+	+	+		+	+	+		+	+	+	+	+	+	+	+	+	+	+	+
9. Infant games	+	+	+	+	+	+	+	+	+	+			+					+	+	+	+		+	+	+	+	+
10. Qualities	+	+	+	+	+	+	+	+	+			+	+					+	+	+	+	+	+		+	+	
11. Compound verbs							+	+	+			+							+	+	+	+	+		+	+	
12. Hypocorism	+	+	+	+	+	+	+	+	+	+	+	+	+	+		+	+	+	+	+	+	+	+	+	+	+	+
PHONOLOGY																											
13. Cluster reduction		+					+	+	+	+	+							+	+	+	+		+		+	+	
14. Liquid substitution	(+)	(+)		+	+		+	+	+	+		+		+				+	+	+	+		+	+	+	+	
15. Reduplication	+	+		+	+		+	+	+	+		+	+	+			+	+	+	+	+	+	+	+	+	+	+
16. Special sounds	+	+		+	+		(+)	+	+	+		+	+	+			+	+	+			+	+			+	+
DISCOURSE																											
17. Questions							+	+							+			+		+		+		+	+	+	
18. Pronoun shift				+			+	+					+					+		+		+	+	+	+	+	
EXTENDED USES																											
19. Child speech								+						+		+	+	+		+			+				
20. Animals					+			+			−						+		+	+	+						
21. Adult intimacy		+		−				+			−						+	+	+	+	+						
VARIATION IN DEGREE	+						+	+				+		+	+		+	+	+	+		+		+	+	+	+

*Languages are abbreviated and arranged in alphabetical order; see Appendix for their full names.

discoursal (e.g. greater proportion of questions). Such modifications have an innate basis in pan-human child-care behaviors, but
the details in every speech community are largely conventionalized
(i.e. culturally shaped) and in part arise directly from interactional
needs and imitation of children's behavior. The modificational features are variable in incidence, but constitute a surprisingly cohe-
sive set of linguistic features that may be regarded as a 'register'
in the language user's repertoire. This 'baby talk' register is an
important factor in the socialization of children, apparently assist-
ing in the acquisition of linguistic structure, the development of
interactional patterns, the transmission of cultural values, and the
expression of the user's affective relationship with the addressee.

3.2 The baby talk register in every speech community tends to
be extended to uses other than addressing young children, such as
reporting child speech, sarcastic attribution of childishness, and
talk between lovers or to animals; such extensions are typically
conventionalized and vary in detail from one community to another.

Structural features of the baby talk register tend to occur in
other registers that share features of function or use. Thus, baby
talk features that are related to the limited language competence
of the child who is addressed may occur in registers addressed to
others who lack such competence (e.g. speakers of other languages,
people with impaired hearing) and baby talk features that are related to the adult-child affective relationship may occur in registers
addressed to people being tended (e.g. nurse to patient, counselor
to client).

3.3 The baby talk register is variable along the dimension between normal speech and the most extreme deviation from normal,
and this variation tends to reflect the speaker's estimate of the
communicative competence of the child addressed and the strength
of the affective bond between them; aspects of the register may
vary in this dimension very subtly in 'fine tuning' with slight changes
in the child's behavior.

3.4 Children's ability to use aspects of this register in addressing younger children begins very early -- at the latest in the third
year -- and develops along with their whole communicative competence.

3.5 The conventionalized details of the register for talking to
young children are transmitted from one generation to the next
much as the rest of language is, and the special lexicon may be
very conservative, remaining essentially the same for long periods

of time; it is possible and instructive to reconstruct earlier baby
talk and to investigate the etymologies of baby-talk words.

The description of a special register used in talking to young
children seems far from our original goal of finding language universals. Instead of discovering phonological or syntactic universals
of human language, we seem to have ended with the discovery of a
universal way of modifying language for interactional purposes,
which cuts across the usual components of the linguist's grammar.
In fact, however, our discovery suggests a different kind of language universals, a kind that ethnographers of communication take
for granted, but are less appreciated by most linguists. From the
universal statements about talk to children of each of the five preceding paragraphs, it is possible to extrapolate to register variation
in general. In this spirit five universals are proposed for serious
consideration as characterizing the nature of human language.

1. Every language has register variation.

A part of the language user's competence is the ability to vary
the structure of the language in accordance with conditions of use,
such as the addressee, the occasion, the topic, or the speaker's
role.

2. Any register may be extended to secondary uses.

Any register may be extended, just as any lexical item, grammatical category, or genre of discourse may be used metaphorically
or in derived senses, and such extensions may become conventionalized.

3. A given register is variable in extent of deviation from the
least marked 'natural' form of the language.

The structural and functional boundaries of a register are often
blurred, and the degree of its implementation may vary. This
variation in degree of deviation may itself be used as a marker of
adjustment to the situation, and such use may be conventionalized.

4. Children acquire competence in register variation as they
acquire the basic grammatical structure of their language.

Register variation is not something added on to the grammar or
a way of using the grammar, acquired separately; it is an integral
part of language that is acquired simultaneously. Individuals may

acquire some registers late in life, but register variation as such begins as soon as the child produces recognizable language.

5. Registers are transmitted and changed as part of the total structure of a language.

Patterns of register variation continue through time and are subject to structural and functional change in much the same way phonological, syntactic and lexical structures continue and change.

Language universals of this kind characterize human language just as much as the usual structural universals do, and they raise the same kind of questions concerning how much is innate or acquired and how much is uniquely human or shared with other animals. In a recent paper I pointed out that all human societies seem to have verbal greetings, and that all primate species also exhibit greeting behaviors (Ferguson 1977a). Many of the functions (e.g. showing deference) and many of the actions (e.g. bowing) are similar, but human societies have, in addition, verbal routines of greeting that share in the syntactic and phonological structure of the language(s) of the society. We might hazard the guess, then, that some of our nonverbal greeting behavior has a significant biological substrate, i.e. is in some sense 'wired' into the organism at birth, and that even some aspects of the verbal greeting behavior of human beings are innate in the sense that human beings do some of the same things with language that they and their primate cousins do with nonverbal behavior on occasions of greeting. The same judgment can be made about the register for talking to children, if we can show that other primates adjust their communicative behavior while interacting with not fully competent individuals. And indeed, just this kind of behavior is well attested for chimpanzees who have learned to use sign language. It is somehow reassuring to know that when Koko, the Stanford gorilla who has learned to sign, is communicating with Mike, the young novice signer, she makes her signs more slowly and carefully, in effect using her version of a baby talk register. In adjusting our speech for talking to children — even though we do it in a uniquely human way with our linguistic structure -- we are essentially exercising deep-seated biological capabilities even more universal than we thought.

APPENDIX
List of sources by language

ARABIC (SYRIAN)	Ferguson 1956
ARAMAIC (NEO-)	Sabar 1974
BENGALI	Dil 1975
BERBER	Bynon 1968
COCOPA	Crawford 1970, 1974
COMANCHE	Casagrande 1948
DUTCH	Beheydt 1976; Snow et al. 1976; Vorster 1974
ENGLISH	Blount and Padgug 1977; Ferguson 1964; Garnica 1977a, b; Read 1946; Snow 1972, 1977 (review of others)
GERMAN	Zoeppritz 1976
GILYAK	Austerlitz 1956
GREEK	Drachmann 1973
HIDATSA	Voegelin and Robinett 1954
HUNGARIAN	MacWhinney 1974
JAPANESE	Chew 1969; Fischer 1970; Takahashi 1977
KANNADA (HAVYAKA)	Bhat 1967
KIPSIGIS	Harkness 1977
LATVIAN	Rūķe-Draviņa 1959, 1961, 1977
LUO	Blount 1972
MALTESE	Cassar-Pullicino 1957
MARATHI	Kelkar 1964
POMO	Oswalt 1976
PORTUGUESE (BRAZILIAN)	Stoel-Gammon 1976
ROMANIAN	Avram 1967
SAMOAN	Blount 1972
SERBO-CROATIAN	Jocić 1975
SPANISH	Blount and Padgug 1977; Ferguson 1964
TZELTAL	Stross 1972

BIBLIOGRAPHY

Austerlitz, Robert. 1956. Gilyak nursery words. Word 12. 200-279.

Avram, A. 1967. De la langue qu'on parle aux enfants roumains. To honor Roman Jakobson, vol. I: 133-140. The Hague: Mouton.

Beheydt, L. 1976. Nederlandse baby talk. Paper presented at the colloquium Psycholinguistisch Onderzoek, in België, Gent 25-26, Nov. Preprint, Louvain: Department of Linguistics, Katholieke Universiteit te Leuven.

Bell, Alan. (in this volume) Language samples.

Bhat, D.N.S. 1967. Lexical suppletion in baby talk. Anthropological Linguistics [AL] 9. 33-36.

Blount, Ben G. 1972. Parental speech and language acquisition:
some Luo and Samoan examples. AL 14. 119-130.

_____ and Elise J. Padgug. 1977. Prosodic, paralinguistic
and features in parent-child speech: English and Spanish.
Journal of Child Language 4. 67-86.

Brown, Roger. 1977. Introduction. In C.E. Snow and C.A. Ferguson 1977: 1-27.

_____ and Albert Gilman. 1960. The pronouns of power and
solidarity. Style in language, ed. by T.A. Sebeok, 253-276.
Cambridge, Mass.: M.I.T. Press.

Bynon, J. 1968. Berber nursery language. Transactions of the
Philological Society (1968), 107-161.

Casagrande, Joseph B. 1948. Comanche baby language. International Journal of American Linguistics [IJAL] 14. 11-14.

Cassar-Pullicino, J. 1957. Nursery vocabulary of the Maltese
Archipelago. Orbis 6. 192-198.

Chew, John J., Jr. 1969. The structure of Japanese baby talk.
Journal-Newsletter of the Association of Teachers of Japanese
6. 1. 4-17.

Crawford, James M. 1970. Cocopa baby talk. IJAL 36. 9-13.

_____. 1974. Baby talk in an American Indian language. Draft
of paper for Conference on Language Input and Acquisition, Boston.

Cross, Toni G. 1977. Mothers' speech adjustments: the contribution of selected child listener variables. In C.E. Snow and C.A.
Ferguson 1977: 151-188.

Crothers, John. (in this book, vol. II) Typology and universals of
vowel systems.

Dil, Afia. 1975. Bengali baby talk. Child language-1975, ed. by
W. von Raffler Engel (Word 27), 11-27.

Drachmann, Gaberell. 1973. Baby talk in Greek. Ohio State University Working Papers in Linguistics 15. Columbus, Ohio.

Ervin-Tripp, Susan. 1977. A psychologist's point of view. In C.E. Snow and C.A. Ferguson 1977: 335-339.

Farwell, Carol B. 1975. The language spoken to children. Human Development 18. 288-309.

Ferguson, Charles A. 1956. Arabic baby talk. For Roman Jakobson, ed. by M. Halle. The Hague: Mouton.

_____. 1964. Baby talk in six languages. American Anthropologist 66. 6, part 2, 103-114.

_____. 1975. Applications of linguistics. Survey of American linguistics, ed. by R. Austerlitz, 63-75. Lisse: De Ridder.

_____. 1977a. Structure and use of politeness formulas. Language in Society 5. 137-151.

_____. 1977b. Baby talk as a simplified register. In C.E. Snow and C.A. Ferguson 1977: 209-235.

_____, David B. Peizer and Thelma E. Weeks. 1973. Model-and-replica phonological grammar of a child's first words. Lingua 31. 35-65.

Fillmore, C.J. and W. S-Y. Wang (eds.) (forthcoming) Individual differences in language ability and language behavior. New York: Academic Press.

Fischer, John L. 1970. Linguistic socialization: Japan and the United States. Families in East and West, ed. by R. Hill and R. König. The Hague: Mouton.

Garnica, Olga K. 1977a. Some characteristics of speech to young children. Ohio State University Working Papers in Linguistics 22. 11-72. Columbus, Ohio.

_____. 1977b. Some prosodic and paralinguistic features of speech to young children. In C.E. Snow and C.A. Ferguson 1977: 63-88.

Greenberg, Joseph H. 1966a. Some universals of grammar with particular reference to the order of meaningful elements.

Universals of language, ed. by J.H. Greenberg, 73-113. Cambridge, Mass.: M.I.T. Press, 2nd ed.

_____. 1966b. Synchronic and diachronic universals in phonology. Language 42. 508-517.

Harkness, Sara. 1975. Cultural variation in mothers' language. Child language -1975, ed. by W. von Raffler Engel (Word 27), 495-498.

_____. 1977. Aspects of social environment and first language acquisition in Africa. In C.E. Snow and C.A. Ferguson 1977: 309-316.

Helvicus, Christophorus (Helwig, Christopher). 1619. Libri didactici, grammaticae universalis, Latinae, Graecae, Hebraicae, Chaldaicae.

Holzman, Mathilda. 1974. The verbal environment provided by mothers for their very young children. Merill-Palmer Quarterly 20. 33-42.

Ingram, David. (in this book, vol. III) Typology and universals of personal pronouns.

Jakobson, Roman. 1960. Why 'mama' and 'papa?' Perspectives in psychological theory, ed. by B. Kaplan. New York: International University Press.

Jocić, M. 1975. Modifications in adults' speech in adult-child communication. Paper presented at the Third International Child Language Symposium, London.

Kelkar, Ashok R. 1964. Marathi baby talk. Word 20. 40-54.

MacWhinney, Brian. 1974. How Hungarian children learn to speak. Doctoral dissertation, University of California, Berkeley, 446-457.

Moskowitz, Breyne Arlene. 1972. The acquisition of phonology and syntax: a preliminary study. Approaches to natural languages, ed. by K. Hintikka et al. Dordrecht, Netherlands: Reidel.

Newport, Elissa. 1976. Motherese: the speech of mothers to young children. Cognitive theory, ed. by N. Castellan et al., vol. II. Hillsdale, N.J.: Lawrence Erlbaum Associates.

222   Charles A. Ferguson

Newport, Elissa, Henry Gleitman and Lila R. Gleitman. 1977.
Mother, I'd rather do it myself: some effects and non-effects
of maternal speech style. In C.E. Snow and C.A. Ferguson
1977: 109 -149.

Oswalt, Robert L. 1976. Baby talk and the genesis of some basic
Pomo words. IJAL 42. 1-13.

Read, Allen Walker. 1946. The social setting of hypocoristic
speech (so-called baby talk). Paper presented at the annual
meeting of the Modern Language Association, Washington, D.C.

Rūķe-Draviņa, Velta. 1959. Ammensprache. Chapter V, § 2 of
Diminutive im Lettischen (Acta Universitatis Stockholmiensis,
Etudes de Philologie Slaves 8. 25-34.) Lund: H. Ohlssons
Boktryckeri.

_____. 1961. Ns. lastenhoitajain kielestä ("On so-called nur-
sery language"). Virittäjä 1. 85-91.

_____. 1976. Gibt es Universalien in der Ammensprache?
Akten des 1. Salzburger Kolloquiums über Kindersprache (=Salz-
burger Beiträge zu Linguistik 2), 3-16. Tübingen: Verlag
Günther Narr.

_____. 1977. Modifications of speech addressed to young chil-
dren in Latvian. In C.E. Snow and C.A. Ferguson 1977: 237-
253.

Sabar, Yona. 1974. Nursery rhymes and baby words in the Jewish
Neo-Aramaic dialect of Zakoh (Iraq). Journal of the American
Oriental Society 94. 329-336.

Sachs, Jacqueline. 1977. The adaptive significance of linguistic
input to children. In C.E. Snow and C.A. Ferguson 1977: 51-61.

Savić, Svenka. 1974. Aspects of adult-child communication: the
problem of question acquisition. Paper presented at the symposium: Structure and Function of Utterances, Cracow, Poland,
October 1974.

Sinclair, J.M. and R.M. Coulthard. 1975. Towards an analysis
of discourse; the English used by teachers and pupils. London:
Oxford University Press.

Slobin, Dan I. 1975. On the nature of talk to children. Foundations of language development, vol. I, ed. by E.H. Lenneberg and E. Lenneberg, 283-297. New York: Academic Press.

Snow, Catherine E. 1972. Mothers' speech to children learning language. Child Development 43. 549-565.

_____. 1977. Mothers' speech research: from input to inter-action. In C.E. Snow and C.A. Ferguson 1977: 31-49.

_____ and Charles A. Ferguson (eds.). 1977. Talking to chil-dren. Cambridge, Eng.: Cambridge University Press.

_____, A. Arlman-Rupp, Y. Hassing, J. Jobse, J. Joosten, and J. Vorster. 1976. Mothers' speech in three social classes. Journal of Psycholinguistic Research 5. 1-20.

Steele, Susan. (in this book, vol. IV) Word order variation: a typological study.

Stoel-Gammon, Caroline. 1976. Baby talk in Brazilian Portuguese: Papers and Reports on Child Language Development 11. 83-88.

Stross, Brian. 1972. Verbal processes in Tzeltal speech sociali-zation. AL 14. 1-13.

Takahashi, Kunitoshi. 1977. Some characteristics of baby talk in Japanese. Unpublished paper, University of Tsukuba, Ibaraki, Japan.

Ultan, Russell. (in this book, vol. IV) Some general characteris-tics of interrogative systems.

Voegelin, C.F. and Florence M. Robinett. 1954. 'Mother language' in Hidatsa. IJAL 20. 65-70.

Vihman, Marilyn May. 1977. A reference manual and users' guide to the Stanford Phonology Archive, part I. Department of Lin-guistics, Stanford University.

_____. (in this book, vol. II). Consonant harmony: its scope and function in child language.

Vorster, Jan. 1974. Mothers' speech to children: some methodo-logical considerations (= Publikaties van het Instituut voor Al-gemene Taalwetenschap 8). Universiteit van Amsterdam.

Wills, Dorothy Davis. 1977. Participant deixis in English and
    baby talk. In C.E. Snow and C.A. Ferguson 1977: 271-295.

Zoeppritz, Magdalena. 1976. Babysprache im Deutschen. A bunch
    of mayflowers (Broder Carstensen zum 50. Geburtstag am 27.
    Mai 1976), ed. by D. Lehmann et al., 264-272.

Universals, Relativity,
and Language Processing

EVE V. CLARK & HERBERT H. CLARK

ABSTRACT

Language is above all a tool, and as a tool it must conform to
the uses required of it. Whether the language is ENGLISH, HUN-
GARIAN, or TOK PISIN, it must be capable of expressing certain
ideas —perceptual experiences, social relationships, and techno-
logical facts. At the same time it must conform to people's limitations --to their limited memory and even to the way their ears
and mouths are constructed. So language is constrained to take
only certain forms, and these are reflected in the universals of
language. For example, the basic color terms in all languages
are drawn from a hierarchy of only eleven color words. This
hierarchy reflects the physiological salience of certain colors in
the visual system. The names for natural and man-made objects
in all languages belong to hierarchies of categories. These hierarchies reflect the mental processes by which objects are classified according to shared features. The shape names and spatial
terms in languages reflect still other characteristics of the perceptual system. Other universals reflect abstract thought processes that favor singular over plural, positive over negative,
present tense over past or future tense, and so on. Still other
universals, like those of kinship terms and pronouns, reflect in-
variant social realities. Finally, the universals of word grouping,
word order, and paradigms arise from the processes by which
people understand and produce ongoing speech.

CONTENTS

Language does not exist in a vacuum.   It serves and is molded by other systems in the human mind.   Because it is used for conveying ideas, its structure and function must reflect these ideas. Because it must be spoken and understood easily and efficiently, its structure and function are forced to stay within the limits imposed by people's processing capacities.   Because it is used for communication within a complex social and cultural system, its structure and function are molded by these forces as well.   Yet once people have learned how to use language, it wields a power of its own.   It aids them in thinking about others.   It molds many aspects of their daily affairs.

Over the centuries these forces have been recognized and taken up within two fields of study, linguistic universals and linguistic relativity.   If languages are molded in part by the ideas, processing capacities, and social factors all people have in common, they should have certain features in common—linguistic universals. Since people need to refer to objects, every language has nouns. But to the extent that languages are molded by accidental properties of thought, technology, and culture, features will also differ from language to language.   Since the Garo of Burma need to distinguish among more kinds of rice than Russians do, GARO has more words for rice than RUSSIAN does.   In the opposite direction, if language molds people's ideas and culture, these language-specific features should lead people who speak different languages to think differently.   The Garo may be able to think about rice in ways Russians can't simply because GARO has more words for rice than RUSSIAN.   This is known as linguistic relativity.

Although linguistic relativity was proposed in the eighteenth century by Johann Herder and later refined by Wilhelm von Humboldt and Edward Sapir, it is most closely associated in the twentieth century with Benjamin Lee Whorf, who stated the hypothesis in its strongest form (1956: 213-14):

> We dissect nature along lines laid down by our native
> languages.   The categories and types that we isolate
> from the world of phenomena we do not find there be-
> cause they stare every observer in the face; on the
> contrary, the world is presented in a kaleidoscopic
> flux of impressions which has to be organized by our
> minds --and this means largely by the linguistic sys-
> tems in our minds.   We cut nature up, organize it
> into concepts, and ascribe significances as we do,

> largely because we are parties to an agreement to orga-
> nize it in this way--an agreement that holds through our
> speech community and is codified in the patterns of our
> language. The agreement is, of course, an implicit
> and unstated one, but its terms are absolutely obligatory;
> we cannot talk at all except by subscribing to the organi-
> zation and classification of data which the agreement
> decrees.

Here Whorf claims that language influences the very way people
perceive and organize the world around them. It is, then, an
important hypothesis about the relation between language and
thought.

Logic, however, won't let us examine linguistic relativity
without at the same time examining linguistic universals. Imagine
how people would describe three shirts. They would probably
stress their differences. Number one is cotton, two is silk,
and three is wool. Or number one is plaid, two is polka-dotted,
and three is plain. Or number one has short sleeves while two
and three have long sleeves. And so on. But note that each
comparison presupposes something universal about the three
shirts. Each is made from cloth, and what varies is the kind
of cloth. Each has a pattern, and what varies is the kind of
pattern. Each has sleeves, and what varies is the length of
sleeve. Differences can be described only with respect to
constancies. The same goes for languages. GARO may have
more nouns for rice than RUSSIAN, but to say this presupposes
that both languages have nouns. It also presupposes that one
can identify that aspect of the conceptual domain, here rice,
that the two languages name differently. In short, linguistic
relativity presupposes linguistic universals.

Linguistic universals, though of concern for centuries, have
recently been taken up with renewed interest. The reasons are
clear. The variation that occurs in languages has obvious limits,
and these limits ought to tell us something about the nature of language. A priori, every human language must be susceptible of:

(1) Being learned by children.
(2) Being spoken and understood by adults easily and
    efficiently.
(3) Embodying the ideas people normally want to convey.
(4) Functioning as a communication system in a social and
    cultural setting.

Consider ENGLISH and NAVAHO.   One might well be sur-
prised to discover that they have features in common.   They
are historically unrelated and until recently have not been in
contact with each other.   The features they have in common,
if not accidental, must therefore be there because it is a requirement of a human language that they be there.   They are
just the features that fulfill the four conditions placed on human
languages.   Thus, if we knew what is common to all languages,
it might be possible to characterize what is inherent in the
human capacity to speak, to understand, and to acquire
language.

Linguistic universals, according to Noam Chomsky (1965,
1968) have a special interest because they reflect the human's
innate predisposition to learn language.   His argument goes
like this.   In learning a language, children hear a sample of
sentences that is quite inadequate for them to acquire the language in all its complexity.   Many of its structures are unob-
servable, and yet they somehow get learned.   It must be that
children have some "hypothesis" about what language is like,
some innate predisposition to look for certain language features
and not others.   The features they look for will therefore be
precisely those that are common to all languages.

It is not very helpful, however, to stop with the conclusion
that linguistic universals spring from innate predispositions.
This point has been made by Lehrman (1953), who years ago
criticized the widespread use of "innate" explanations for animal
behavior.   At the time he wrote, many investigators had concluded, for example, that the pecking of the chick immediately
after it emerged from the egg was "innate," or "instinctual."
After all, the chick didn't have to be taught how to peck.
Lehrman noted, however, that on a closer look, pecking consists of a coordinated pattern of dipping the head, opening the
beak, and swallowing that develops out of separate behavior
patterns that combine while the chick is still in the egg.   As
Lehrman put it, "The statement that 'pecking' is innate, or
that it 'matures,' leads us <u>away</u> from any attempt to analyze
its specific origins.   The assumption that pecking grows <u>as</u> a
pecking <u>pattern</u> discourages examination of the embryological
processes leading to pecking.   The elements out of whose
interaction pecking emerges are not originally a unitary pattern;
they <u>become</u> related as a consequence of their positions in the
organization of the embryonic chick (1953, p. 344)." Lehrman con-

cluded: "The use of 'explanatory' categories such as 'innate' and 'genetically fixed' obscures the necessity of investigating developmental processes in order to gain insight into the actual mechanisms of behavior and their interrelations (p. 345)." In this chapter we will try to follow Lehrman's example. Not only will we take up features of language that are thought to be universal, but we will also suggest plausible psychological processes to account for their universality. Linguistic universals may not be as mysterious as the concept of "innate predispositions" makes them seem (Schlesinger 1967; Levelt 1975).

In this chapter our goal is to see how thought influences language and how language influences thought. We take up selected linguistic universals and look at the thought processes they might plausibly reflect. These universals are divided into those that derive from perception, general cognition, social systems, and processing capacities--although these divisions are not hard and fast. We conclude by returning to variation in languages and the question of how language may influence thought.

Perceptual Categories

What are the ties between cognitive abilities and language? This question is best answered through an examination of language universals. Many features common to languages are not specific to language per se, but are derived from the human capacity to perceive, categorize, and socialize. The first universals to be taken up are those that probably derive from the human capacity to organize and categorize perceptual information. For example, because the human visual apparatus finds certain colors more salient than others, languages are extraordinarily consistent about which few of the infinite number of colors are named. Other aspects of the human perceptual and cognitive system lead to universal ways of treating names for such things as natural categories, names for shapes, and spatial terms.

Complexity of Expression

The features of language that are universal, of course, are not sounds, words, or phrases, but something far more abstract. The first universals to be examined all deal in a commodity called complexity of expression. It is central to one of the most important hypotheses about the relation of language to thought:

The complexity principle: Complexity in thought tends to be reflected in complexity of expression.

Broadly speaking, the more complex the expression, the more complex the thought it reflects.

But when is an expression complex? This question has been discussed extensively by Greenberg (1966) under the rubric of markedness. He has proposed several criteria for deciding which of two categories of thought--usually two contrasting categories-- is given the more complex expression or, in his terminology, is more marked. The following are two of his main criteria.

(1) Added morphemes. If expression B consists of expression A plus an added morpheme, then B is more complex than A. The word dogs, for example, consists of dog plus an added morpheme, the suffix -s, which is said to "mark" dogs as plural. Dogs is therefore a more complex expression than dog. In English generally, plurals are marked by an added morpheme (with exceptions like deer and sheep), while singulars never are. In Greenberg's terminology, then, the category plural is marked with respect to the category singular in English: that is, plural is given a more complex expression than singular. In English, added morphemes can be of various kinds, as in these pairs:

happy	unhappy	sleep	will sleep
oak	scrub oak	father	grandfather
blue	light blue	complex	complexity

(2) Contextual neutralization. If expression A can neutralize in meaning in contexts that the almost equivalent expression B cannot, then B is more complex than A. In most contexts, for example, actor is male and actress female. In some contexts, however, actor but not actress can be neutralized in meaning to cover both males and females. Actress is therefore a more complex expression than actor. In English generally, the category female is marked with respect to the category male. Note that actress would be considered marked by the first criterion too, since it consists of actor plus the added morpheme -ess. The different criteria for markedness almost always lead to the same judgment of what is simple and what is complex. When they don't, one should be cautious about calling either category marked.

Using these and other criteria, investigators like Greenberg have sifted through many genetically unrelated languages for categories that are universally, or almost universally, given the least complex expression. These criteria have been especially successful in discovering the fundamentals of color terminology.

Basic Color Terms

For many years scholars believed that languages divided up the color spectrum arbitrarily. For these people, it was conceivable that some language had a color term like binkle that

straddled the English terms <u>blue</u> and <u>red</u> and had its center in
purple. Recently, however, Berlin and Kay(1969; Kay 1975), two
anthropologists, discovered that color naming is far from arbitrary. They did so by examining languages for what they called
<u>basic color terms</u>. These are the terms in a language that have
the least complexity of expression yet cover all parts of the color
spectrum. Berlin and Kay used four main criteria to identify the
basic color terms of each language, one of which is equivalent to
"added morphemes." For a color term to be basic:

(1) It must consist of only one morpheme, like <u>red</u>, and not
    two or more, as in <u>light red</u> or <u>blood-like</u>.

(2) It must not be contained within another color, as <u>scarlet</u>
    is contained within <u>red</u>.

(3) It must not be restricted to a small number of objects, like
    <u>blond</u>, which applies only to hair and a few other objects.

(4) It must be common and generally known, like <u>yellow</u> and
    not <u>saffron</u>.

From their survey, Berlin and Kay found that every language takes
its basic color terms from the following list of only eleven color
names: <u>black</u>, <u>white</u>, <u>red</u>, <u>yellow</u>, <u>green</u>, <u>blue</u>, <u>brown</u>, <u>purple</u>,
<u>pink</u>, <u>orange</u>, and <u>gray</u>. Far from being chaotic, the world's lan-
guages are remarkably uniform in their treatment of color.

Even more surprisingly, Berlin and Kay found that these eleven
basic color terms formed a hierarchy. Some languages, like
English, use all eleven, while others use as few as two. When a
language has only two, it picks not just any two at random, but
<u>black</u> and <u>white</u> (sometimes translated as <u>dark</u> and <u>light</u>). When
a language has three colors, it always picks <u>black</u>, <u>white</u>, and <u>red</u>.
In general, each language selects its terms from this hierarchy:

$$
\begin{bmatrix} \text{black} \\ \text{white} \end{bmatrix} \rightarrow \text{red} \rightarrow \begin{bmatrix} \text{yellow} \\ \text{green} \\ \text{blue} \end{bmatrix} \rightarrow \text{brown} \rightarrow \begin{bmatrix} \text{purple} \\ \text{pink} \\ \text{orange} \\ \text{gray} \end{bmatrix}
$$

Thus a language with six color terms will take the first six terms
from the left: <u>black</u>, <u>white</u>, <u>red</u>, <u>yellow</u>, <u>green</u>, and <u>blue</u>. To put
it another way, if a language has <u>blue</u> as one of its basic color
terms, it will also have every term to its left in this hierarchy,
namely <u>red</u>, <u>black</u>, and <u>white</u>. The terms within brackets can be
selected in any order. The hierarchy also carries a historical
implication: if a language acquires a new basic color term, it always acquires the next one to the right of the ones it already has.
This is a powerful statement about color terminology. If combi-

nations of the eleven basic color terms were random, there would
be 2,048 possibilities. The hierarchy restricts that number to
thirty-three.

Focal Colors. The hierarchy could not have been constructed
if Berlin and Kay had not hit on what they called focal colors. To
study color terms, they had prepared a chart of 320 small squares
called "color chips." This chart covered more or less evenly all
the saturated hues people can see. Speakers of various languages
were asked to point to the color chip that best represented each of
the basic color terms in their language. The ones people selected
as the best red, green, yellow, and so on were virtually the same
from language to language. The major exception came in languages with only two terms. For them, white covered all the
warm colors and had its focal color in white, red, or yellow,
while black covered all cool colors and had its focal color in
black or brown. Against the high degree of consistency with focal
colors, people were not at all consistent in drawing boundaries
between the basic terms. It is the focal colors that make it possible to match color terms across languages--to say that JAPA-
NESE aka is the same as ENGLISH red, NAVAHO lichi, and
ESKIMO anpaluktak.

Why these particular eleven colors? It must be because they
are perceptually the most salient of all colors in the spectrum.
Rosch (formerly Heider) set out to demonstrate just that. In one
study (Heider 1971), three-year-old children were presented with
an array of color chips and, when the experimenter's back was
turned, were asked, "Show me a color." They overwhelmingly
preferred focal to nonfocal colors. And when four-year-olds were
asked to pick from an assortment of color chips the one that
matched a test chip, they matched focal colors more accurately
than nonfocal ones (see also Mervis, Catlin, and Rosch 1975).
In a study with adults from twenty-three different language groups
(Heider 1972), focal colors were named faster and with shorter
expressions than nonfocal ones. And in a memory task, adults
from two language groups were shown a single color chip for five
seconds, and after thirty seconds were presented with 160 color
chips from which they were to select the one they had just seen.
They matched focal colors more accurately than nonfocal ones.
In brief, focal colors are easier to remember, named more
quickly, given shorter names, and are more "eye-catching"--
proof enough of their perceptual salience.

Rosch's most remarkable studies were carried out with the
Dani, a New Guinea people whose language has only two basic
terms, mili ("black") and mola ("white") to cover all the colors of

the spectrum. Because the Dani had no basic color terms for red, green, yellow, and the rest, it was possible to see how quickly they could learn names for these focal colors. One group was taught arbitrary names for eight <u>focal</u> colors, and another group, arbitrary names for eight <u>nonfocal</u> colors. The first group learned much faster than the second (Rosch 1973). In a memory study (Heider 1972), the Dani were found—just like English speakers--to remember focal colors more accurately than nonfocal ones. In a study requiring judgments of color similarity (Heider and Olivier 1972), the Dani were found to represent colors in memory the same way English speakers do, in spite of the great difference between the two systems of color naming. Evidently, focal colors are salient regardless of whether or not people have names for them.

The Visual System. But why the sensitivity to focal colors? The answer undoubtedly lies in the physiology of the human visual system (McDaniel 1974). The Hering "opponent" theory of color vision holds that the eye has three opponent processes: one for brightness (black-white) and two for hue (red-green and yellow-blue). When light strikes the eye, each opponent pair responds with a value varying from positive to negative, and the combination of the three values produces the sensation of the appropriate color. The system thus has six unique points of response, one for each point at which two of the systems are neutral (with zero response) and the third is maximally positive or negative (Hering 1920; Jameson and Hurvich 1955; de Valois and Jacobs 1968). Significantly, these six points correspond to the first six colors of the hierarchy: black, white, red, green, yellow, and blue. It seems likely that the remaining five colors correspond to other "maxima" in the visual system.

The universality of color terms, therefore, has a plausible explanation. The very physiology of the human visual system makes some colors more salient than others. Children find these colors eye-catching and easy to remember. Because of this, they take these colors to be the ones adults talk about whenever they refer to colors and therefore find terms denoting them easy to learn (Dougherty 1976). Adults maintain these preferences for the same reasons. There is more occasion to talk about salient colors, and listeners assume that speakers are more likely to be talking about them. Color terminology is universal because the human visual system is universal.

Basic Category Names

Roger Brown (1958) once observed that although all objects have

more than one name, people often talk about the name of an object,
as if it had just one. An apple is an apple, even though it is also a
fruit, a thing, an object, a Golden Delicious apple, and Amanda's
dessert. Apple is somehow primary, or basic, the name that
seems to fit best. But why? According to Brown, apple is at a
level of abstraction with the greatest utility in most contexts.   To
call an apple merely a fruit would generally do too little, failing
to distinguish it from bananas, pears, and other fruit. And to call
it a Golden Delicious apple would generally do too much, distinguishing it from other minor varieties of apples. But what determines the most useful level of abstraction? What are its origins?

Levels of Abstraction.   In their study of "folk biology"--the
way people of the world name plants and animals--Berlin and his
colleagues (Berlin 1972; Berlin, Breedlove, and Raven 1968, 1973)
have concluded that all people divide the plant and animal kingdom
into categories, each of which is given a name. These categories
are hierarchically organized with five (and sometimes six) levels
of abstraction:

(1) Unique beginner: plant, animal

(2) Life form: tree, bush, flower

(3) Generic name: pine, oak, maple, elm

(4) Specific name: Ponderosa pine, white pine, jack pine

5) Varietal name: northern Ponderosa pine, western
              Ponderosa pine

At each level, the categories are mutually exclusive--they don't
overlap. Nothing is both a pine and an oak. And each category
belongs to a category at the next higher level of abstraction.
Pines, oaks, maples, and elms are all trees. It is not a foregone
conclusion that all people should classify and name their world
this way.

Berlin and his colleagues argues that the generic level, level 3,
is the most basic. For one thing, in each language it has around
500 categories, which is more than any other level. It is more
useful than level 2 and better developed than level 4. It is also
distinguished from levels 4 and 5 linguistically. Note that in
English the generic level uses simple names like pine, oak, elm,
and maple, whereas the next level down, the specific, uses complex names like white pine, jack pine, and Ponderosa pine. The
names at level 4 usually contain more than one word, often a
superordinate level 3 term, like pine, combined with a modifier,
like Ponderosa. The same difference between levels 3 and 4 shows
up in all languages. Why should level 4 use complex terms?   Its
categories must belong to a more complex classification system,

one in which the divisions are not as natural or as easy to identify. The generic level, with its simple names, represents a relatively natural way of dividing up the world. Indeed, Berlin and his colleagues found that people felt generic names to be primary, and these names were the first ones learned by children in the cultures they studied. The name of an object, in Brown's sense, seems to belong to this basic level of categorization.

Basic-level Categories. But how do people slice up the world into categories? Rosch and her colleagues have argued that natural categories are a product of the human perceptual and cognitive apparatus for dealing with the world. Objects are perceived in terms of attributes and, in nature, these attributes come in clusters. If an object is feathered, it is a good bet that it sings, flies, has a beak, and a particular shape. It is also a good bet that it doesn't roar, bear live young, or have four legs. Attributes that go together, like feathered, singing, flying, beaked, and bird-shaped, define a natural category, like bird. The objects within a single category share attributes with each other, bear a "family resemblance" to each other. At the same time, they share few attributes with objects in other categories, bear little family resemblance to other objects.

Rosch and Mervis (1975) have demonstrated that natural categories are formed by the clustering of perceived attributes. In one study people were asked to list attributes for a variety of objects. As expected, each object shared a good many attributes with others in the same category, but few attributes with those in other categories. Other people were asked to rate each object as to how typical, how good an example, it was of the category. The more typical an object was judged to be, the more attributes it shared with members of the same category--and the fewer attributes it shared with members of other categories. Consider oranges and blueberries, typical and atypical fruits, respectively. Oranges share more attributes with all other fruits than do blueberries, but they share fewer attributes with all vegetables than do blueberries. From these and other findings, Rosch and Mervis have argued that categories are "out there" in nature. The human perceptual apparatus is geared to deal with certain attributes, and in nature those attributes go together to form certain categories (Rosch 1977).

The reason why Berlin's generic level is basic, Rosch and her colleagues would argue, is that it is the level at which categories are the tightest. Take, for example, the categories furniture, table, and kitchen table. Members of the category furniture (such as chairs, bookcases, rugs, and vases) have few attributes in common; however, members of the category table (dining room tables, kitchen tables, and side tables) have many. So do members of the category kitchen table (Aunt Martha's, the neighbor's, and grandfather's), although they have very few more attributes in common than do members of the category table. By the criterion <u>common attributes</u>, table and kitchen table are very good categories. On the other hand, since kitchen tables have many attributes in common with other types of tables, the category kitchen table is hard to distinguish from other categories at the same level, while the category table is easy to distinguish from other categories at the same level. So by the criterion of <u>distinguishability</u>, table is a good category and kitchen table a bad one. Table, then, is the "tightest" category. Its members are all very similar to each other yet all very different from members of other categories at the same level. Rosch et al. (1976) have confirmed these impressions for objects in a variety of categories.

<u>Expertise.</u>   One caution: not everybody sees the same categories as loose or tight. It depends on how much each person "knows" about the objects in each category. A car novice sees all cars pretty much the same, but a car fanatic pays attention to all kinds of differences the novice doesn't even notice. The category car is therefore tighter for the novice than for the fanatic, while the subcategories of car are each tighter for the fanatic than for the novice. If the tightness of a category depends on expertise, then so does what people take as a basic category. Rosch et al., for example, found that their city-born subjects treated tree as a basic category, whereas Berlin et al. found that the mainly agricultural peoples they studied treated oak, elm, and pine as basic categories. As Berlin argued (see Rosch et al. 1976), this difference probably reflects a difference in expertise. The ENGLISH names <u>oak</u>, <u>elm</u>, and <u>pine</u>, all simple generic names, are in the language because at one time most people knew their trees, just as car fanatics know their cars. Here, then, is a place for cultural relativity. Basic categories vary with the expertise of the culture or subculture of people naming the objects.

Berlin et al.'s universals of naming categories, therefore, seem to arise from people's perceptual experience with objects. In nature, the attributes people perceive and pay attention to come in clusters and lead people to form natural categories. These for most people are tightest at the generic level of abstraction and are called basic categories. When it comes to naming, this level is very useful, and its categories are given simple names. Since these categories will also be among the earliest that children form, they will generally be among the first that children acquire names for (Brown 1958; Rosch et al. 1976; Stross 1973). As for Brown's observation that people think objects have a best name, the name of an object is the name of the tightest category it belongs to, the name of its basic category.

Shape Names

In English some geometrical shapes get named and others do not. The most common one- and two-dimensional shape names (Kučera and Francis 1967) are these:

Single lines	Closed figures
line	square
curve	circle
angle	oval
	triangle
	rectangle

Most other simple shape names are so uncommon that they are virtually technical terms in geometry. How, then, do people describe shapes not covered by this list? One way is to resort to complex expressions like square with a corner cut off or flower-shaped or pear-like. Another is to use the nearest shape name in the above list as an approximation good enough for practical purposes. In any event, there seem to be basic shape names, following Berlin and Kay's (1969) criteria for basic terms, and they correspond to only certain shapes.

Good Figures. To the Gestalt psychologist it is obvious why these are the shapes with basic names. They are just those shapes that form good Gestalts, or "good figures" (see Boring 1942). A figure has more characteristics of a "good figure" when it is closed, when it is symmetrical, when it has the fewest changes in curvature, and so on. On principles like these, lines, curves, and angles are better figures than squiggles, esses, and ogives. Circles and squares turn out to be the best closed figures, followed closely by ovals, triangles, and rectangles. These are all better figures than hexagons, quadrilaterals, and rhombuses, to say nothing of all the figures that require complex names. Although the shape names have not been systematically studied in various languages, it is difficult to imagine that the same Gestalt principles wouldn't predict what is and isn't named in those languages, too.

Rosch (1973), however, found that the Dani did not have basic names for the common shapes named in English. To describe geometrical figures, they resorted to circumlocutions like pig-shaped or fence-shaped. So Rosch had them learn arbitrary names for a variety of shapes. One group of Dani learned one name for a circle and variations of it, another name for a square and variations of that, and a third name for a triangle and variations of that. Other groups learned names for variations of three shapes that are not as good by Gestalt principles. The Dani who learned names for the best figures--the variations of circle, square, and triangle-- did so the fastest. Those who learned names for less good figures did correspondingly less well. So it may not be accidental that English and other languages have basic names for these particular shapes. They are good Gestalts that other people find easiest to learn names for too.

Classifiers. Many languages have a system of so-called classifiers, and in them shape plays an important role. To talk about more than one ball in some languages, for example, one cannot use the equivalent of the ENGLISH six balls. One must instead attach six to a classifier used with the noun ball, as in six round-things ball. The classifier (here, round-thing) is usually a single word that categorizes the object in some way (Berlin 1968; Denny 1976; Greenberg 1972). There is a comparable categorization in the English expressions a blade of grass, three sheets of typing paper, and three rolls of wall paper. The words blade, sheet, and roll help pick out the shape and dimensionality of the objects named. In some languages, the classifier makes up part of the verb instead, as in he caused-round-solid- thing -to-move-upward stone ("he lifted the stone") and the man animate-thing-moved away ("the man left"). Classifiers like these are common in languages throughout Southeast Asia (such as MANDARIN CHINESE, VIETNAMESE, and LAOTIAN) and in languages of North and Central America (such as HOPI, NAVAHO, and TZELTAL).

How do classifiers classify? According to K. Adams and Conklin (1973), they usually distinguish first between animate and non-animate objects and often then divide the animate objects into humans versus animals, with some further subcategorization. More significantly for our purpose, they frequently classify objects on the basis of shape. The shapes most often picked out are round, long, and (less frequently) flat. Objects are classified by these shapes either alone or in combination with some secondary property like orientation, rigidity, or use. For example, a long object might be classified as a long vertical thing (like a pole) or as a long horizontal thing (like a log), and a flat object might be classified as a flat rigid thing (like a board) or as a flat flexible thing (like a rug). These three shapes--long, flat, and round--are again perceptually simple. Long denotes simple one-dimensional extension (as in lines), flat simple two-dimensional extension (as in rugs), and round simple three-dimensional extension (as in spheres). These are all good Gestalts.

Table 1: Types of Gestalt Figures

	OPEN	CLOSED
GOOD FIGURES	/ (	◯ □
LESS GOOD FIGURES		

What is remarkable is that the shapes selected by classifiers are most often the very shapes children use in overextending their first nouns (E. Clark 1977a). For example, just as classifier systems commonly categorize objects by their round shape, so do children in their overextensions. And just as classifiers categorize objects as long (extending in one dimension), so do children in their overextensions. These two parallels are illustrated in Table 2. There seem to be no clear instances of flat objects being grouped together in overextensions, but this may be because flat is really only a special case of long, as Adams and Conklin (1973) suggested. Children also use animacy or movement as a basis for overextension, and this parallels the nonshape categories of classifier systems. One final note: classifier systems never categorize on the basis of color, and neither do children in their overextensions.

The shapes people pick out for basic names or classifiers, therefore, have a plausible origin in human perceptual capacities. People have a predilection for good Gestalt figures perceptually, and these are the shapes that are named. Children appear to find some shapes more salient than others and use these in their first hypotheses about what nouns pick out. Names for these shapes will therefore be easy to learn, and with the adult predilection for the same shapes, they will also be maintained in the language. Basic shape names, then, are determined by principles that are built onto the human perceptual system.

Spatial Terms
    All languages appear to make reference to such spatial dimensions as height, width, distance, and thickness. In ENGLISH, dimensions are described with adjectives like high and low, wide and narrow, far and near, and thick and thin. In each pair the first adjective describes extent along the dimension, and the second adjective describes lack of extent. But there is an extraordinary consistency among these adjectives. The terms that describe "having extent" are all linguistically unmarked and positive; the terms that describe "lacking extent" are linguistically

Table 2: Parallels between Classifier Categories and Children's Overextensions*

SHAPE	CLASSIFIER CATEGORY	CHILDREN'S OVER-EXTENSIONS
ROUND	*Indonesian:* fruit, pea, eye, ball, stone	*English:* moon, cakes, round marks on windows, round marks in books, round tooling on book covers, round postmarks, letter 'O'
	Laotian: sun, moon, plate, pot, eye, stone	
	Thai: bead, stone, seed, globe, fruit	*French:* nipple, point of bare elbow, eye in portrait, face in photo
		Serbian: coat button, collar stud, round light switch, anything small and round
LONG	*Nung:* tree, bamboo, thread, nail, candle	*English:* stick, cane, folded umbrella, ruler, old-fashioned razor, board of wood
	Trukese: tree, canoe, stick, pencil, cigarette	*English:* bars of cot, abacus, columned facade of building

*Based on E. Clark (1977a).

marked and negative. What is even more remarkable is that, according to Greenberg (1966), this is true in all languages (unless the language treats them equally). In many languages, the terms for "lacking extent" are expressed with an overt negative, the equivalent of unlong, not-deep, or non-far. FRENCH, ITALIAN, and SPANISH, for example, lack words for shallow and are forced to use the equivalent of little deep, a more complex expression than deep.

One obvious source for this universal is perception. Take length. In nature it is asymmetrical: a line remains a line, for example, as it grows longer, but it eventually decreases to nothing as it grows shorter. It is only natural, then, to conceive of "having extent" as positive and "lacking extent" as negative. Moreover, children seem to attend more to objects that "have extent" than to those that "lack extent" and this appears to explain why they typically learn the words for the positive ends of such dimensions first.

Natural Dimensions. The dimensions languages pick out are far from arbitrary: they appear to be just those dimensions the human perceptual apparatus is tuned to pick out (H. Clark 1973). This can be illustrated for the ENGLISH spatial terms listed in Table 3. In nature, there is a dimension defined by the pull of gravity, namely verticality, and there is also a natural plane of reference, namely ground level. When describing spatial relations, it is convenient to use these two perceptual invariants.

Table 3: Dimensions Described by English Spatial Terms

REFERENT OBJECTS	DIMENSION	ADJECTIVES	PREPOSITIONS
Gravity	Verticality	high-low	up-down, above-below
People	Verticality	tall-short	up-down, above-below
	Visibility		front of-back of, ahead-behind
	Laterality		left of-right of, at the side of
	Corpulence	fat-thin	
Directed	Verticality	tall-short	up-down, above-below, top of-
objects			underneath
	Visibility		front of-back of, ahead-behind
	Laterality	wide-narrow	left of-right of, at the side of
Undirected	Length	long-short	at the end of
objects	Width	wide-narrow	at the side of
	Thickness	thick-thin	
	Size	large-small	
Points	Distance	far-near	at, to-from, near
Containers	Internality	deep-shallow	in-out, inside-outside
Surfaces	Support		on-off

Gravitational verticality is used in adjectives like high, low, tall,
and short, in prepositions like up, down, above, and below, and
even in verbs like rise, fall, raise, lower, lift, and drop. Ground
level is used in judging something as high or low, unless some
other plane of reference supersedes it.   It is normally taken to be
zero height.

   Common objects have natural dimensions as well. The human
body has a biologically defined and perceptually obvious plane of
symmetry--the sagittal plane that splits the left and right sides of
the body in half. This defines the dimension underlying left and
right. The line running from head to toe in the sagittal plane defines another perceptually salient dimension, body verticality, and
perpendicular to that plane is front and back. The terms used
with these two dimensions have natural origins. When people are
in their normal standing position, body vertical coincides with
gravitational vertical, hence it is convenient to use the same terms
for both. Up and down, for example, are used for both gravitational and body verticality, even when these two dimensions don't
coincide. ENGLISH, like so many other languages, builds many of
its relational terms for the up-down, front-back, and left-right dimensions around appropriate body-parts, such as head, front, back,
top, and side, as in ahead, in front, in back, on top, and beside
(see Friedrich 1970). These terms are then transferred to the
vertical, front-back, and lateral dimensions of other "directed"
objects like cars, trains, chairs, and houses, objects that all have
a normal orientation.

These natural dimensions have natural directions. When people stand, the space in front of them and above the ground is optimal for perception by eye, ear, and touch, hence upward and forward should be "positive" directions. In English, upward is positive, as in high versus low opinion, and so is forward, as in forward versus backward policies. So even though neither up nor down, for example, is linguistically marked, up denotes movement in a positive direction and should be easier to handle conceptually. Indeed, up has been found to take less time to process than down (H. Clark and Brownell 1975), and the same has been found for above and below, in front of and in back of, ahead of and behind, into and out of, and to and from (H. Clark 1974). Left and right are quite another matter. The left and right sides of the body are symmetrical about the sagittal plane, and that predicts no asymmetry. But since most people are right-handed, right should be positive, as it is in perhaps all languages. For example, dexterous comes from the Latin word for right, and sinister from the word for left. Consistent with this view, Olson and Laxar (1973, 1974) found that right-handers processed right faster than left, but left-handers processed left about as fast as right.

Dominance Relations Among Dimensions. In English some dimensions "dominate" others. Height and length, for example, dominate width, and width dominates thickness (Bierwisch 1967). With a vertically oriented block of wood, the vertical dimension is called height, the more extended of the two remaining dimensions width, and the final remaining dimension thickness. And with an arbitrarily oriented block of wood, the most extended dimension is called width, and the final remaining dimension thickness.

These dominance relations turn up in children's first perceptual tactics. Very early in life, they pay attention to the natural directions vertical and horizontal, orienting most strongly to the vertical, especially the upper end. As Rudel and Teuber (1963) showed, they are able to learn a contrast between | and — more easily than between \ and ╱. Diagonal lines are not natural dimensions for children. In addition, they can learn to distinguish ⊔ from ⊓ more easily than ⌐ from ⌐ , showing that they can deal with vertical asymmetries more easily than horizontal ones. These two findings are surely perceptual in origin, for they appear to hold even for octopuses (Sutherland 1957, 1960). Children also look at the upper parts of figures in preference to the lower parts (Ghent 1960, 1961). Here, then, the vertical seems to be dominant. In the well-known Piagetian conservation tasks, children are asked to say whether or not the amount of water in two beakers is the same, or whether or not the amount of clay in two rope-like forms is the same. In these judgments, young children attend to the height and

ignore the width of the water beakers, and they attend to the length
and ignore the width of the clay ropes (Piaget 1953; Farnham-
Diggory and Bermon 1968; see also Lumsden and Poteat 1968).
In both instances they pick out natural dimensions according to
the dominance relations reflected in language.

Unfortunately, unrelated languages have not been systematically
examined for the dimensions they make use of. Yet most languages
appear to express height, length, distance, depth, and other dimensions, express binary relations with respect to the body's up-
down, front-back, and left-right directions, and express verticality
in a variety of other terms. It is difficult to imagine a language
with a preposition meaning "in a left-ward, upward, and outward
direction from," one that does not reflect a natural dimension.
Here again it appears that languages pick their terms for perceptual
reasons. Dimensions that are perceptually salient are the easiest
for children to acquire terms for. They are also the most useful
for adults to refer to, hence are maintained better and with greater
accuracy.

Extensions of Spatial Terms

People make extensive use of their conception of space in many
other language domains. To describe change of spatial position
one might say The balloon went up, and to describe change of temperature one might use the identical words The temperature went
up. Apparently, people conceive of height as an analogue for temperature and can therefore use it as a metaphor for temperature.
They simply transfer all vocabulary for height and change of height
to the domain of temperature and change of temperature. Temperature goes up and down, rises, falls, drops, lowers, and is high or
low. ENGLISH and other European languages have an extraordinary variety of metaphors based on space, suggesting that people's
conception of space plays a central role in their use of language.
The following is just a sampling of these metaphors.

(1) States and changes of state. States are analogous to places,
and changes of state analogous to movement from place to place
(Gruber 1976; Jackendoff 1976), as in English Her face went from
red to white (like She went from London to Paris), Melvin stayed
calm (like Melvin stayed in Paris), or The caterpillar turned into
a butterfly (like The car turned into an alley).

(2) Case relations. For centuries many linguists have argued
that each case relation could be thought of as analogous to a spatial
relation, and they called their theory the "localist" theory of case
(Hjelmslev 1935; Anderson 1971). The case relation Fillmore (1968)
called Experiencer, for example, might be considered analogous to

a place to which something goes. So King George told Wellington a story is like King George sent Wellington a medal. Wellington, the noun in the Experiencer case, receives the story in the first instance just as he receives the medal in the second. This is why people speak of the king telling the story to Wellington. This to is a metaphorical usage based on the to for physical direction.

(3) Possession. In most, perhaps all, languages the possessor is treated analogously to a place, and the object possessed is analogous to an object at that place (E. Clark 1970; Lyons 1967). As in many other languages, in FRENCH one says L'enfant est à la maison ("The child is at the house") for location, and analogously, Le livre est à moi ("The book is at me/mine") for possession. In English, one has the same metaphor in The house went from father to son (like The train went from London to Brighton) and Mary got the house from the Fords (like Mary got the car from the garage).

(4) Normal states. In certain English idioms, normal states are treated as analogous to "here," and abnormal states as analogous to "there" (E. Clark 1974). It is normal, for example, to be conscious and abnormal to be unconscious. Hence one says John came to his senses or John came out of a coma (like John came here), but John went into a daze (like John went there).

(5) Definite reference. According to linguistic evidence discussed by Thorne (1972,1974), the definite article the is basically locative. The man, Thorne suggests, means "man who is there." Many languages have no definite articles, and when they want to mark something as definite, they use a demonstrative pronoun like that, as in that man (Moravcsik 1969). That, of course, is locative, literally meaning "the one there." Note that if Thorne is right, there is a relation between space and given information, since definite articles mark information as given (H. Clark and Haviland 1977).

(6) Time. In ENGLISH and many other languages, time is analogous to a line running from front to back, and the concept of "now" moves along this line in a forward direction (H. Clark 1973; Traugott 1974,1976). Hence in, on, to, from, go, come, pass, ahead, behind, before, after, long, short, and a variety of other spatial terms are used in expressions for time, as in ahead of time, on Tuesday, in the afternoon, long before noon, from Friday onward, in time gone by, and noon came and went.

(7) Temperature. Temperature is analogous to height, with positive direction in temperature (warmer) corresponding to positive direction in height (higher). Some expressions of temperature have already been given.

(8) <u>Status</u>.   Like temperature, status is analogous to height, with greater status corresponding to higher positions. Hence <u>high</u> and <u>low status</u>, <u>status going up</u> and <u>down</u>, and <u>status being raised</u> or <u>lowered</u>.

(9) <u>Pitch</u>.   A number of perceived but nonspatial dimensions have analogues in space too. One of them is pitch, which in English is analogous to height, as in <u>high</u> and <u>low pitch</u>, <u>raised</u> and <u>lowered pitch</u>, <u>going up from C to G</u>, and <u>dropping from G back down to C</u>. There is a curious illusion associated with this analogue. A tone of higher pitch heard in a dark room is misperceived as being higher spatially than it actually is (Harvey 1973).

(10) <u>Emotion</u>.   Emotion, at least in English, is treated as analogous to a substance in a container with depth. One can say <u>His emotion was deep</u>, <u>Victoria was in deep sorrow</u>, and <u>Dick is a shallow person</u>.

(11) <u>Mind and ideas</u>.   Closely related to the analogue for emotion is the English analogue for the mind and ideas. The mind is a receptacle, and ideas are objects put in, taken out, and moved around in this receptacle. One says, for example, <u>That idea was in the back of my mind</u>, <u>He had this idea in mind</u>, <u>Her mind is filled to overflowing with good ideas</u>, <u>He kept count</u>, and <u>He lost count</u>.

Where do these metaphors come from? We, as humans, have a common conception of space as something characterized by directed dimensions (like height) and occupied by objects (like rocks and cars). Within space there are places, distances between places, and movement from place to place. Because children know a lot about dimensions, objects, and movement from early on, they find it easy to learn terms for them. When they come to know about more abstract concepts like time, possession, normal states, and ideas, they are apparently able to see analogues to their spatial knowledge and apply the spatial terms they already know to these new domains without difficulty. For instance, children are able to use locative expressions like <u>in the house</u> before analogous expressions for time like <u>in the afternoon</u>. Because adults know the analogues too, they find it easier to extend their spatial vocabulary than to remember technical names in these special domains. This maintains the metaphors. The widespread and perhaps even universal use of some of these metaphors suggests that the analogical extension of spatial terms is a basic process in language use.

Cognitive Categories

So far the universals discussed have plausible origins in perception. People have natural, built-in ways of perceiving and representing color, objects, shapes, distances, and spatial relations, and this is reflected in the basic names given them. The universals to be taken up next, the <u>cognitive</u> categories, seem to arise from more abstract conceptions of events and relations, although there may be no principled way to distinguish these from perceptual categories. A degree of speculation was often necessary in suggesting accounts for perceptual categories, and this will happen even more often with the cognitive categories. Much remains to be learned about the origins of these universals.

The categories to be examined cover number, negativity, cause and effect, and time. Most of them come from the work of Greenberg (1966), who, using his two criteria for complexity of expression ("added morphemes" and "neutralization"), searched a large number of unrelated languages for regularities in complexity. He concentrated on pairs of categories, one of which he could identify as universally "marked," or more complex, compared with the other.

Number

Most languages have ways of expressing singular and plural in nouns, as in the English <u>dog</u> and <u>dogs</u>. Some languages even have "dual" form for denoting two objects, which would mean "two-dogs." (When a language has a dual, its plural means "more than two" instead of "more than one.") As Greenberg noted, in languages where these forms differ in complexity, plural is always marked with respect to singular, and dual is always marked with respect to plural. Or to use a shorthand to denote increasing complexity of expression:

singular : plural : dual

Most languages also distinguish cardinal numbers (<u>one</u>, <u>two</u>, <u>three</u>, etc.) from ordinal numbers (<u>first</u>, <u>second</u>, <u>third</u>, etc.) As Greenberg found:

cardinal : ordinal

In English this shows up in words like <u>twentieth</u>, which consists of <u>twenty</u> plus an added suffix -eth.

The singular-plural-dual progression very likely derives from the primacy of the individual object in perception. Each object is perceived as an individual with an identity of its own, constant over time. Collections are conceived of as groupings of individual objects in which each object has its own identity. Hence the basic contrast is between an individual and a collection of individuals, between singular and plural.   Dual denotes a particular kind of collection—one with exactly two members—and is therefore more complex.   Cardinals and ordinals fit another progression of cognitive complexity.   Ten objects can be counted in any order, but the ordinal position of each requires two notions: counting and order of counting.   Hence cardinals, which are mere counts, depend on less complex conceptual requirements than ordinals, which are ordered counts (see Piaget and Szeminska 1952).

Negation

One of the most conclusive universals Greenberg found was that negatives are marked with respect to positives:

positive   :   negative

In ENGLISH, the complexity of negatives shows up in the material added to sentences (John is here versus John isn't here), verbs (tie versus untie), adjectives (able versus unable), adverbs (ever versus never), and even pronouns (one versus none).

Negation is probably expressed in a complex way because it takes more specification to say what something is not than to say what something is.   The color of a car wouldn't be described in terms of what colors it is not—blue, yellow, green, orange, black, gray, white, and purple.   It would be described positively as red. People normally use positive rather than negative representations so that they can represent knowledge as simply and directly as possible.   This, of course, is reflected in the representation of x isn't red as two propositions: False(Red(x) .   In the positive case only the specific category, red, is represented, as in Red(x). There is good reason to consider negation complex.

Positive, Good, and Normal.   Positive and negative serve to divide domains like color into two parts, such as red and not red. Many domains divide in half naturally, and then it seems arbitrary to call one half positive and the other negative.   Yet there is almost always a conceptual asymmetry between the two halves, and languages often seize on the asymmetry just to be able to express one half positively and the other half negatively.   This happens, for example, with dimensional terms like high and low or deep and shallow.   In all languages, apparently, extent is taken to be positive and lack of extent negative.   It also happens with evaluative terms.   Good is always expressed positively and bad negatively, but never the reverse (Greenberg 1966):

good   :   bad

The relation between good-bad and positive-negative is very close.
In many languages <u>bad</u> is expressed explicitly as "not-good" or
"ungood." And Zimmer (1964) and Boucher and Osgood (1969) found,
for a variety of languages, that it is almost never possible to add
negative prefixes or suffixes to bad evaluation words to produce
terms like <u>unbad</u>, <u>unsad</u>, or <u>unugly</u>, although these prefixes are
often added to good evaluative words to produce terms like <u>ungood</u>,
<u>unhappy</u>, and <u>unbeautiful</u>.

Why should goodness be expressed positively and badness negatively? That is, why are good and bad often expressed as <u>good</u>
and <u>ungood</u>, but never as <u>unbad</u> and <u>bad</u>? Boucher and Osgood
(1969) have argued for a "Pollyanna hypothesis": people tend to
"look on (and talk about) the bright side of life (p. 1)." If this is
so, words like <u>good</u> should occur more frequently in languages
than words like <u>bad</u>, and this has been amply demonstrated by
Zajonc (1968) at least for English and several other European languages. But the Pollyanna hypothesis doesn't explain why good
words get positive expression and bad words negative expression.
All it implies is that good words should occur more often. Zajonc
(1968) has argued for the opposite hypothesis, that frequently encountered objects come to have a positive evaluation, but his hypothesis suffers from the same defect. It may explain why good
words occur more often, but not why they get expressed positively
and bad words negatively.

The answer more likely lies in the notion of normality. Normal
states are conceived of positively, abnormal states as the absence
of normal states, as negative states. Now, as Bierwisch (1967)
has noted, goodness itself is conceived of as a normal state, and
badness as an abnormal state. Note that milk in its ordinary state
is "good milk," but in its abnormal state has "gone bad." Goodness is considered normal because it is what is expected--what
should be--and so badness is abnormal. Thus, because normal is
positive and abnormal negative, goodness is expressed positively
and badness negatively. The normality hypothesis is consistent
with the Pollyanna hypothesis and Zajonc's findings, but it gives
a reason for expressing one state as the negative of the other.
Moreover, it accounts for the linguistic form of such pairs as
<u>mortal-immortal</u>, <u>usual-unusual</u>, and <u>finite-infinite</u>, words that do
not differ in good and bad evaluation (Zajonc 1968) but do differ in
positive and negative expression. Dimensional terms like <u>high</u>
and <u>low</u> fit here too. <u>High</u>, the positive term, describes measurement in the normal direction on the height scale, and <u>low</u>, the
negative term, measurement in the abnormal direction. Whenever

possible, languages treat the normal positively and the abnormal
negatively, and goodness and badness are just one domain where
they do this.

Cause and Effect

According to Greenberg, if a language has expressions that
differ in complexity for state, change of state, and cause of
change of state, as in dead, die, and kill, then they are given
increasingly complex expression:

state   :   change of state   :   cause of change of state

In ENGLISH change of state often takes an added morpheme compared
with state--as in such pairs as solid-solidify, red-redden, and long-
lengthen. The same goes for cause of change of state compared with
state in such pairs as sharp-sharpen, legal-legalize, large-enlarge.
Many languages add a regular 'affix' to form cause of change of state
from change of state, as TURKISH öl versus öldür for "die" versus
"kill" (cause to die). FRENCH makes causative verbs out of change-
of-state ones by adding the verb faire as in tomber versus faire
tomber for "fall" versus "cause to fall."

Why? Intuitively, states are simpler than changes of state. Being
solid is a constant state, whereas solidifying involves an initial state,
a final state, and a change from the first to the second. Causing
a change of state is still more complex. It requires not only an
initial state, a final state, and a change from one to the other, but
also an event that causes the change to come about. This increase
in complexity is reflected quite naturally in the functional notation
for these three notions: Solid(x), Come-about(Solid(x)), Cause(y,
Come-about(Solid(x))). Children seem to build verbs in this order
too, making change-of-state verbs out of state expressions, and causative verbs out of both change-of-state verbs and state expressions.
How these notions develop prior to language is not well understood.

In English two events that occur in succession can be described
with the first event subordinated to the second, or with the second
event subordinated to the first, as in 1 and 2:

1. John left after Mary insulted Bill.
2. Mary insulted Bill before John left.

But if the first event is the cause of the second, one has to use an
expression similar to 1 in which the first event (here the cause)
is subordinated to the second, as in 3:

3. John left because Mary insulted Bill.

That is, the conjunction because is analogous to after, and there
is no subordinating conjunction expressing cause in English analogous to the before in 2. According to Talmy (1976), this asym-

metry seems to hold for all languages.   Effects are seen and
expressed with respect to causes, not vice versa.   If true, this is
a powerful universal that should be founded in the human concept
of cause and effect.   It may have its roots in the child's acquisition
of notions of causation, but just how is as yet unclear.

Time

All languages have ways of distinguishing among the present,
past, and future, but according to Greenberg, the past is usually
marked with respect to the present, and the future always is:

present : past   present : future

In English the markedness of past over present shows up in the
added morphemes in such pairs as work versus worked and work
versus have worked, and the markedness of future over present in
work versus will work.   In many languages the future is expressed
as a hypothetical event, as distinguished from an actual event.
Certain linguists (Boyd and Thorne 1969) have argued that this is
the case for English: the auxiliary verb will in will work expresses an intention to work and hence is a hypothetical.   In any
case, as Greenberg noted, hypotheticals like would work are invariably marked with respect to actuals like work:

actual   :   hypothetical

It is easy to see where these universals might come from.
Children begin their speech careers by talking solely about the
here and now—objects and events in the present moment.   It takes
time for them to acquire the notion of non-present.   When they do,
they first seem to acquire the notion of past, events they have already experienced, and a bit later the notion of future, events they
have not yet experienced.   For instance, when children begin
learning words like yesterday and tomorrow, they often confuse
them (Decroly and Degand 1913; Stern and Stern 1928).   Harner
(1975) studied two- to four-year-old children who began by inter-
preting yesterday as both past and future, that is, as "not present."
Next they got yesterday right, then finally learned to use tomorrow.   The child's understanding of hypothetical events is acquired
even later than the notions of present, past, and future (Slobin 1973).

Social Categories

The universals included under the term social categories seem
to have their roots in the social and cultural conditions in which
people live.   The two main classes of social categories to be considered probably derive from the universal characteristics of
families and human conversations.

Kinship Terms

Kinship terms -- the terms used to name one's relatives --
have been studied intensively by anthropologists for many languages
and cultures. These terms are especially amenable for study because the anthropologist can set out an objective list of the people
to which each term applies (Burling 1970). The English term uncle,
for example, applies to one's father's brother, one's mother's
brother, the husband of one's father's sister, and the husband of
one's mother's sister. Once the relatives for each term in each
language have been listed, it is relatively straightforward to compare languages in search of the universals of kinship systems.
This is precisely what Greenberg (1966) did, and he turned up a
number of important universals.

All languages distinguish at least three characteristics in relatives: generation, blood relationship, and sex. All languages keep
the generations apart: they have different terms for parents, grand-
parents, children, and grandchildren, even though they may use
only one term for both father and father's brother or one term for
all four grandparents. In addition, all languages distinguish between blood relatives and spouse's relatives, as in ENGLISH
mother versus mother-in-law. And all languages distinguish the
sex of at least some relatives, as in ENGLISH mother versus
father and sister versus brother. Other characteristics are distinguished in some languages but not others.

But languages treat relatives unequally. They favor ancestors
over descendants, near relatives over far relatives, and blood
relatives over spouse's relatives. These biases show up in the
markedness of kin terms:

　　　ancestor : descendant

　　　one generation away : two generations away : three
　　　generations away : ...

　　　blood relative : spouse's relative

In many languages the terms referring to children and other descendants are more complex than the terms referring to parents
and other ancestors, although this does not show up in English.
As for generations, in English there is a progression from father
to grandfather to great grandfather and so on. There is increasing complexity of expression with the addition of grand and
great the more distant the generation the relative belongs to. This
applies to descendants as well, as in grandchild, great grandchild,
and great great grandchild. As for spouse's relatives, these are

clearly marked in English with respect to blood relatives, as in mother-in-law versus mother and sister-in-law versus sister. The added morphemes -in-law mark a relative as belonging to one's spouse.

It seems fairly clear why these distinctions and biases should exist. Humans, by their biological nature, have parents and grand-parents, and--with the usual systems of stable marriage--they may have brothers and sisters, aunts and uncles, cousins, and children. It seems only natural to distinguish the care-taking generations from those being taken care of, and to give one's ancestors, who are necessarily there, priority over one's descendants, who aren't. The relatives most closely associated with a person, either bio-logically or as caretakers (and often both), will be near relatives, hence it is the distant relatives who should be marked. In-laws are acquired only by marriage, so they too are out of the ordinary and should be marked. Put simply, languages will develop kin terms useful for everyday purposes, and this favors ancestors, near relatives, and blood relatives.

A widespread though not universal bias in language is the one favoring male over female:

$$male \ : \ female$$

In English the markedness of female is especially visible. Female terms are formed by the addition of suffixes, as in actor-actress, or major-majorette, and it is the male term that neutralizes to cover both sexes, as in such terms as workman, chairman, fore-fathers, mankind, and even he and man. Although one can only speculate here, sexism in language seems to have its roots in society. Men have often been viewed as dominant, and languages have therefore developed simpler terms to denote them. Note how in English-speaking societies, the dominance of men over women varies with profession, and the complexity of expression follows suit. Doctors, judges, and senators are too often assumed to be men, and nurses and secretaries to be women. Newspapers, then, often mark the out of the ordinary people in these professions as woman doctor, lady judge, lady senator, male nurse, and male secretary where they would never use the terms man doctor, gentleman judge, gentleman senator, female nurse, or female secretary except under special circumstances. These examples show how complexity of expression follows from the assumptions of society, and so the general markedness of female over male terms in ENGLISH probably has the same origins (Miller and Swift 1976). Sexism of this sort seems to be widespread in the languages of the world.

Table 4:   Palaung Pronouns--An Eleven-form System

		SPEAKER INCLUDED	SPEAKER EXCLUDED
ADDRESSEE INCLUDED	Singular	——	mi (*thou* ')
	Dual	ar (*thou and I*)	par (*he or she, and thou*)
	Plural	ɛ (*thou, I, and he, she, or they*)	pɛ (*they and thou*)
ADDRESSEE EXCLUDED	Singular	ɔ (*I*)	ʌn (*he or she*)
	Dual	yar (*he or she, and I*)	gar (*they two*)
	Plural	yɛ (*they and I*)	gɛ (*they, three or more*)

*Thou indicates singular second person pronoun.
Based on Burling (1970).

Pronouns

Although kin terms arise from family and marriage systems,
pronouns are needed in conversation to distinguish the speaker (I)
from the person or persons addressed (you) and from other participants (he or they). Indeed, pronoun systems universally distinguish among these three roles (Forchheimer 1953; Ingram 1971).
And according to Greenberg (1966) and Kuryłowicz (1964), I is
unmarked with respect to you:

                    speaker   :   addressee

Pronoun systems also invariably distinguish the number of participants in one way or another, and may have different forms, for
example, for singular and plural addressees.

Languages may have between four and fifteen pronouns. English
has only five (if gender distinctions are ignored), namely:

                    I   you   he   we   they

In this set, I and he are singular, we and they plural, and you
either singular or plural. I is used for the speaker, you for the
addressee, and he and they for "third persons," other people or
objects. We can be used either "inclusively" for the speaker and
addressee together, or "exclusively" for the speaker and some
third person together. You can be used either for people addressed or for people addressed plus some other people. ENGLISH
does not distinguish between the two wes or the two yous, but many
languages do. One example is PALAUNG, a Mon Khmer language
spoken in Burma, as shown in Table 4. According to Ingram
(1971), this is one of the commonest types of pronoun system found.
Each pronoun specifies whether it denotes one, two, or more than
two people, whether one of those people is the speaker, and whether
one, two, or more than two of these people are the addressees.
The system is perfectly regular and makes good sense.

It seems obvious why languages should universally distinguish role and number in their pronouns. Speech occurs primarily in conversations between a speaker and one or more addressees. It would be highly inefficient to refer to these participants only by expressions like John and Mary, the speaker and the addressee, or the person here and the person there. Pronouns provide a convenient shortcut. Moreover, the one participant essential to every conversation is the speaker. It therefore makes sense to express I in a less complex form than you. Significantly, children generally acquire I before you (E. Clark 1977b). In conversations number is less critical than role and it is also less well developed in pronoun systems. Like the kin terms, then, the pronouns take their universal characteristics from the categories people need for the social and cultural system they are a part of.

Processing Constraints

At first glance there seems to be no consistency from language to language in how words are ordered and grouped in surface structure. For example, the verb normally comes first in SAMOAN and TAGALOG, last in JAPANESE and TURKISH, and in the middle in ENGLISH and FRENCH. This first impression is far from the truth. Only some of the word orders that could conceivably be used in languages actually ever occur, and these have striking characteristics. It appears that the mental processes people have available for speaking and listening exert "forces" on language that favor certain configurations of words over others. The forces to be taken up here have their consequences on the grouping of words, the order of words, and the regularity of paradigms.

Word Groups

It is hard to imagine a language in which an adjective and the noun it modifies are not normally adjacent in the sentence, as in ENGLISH red car, FRENCH voiture rouge, or GERMAN rotes Auto. Since red and car express propositions that make reference to the same entity, they belong together in a single surface constituent. The same goes for other words that reflect closely linked propositions. Indeed, languages appear to conform as closely to this constraint as possible (Greenberg 1963; Sanders 1975; Vennemann 1973, 1974, 1975). The general principle is what Vennemann called Behaghel's First Law:

> Word groups: What belongs together mentally is
> placed close together syntactically.

This principle is nicely illustrated in languages with noun classifiers (Greenberg 1972, 1975). Recall that these languages refer to objects with noun phrases like two flat-things book, in which two is a quantifier (Q), flat-things is a classifier (C), and book is a noun (N). These three constituents "belong together mentally" and always go together to form a single constituent. But as Greenberg argued, the classifier flat-things denotes the objective units that are to be counted, much as grain, spoonful, and pail do in the ENGLISH two grains of sand, two spoonfuls of sand, and two pails of sand. The quantifier therefore goes with the classifier, not with the noun, and should form a surface constituent with the classifier. This is just what Greenberg found. Of the six conceivable orders of Q, C, and N, only four ever occur in languages:

$$(Q + C) + N$$
$$(C + Q) + N$$
$$N + (Q + C)$$
$$N + (C + Q)$$

The two orders that never occur, Q + N + C and C + N + Q, are precisely those in which Q and C do not form a natural surface constituent.

Agreement.   Another device languages have for linking words in surface structure is "agreement." In ENGLISH, the verb is made to agree with the subject in number, as in he works versus they work, and in FRENCH, for example, articles and adjectives are made to agree with their nouns in both number and gender, as in le soleil rond ("the round sun"), in which all three words are masculine and singular, and la lune ronde ("the round moon"), in which all three are feminine and singular. In an extensive survey of unrelated languages, Moravcsik (1971) found that whenever two words agreed like this, they expressed propositions that referred to the same entity. In he works, he refers to the same person that the proposition underlying works refers to. Thus, rules of agreement function very much like word groups. They are used to indicate that two words denote propositions that "go together mentally."

Word groups and rules of agreement are plausibly accounted for as consequences of the way people produce and understand sentences. In noun phrases--which are word groups par excellence--people collect together all the qualifications they want to make about a single entity and pack them into one constituent. In production, they plan all of these qualifications at one time, and so it ought to be easiest to produce them together as a single constituent. In comprehension too it should be easiest to identify the entity referred to when all the qualifications are heard and taken in as part of a single constituent. Most rules of agreement simply reinforce the grouping in noun phrases and underline their coherence as perceptual Gestalts. But rules of agreement can also link words that are compelled by other factors to be widely separated, as with <u>he</u> and <u>works</u> in <u>he scarcely ever works</u>. Here, rules of agreement have an especially critical processing function: they may provide the only way to indicate that two words refer to the same entity.

Word Order

By looking at a diverse sample of the world's languages, Greenberg (1963) discovered a remarkable series of facts about word order. Every language has declarative sentences that express subject (S), verb (V), and object (O), and although many languages (like LATIN), allow S, V, and O to occur freely in any order, they all have a preferred, or normal, order for these three elements. In ENGLISH the order is SVO, as in <u>Maxine picked the flower</u>. Greenberg's first discovery was that of the six conceivable orders of S, V, and O, only four occurred in the world's languages, and one of those was exceedingly rare:

VO-Languages		OV-Languages	
SVO	35%	SOV	44%
VSO	19%		
VOS	2%		

These percentages, taken from Ultan (1969), are only a rough guide to the relative frequency of these four types. Greenberg found no examples of OVS or OSV languages, a point corroborated by others (Pullum 1977).

As if this weren't remarkable enough, Greenberg noted that the ordering of many other elements in surface structure generally goes along with having the object before the verb (an "OV-language") or the verb before the object (a "VO-language"):

VO-Languages	OV-Languages
Verb + Object	Object + Verb
Auxiliary + Main verb	Main verb + Auxiliary
Preposition + Noun	Noun + "Postposition"
Noun + Relative clause	Relative clause + Noun
Noun + Possessive	Possessive + Noun
Noun + Adjective	Adjective + Noun
Noun + Demonstrative	Demonstrative + Noun
Noun + Number	Number + Noun

Although these orders generally all go together, the tendencies aren't perfect. ENGLISH, for example, shows some inconsistency.

As a VO language, it displays the first five constructions (eat apples, may go, at home, man who left, leg of chair), but not the last three (good man, that man, and ten men). This inconsistency may have come about because ENGLISH, like many other Indo-European languages, used to be an OV language and is still in the process of bringing its constructions into harmony as a proper VO-language (Vennemann 1974). Lehmann (1972, 1973) has called languages that fit all the VO patterns "consistent VO-languages," and those that fit all the OV patterns "consistent OV-languages." Classical HEBREW and PORTUGUESE are examples of consistent VO languages, and JAPANESE and TURKISH consistent OV ones.

These consistencies in word order beg for a processing explanation, and that is just what Bartsch and Vennemann (1972; Vennemann 1973, 1974, 1975) have proposed with the "principle of natural serialization." Each of the orderings in consistent VO languages, they argued, is composed of an "operand" followed by an "operator." In the Verb + Object phrase eat apples, for example, apples operates on eat to specify, or determine, just what it was that was eaten, and in the Noun + Relative Clause man who left, who left operates on man to specify which man is being denoted.

In consistent OV languages, the order in all these phrases is just the reverse, with the "operator" before the "operand." So there is a force in languages that might be described like this:

> Natural Order: Constituents in surface structure all tend
> to have the same order, either Operand +
> Operator, or Operator + Operand.

In essence, this is a processing explanation. The claim is that constituents are produced and taken in according to whether they are operators or operands, and the mental processes involved work best when all operators and operands are in the same order.

Subjects and Given Information. Another force at work in languages is one that places the subject at or near the beginning of the sentence. Note that the subject (S) comes first in the two commonest language types, SVO and SOV (about 80 percent of Ultan's sample), and it precedes the object in all but the rarest type, VOS (less than 2 percent of Ultan's sample). Why subjects are placed early seems fairly clear. People tend to express given information, what is already known, to the listener, before new information, what is not already known. This tendency appears to be universal. Languages overwhelmingly prefer to place definite noun phrases (given information) before indefinite noun phrases (new information). In some instances, the only way to indicate that a noun is definite is to place it before any indefinite noun, or to place it

before the verb and to place any indefinite noun after the verb
(E. Clark 1970; Kuno 1971; Li and Thompson 1974). Thus:

> Given Information: Given information should appear
> before new information.

In the normal case, however, it is the subject that is preferred as
given information (Keenan 1976):

> Subjects: As given information, subject are preferred
> over objects, objects over indirect objects,
> and indirect objects over other noun phrases.

Together, these two forces lead to subjects being mentioned early
in utterances.

The "given-new strategy" provides some explanation for the
forces called Given Information and Subjects (see H. Clark and
Haviland 1977). By that strategy, listeners first search memory
for an antecedent to given information--for example, a referent for
a definite noun--then attempt to attach the new information to this
antecedent. They must find the antecedent in memory before they
can attach the new information to it. Thus it is optimal to take in
the given information before the new information; otherwise, they
have to hold the new information temporarily while they search for
the antecedent to which it is to be attached. As for the subject, it
is in some sense already formulated when people begin to speak,
for it normally reflects the matter that provoked the speech in the
first place. And people may even begin speaking before fully formulating the predicate they want to attach to it. It is plausible,
then, that because subjects are planned before predicates, they
should be expressed first too.

Objective Content. Some words tend to be given more prominence in surface structure than others. In The man wouldn't have
captured the elephant, the words man, capture, and elephant are
most prominent: they are central syntactically and get major
stress. The remaining words are less prominent: they depend on
the presence and position of man, capture, and elephant. Langacker (1974) has argued that what tends to get prominence is "objective content," the physical objects, events, and attributes being
referred to. What gets put in the background are the elements expressing the less tangible content, for example, past tense (-ed),
completion (have), prediction (would), negativity (not), and defi-
niteness (the). These less tangible ideas, of course, can be made
prominent, as negation is in It is not true that the man would have
captured the elephant, but usually they aren't. Languages have
various devices for placing these elements in the background. The
tendency Langacker described might be characterized like this:

Objective Content: Languages tend to give objective content prominence in surface structure.

As Langacker noted, this force has an obvious function. It places the words that carry the most information, and normally the most important information, in prominent positions. It is natural to suppose that the speaker finds it useful to make this content prominent and that the listener finds it easier to take in and remember this content because it is prominent.

The five "forces" examined so far--Word Grouping, Natural Order, Given Information, Subjects, and Objective Content—each have a relatively independent reason for existence. Each appears to reflect some fundamental process in comprehension and production. Nevertheless, the forces will sometimes be in conflict and have to battle for their effect. At any one time in the history of a language they may collectively compel syntax to take a particular form, but their conflicts may encourage language change. ENGLISH has undergone a change from SOV to SVO, and because of these natural forces, it is still bringing its subsidiary constructions into line. But as each change is made, other forces come into play that change the language in still other directions. Syntax, and its evolution, may well take the form it does in part because of the forces imposed by the mental processes people rely on for producing and understanding speech.

Paradigms

All languages appear to have "paradigms." In ENGLISH, the verbs belong to a paradigm in which each verb has a present and a past tense form. The past tense is normally formed by adding -ed (in spelling) to the present tense, but there are exceptions.

Regular Past Tense		Irregular Past Tense	
work	worked	build	built
bar	barred	eat	ate
add	added	ring	rang

When new verbs are added to the language, like bicycled, helicoptered, or blitzed, they are invariably given the regular past tense -ed. This "force" might be described as follows:

Paradigms: Languages favor regular paradigms.

Exceptions tend to be straightened out as languages change historically. The irregular verbs that remain in ENGLISH come from earlier regular paradigms that have fallen into disuse, and many are being dropped in favor of regular past-tense forms. Work-wrought, for example, has already become work-worked, and in the United States (but not in Britain), spell-spelt has become spell-spelled, and dream-dreamt has become dream-dreamed.

Regular paradigms have clear advantages in production and comprehension. First, a past-tense verb should be easier to plan and
produce if all people have to remember is to add -ed to the present
tense form—and it is (MacKay 1976). Second, in comprehension a
verb should be easier to identify as being in the past tense if there
is an invariable signal, the -ed, indicating past tense. What makes
regular paradigms so advantageous is their economy for memory.
Imagine that ENGLISH had 10,000 verbs. If present and past tense
forms were each as different as go and went, there would be
20,000 different forms to learn. If, instead, the past tense forms
all took -ed, there would be only 10,000 forms to learn plus the
rule, "Add -ed to make the past tense." The latter is more eco-
nomical, and that may be why languages move toward this ideal.

The advantage of regular paradigms shows up clearly in children,
for whom the economics of memory are critical. As Slobin (1973,
1977) has persuasively argued, children look for suffices (like -ed,
-s, -'s) that have a systematic mapping into meaning. Once they
have found the markers, they try to use them without exceptions.
They say buyed instead of bought, foots instead of feet, and him
instead of his, and learn the exceptions only much later. In
TURKISH, where the major paradigms have virtually no exceptions,
children have little trouble learning the complete paradigms, while
in ENGLISH, where there are exceptions, children master the
corresponding paradigms rather later. The force called Paradigms,
therefore, may have its origin in the strategies children apply in
acquisition.

Invented Languages

In many parts of the world, people trading with each other but
speaking different languages have had to invent trading languages,
technically called pidgins, by which they could talk to each other
(see DeCamp 1971). As temporary "contact vernaculars" with
restricted purposes, pidgins need only a rudimentary structure.
They tend to borrow nouns and verbs from one language--commonly
PORTUGUESE, FRENCH, DUTCH, and ENGLISH—and to use a highly
simplified snytax. They tend not to have subordinate clauses, relative clauses, articles, or grammatical morphemes that mark
plurality, present, past, and future tense. They are simplified
semantically as well. They often have just a single locative preposition to take the place of at, in, by, from, on, to, and the rest
(Traugott 1974). Pidgins can get by with this simplicity because
they are used when the communication requirements are fairly
rudimentary.

An extraordinary thing happens, however, when for one reason
or another a pidgin begins to be learned as a first language by the
children of a culture. Suddenly there are rapid and dramatic
changes in vocabulary and syntax, and it becomes what is technically called a creole. As a pidgin becomes a creole, it acquires a
host of syntactic devices to allow it to distinguish present, past,
and future tenses, to distinguish singular from plural, to build
relative and subordinate clauses, and to distinguish among all the
various locative relations. For example, an ENGLISH-based creole
in New Guinea that is called, appropriately enough, TOK PISIN
("Talk Pidgin"), has evolved a device to allow speakers to build
relative clauses, a device that presumably was not there in its
pidgin ancestor (Sankoff and Brown 1976). The relative clause is
formed simply by inserting a sentence into the main clause and by
"bracketing" it on both sides by the word ia, as in this example:

> Na pik ia ol ikilim bipo ia bai ikamap olsem draipela ston.
>
> And this pig ia they had killed it before ia would turn into
> a huge stone.

As Slobin (1977) has pointed out, this is just the kind of device that
allows speakers to separate main from relative clauses easily and
simply, yet is perceptually easy for the listener to take in.

The characteristic ways pidgins turn into creoles may tell us what
a linguistic system has to look like for it to be spoken, understood,
and learned, and for it to fulfill the communicative functions it is
meant to fulfill (Kay and Sankoff 1974; Slobin 1977). Many pidgins,
for example, are fairly effective communication systems, yet one
test they haven't passed is the one that says, "To be a human language, a communication system has to be learnable by children as
their first language." The changes that occur when pidgins become creoles appear to reflect this requirement as much as any.
It is as if children demand of their language that it enable them to
build relative and subordinate clauses, to indicate present, past,
and future tense, to distinguish among locative relations, and the
like. Kay and Sankoff (1974) have suggested that the order in which
creoles invent linguistic devices will tell us what is "psychologically
salient or functionally necessary or both" in language. Indeed, so
far as one can tell, the aspects of language that creoles invent first
are always among the language universals.

Language Variation

Despite the emphasis on language universals, it is all too obvious that languages differ. They differ in their sounds, surface

structure, grammatical categories, and vocabularies. Just how
much can languages vary, in what ways, and why? And what consequences do variations have for the language user?

Language variation has already been examined a little--but under
another guise. Many universals discussed earlier define not a standard that languages must adhere to but a range within which they
may vary. Berlin and Kay's proposal about basic color terms, for
example, really defines thirty-three ways in which languages can
select their color terms. They can choose from two to eleven
terms, which have to fit the color hierarchy. What Berlin and Kay's
proposal does not do is predict how many color terms a language
should select. It sets limits on variation in language, but doesn't
explain the variation that actually occurs. Much the same could be
said of the other universals. What is lacking so far, then, are principles that explain language variation. Unfortunately, there are few
firm principles to be found. Probably the most transparent principles --though even these have not yet been carefully formulated--are
found in vocabulary.

Variation in Vocabulary

Burling (1970) has compared certain parts of the vocabulary of
GARO, a language spoken in Burma, with the corresponding vocabulary in English and has found several obvious differences. GARO,
for example, has many words that correspond to ENGLISH carry.
Their usage depends on how the object is held and conveyed (on the
head, on the shoulders, in the hands, by means of a strap or in a
basket, and so forth) and on the direction in which it is conveyed.
GARO also has many words for the ENGLISH basket, one for each
of several kinds of basket found in Burma. Where English has the
one word rice, Garo has different words for husked and unhusked
rice, cooked and uncooked rice, and   various varieties of rice.
And Garo has names for several different species that would all be
called ant in English. In the opposite direction, ENGLISH has eleven
basic color terms whereas GARO has only four. ENGLISH also
has many more words for the technical innovations of the last century. Of course, English speakers can describe the different ways
of carrying and the different baskets, rice, and ants by using modi-
fiers as in uncooked rice, wicker basket, and red ants, and Garo
speakers can describe the English colors and technical innovations
by similar means. It is just that the basic terms, the simple one-
word descriptions, do not correspond in ENGLISH and GARO.

It seems obvious enough why GARO and ENGLISH should differ
in these ways. Rice is critical to the survival of Garo speakers,
hence distinctions among kinds of rice are economically and so-

cially important. Baskets are a major aid in transportation, and so baskets and modes of carrying objects are important to distinguish. Ants, although not economically important, have a variety in nature that is more central to an agricultural people than to an industrialized society. Color works the other way around. According to Berlin and Kay (1969), the more industrialized the society (and, presumably, the more artificial dyes used), the more basic color terms it is likely to have. In short, proliferation in the vocabulary of any language reflects utility and hence expertise in concepts.

Expertise within Subcultures. What is often not appreciated, however, is that expertise varies as much within as between language groups, and vocabulary size varies accordingly. Beekeepers, farmers, carpenters, miners, surgeons, football players, cooks — each group, through its special expertise, has evolved a wealth of special terms. A person off the street might know a handful of names for the internal organs of the body, but the surgeon knows hundreds. Thus, it is misleading to think of vocabulary as characteristic of a language. It is rather a characteristic of the subgroups who speak the language.

The way expertise leads to proliferation in vocabulary is quite simple. Consider a forester's use of tree versus pine, oak, and elm, versus jack pine, Ponderosa pine, and white pine. After working closely with trees, he begins to think one level down: in terms of Berlin's levels of abstraction, he treats tree as a unique beginner, pine, oak, and elm as life forms, and jack pine, Ponderosa pine, and white pine as generic terms. Because generic terms should be simple one-word names, he speaks of jacks, ponderosas, and whites instead of jack pines, Ponderosa pines, and white pines. He also adds new terms to the specific level, e.g. Rocky Mountain jacks, western ponderosas, and short-needled whites. Anyone familiar with other areas of expertise will recognize this process. Experts distort their worlds by magnifying their own areas of expertise and the words in them out of all proportion.

The process of shortening and proliferation just illustrated makes sense of two observations Zipf (1935, 1949) made some years ago. First, he noted that the most frequent ENGLISH words have one syllable. Indeed, the less frequent the word, the longer it is likely to be. But note that the most common words--the ones people have most use for--will be just those that denote simpler categories--for example, positive instead of negative, singular instead of plural, and

generic instead of specific categories in Berlin's hierarchy--and
these are just the ones that have shorter, less complex names.
Zipf also noted that as a word becomes more frequent--often because
of a technical or cultural change--it tends to get shortened. Most
shortening probably reflects a change of levels in Berlin's hierarchy. For example, when the moving picture was a technical gadget
in Edison's laboratory, it had a specific-level name moving picture.
But when it became common, it was reclassified as a general-level
category, and moving picture was shortened to movie. The same
happened with many other technical innovations:

talking picture	$\longrightarrow$	talkie
gasoline	$\longrightarrow$	gas
television	$\longrightarrow$	TV or telly
omnibus	$\longrightarrow$	bus

Both of Zipf's observations ultimately reflect the law that complexity in thought is reflected in complexity of expression.

Another way people adapt vocabulary to their needs is by borrowing and inventing terms. When ENGLISH speakers were first introduced to the potato, they needed a name and so they adopted the
term the Spanish had taken from the Taino Indians. There are
similar origins for dilettante (ITALIAN), goulash (HUNGARIAN),
sabotage (FRENCH), whisky (GAELIC), tomato (NAHUATL),
Gestalt (GERMAN), and tomahawk (ALGONQUIAN). The need for
new names can also be solved by coining new ones, as ENGLISH
has by using GREEK (pseudopod), LATIN (quadrilateral), language
mixtures (Minneapolis from DAKOTA mini and GREEK polis), dis-
coverers' names (Parkinson's disease), and so on. Apparently,
when people lack a word for a useful concept, they soon find one.

How Does Language Affect Thought?

So far language and thought have been looked at from one direction only: from how thought affects language. But perhaps the most
celebrated hypothesis in this area--the Sapir-Whorf hypothesis of
linguistic relativity--claims just the opposite: that language affects
thought. According to Whorf, each language imposes on its speaker
a particular "world view." As he put it in the passage cited earlier,
"We cut nature up, organize it into concepts, and ascribe signifi-
cances as we do, largely because we are parties to an agreement
to organize it in this way -- an agreement that holds through our
speech community and is codified in the patterns of our language."
He based this view on his comparison of major European languages
with such American Indian languages as HOPI, AZTEC, NOOTKA,
and APACHE. He argued that the world view Indian languages im-

posed on their speakers was different from the view European
languages imposed on theirs.

Most of the evidence Whorf adduced for this hypothesis consisted of anecdotes like this (1956:241):

> We might isolate something in nature by saying "It is a
> dripping spring." A PACHE erects the statement on a verb
> ga: "be white (including clear, uncolored, and so on)."
> With a prefix nō- the meaning of downward motion enters:
> "whiteness moves downward." Then tó, meaning both
> "water" and "spring" is prefixed. The result corresponds
> to our "dripping spring," but synthetically it is "as water,
> or springs, whiteness moves downward." How utterly
> unlike our way of thinking.

It is unlike our way of talking, but is it really so unlike our way of
thinking? The APACHE word for dripping spring contains elements
that denote "white or clear," "moving downward," and "spring,"
but roughly speaking so does the ENGLISH dripping spring.
Dripping means "moving downward in drops," and spring means
"spring." The ENGLISH expression doesn't happen to mention that
the spring is "white" or "clear," although it could. (Perhaps
Whorf should have translated the APACHE expression as clear
dripping spring.) What is striking here is that both languages have
separate elements for "moving downward," "spring," and "clear."
More than that, these elements appear to extend to other domains
along similar lines. In his very next sentence, Whorf noted: "The
same verb, ga, with a prefix that means 'a place manifests the
condition' becomes gohlga: 'the place is white, clear; a clearing,
a plain.'" In ENGLISH too, one takes the verb clear, adding the
suffix -ing, and forms clearing, "a place that manifests the condition of being clear." How utterly like our way of thinking!

Unhappily, the evidence for the Sapir-Whorf hypothesis has been
equivocal. Whorf's own work suffers all too often from the weaknesses evident in the last example. From his anecdotes it is impossible to tell whether Indian and European languages cut up the
world differently or not. Direct tests of the hypothesis have fared
no better. Some of the earliest work, for example, examined how
perception and memory for colors were affected by different color
terminologies (see R. Brown and Lenneberg 1954; Lenneberg and
Roberts 1956). These studies, however, assumed that the way
languages cut up the color domain is arbitrary, and with the work of
Berlin and Kay (1969), this assumption is no longer viable. Other
tests are difficult to interpret for similar reasons (see Rosch
1974).

Differentiation of Vocabulary. As evidence that language affects thought, Whorf often pointed to the fact that one language has
more words in a particular domain than another language. For example, ESKIMO has four words for snow (Boas 1911) where ENGLISH
and AZTEC have only one. But t hese differences probably reflect
differences only in expertise. Eskimos are led by ecological concerns to note and name different kinds of snow, where the Aztecs
in Mexico were not. The same variation can occur within a language. In ENGLISH, expert skiers have specialized words for
snow--powder, corn, ice, and the like--whereas the rest of us
have just snow. It cannot be, then, that just because people speak
ENGLISH they cannot notice differences in snow.

    Yet becoming an expert may well be aided by a well-differentiated
vocabulary.

        To quote Bross (1973:217):

    How did the surgeon acquire his knowledge of the structure of
    the human body? In part this comes from the surgeon's first-
    hand experience during his long training. But what made this
    experience fruitful was the surgeon's earlier training, the
    distillation of generations of past experience which was trans-
    mitted to the surgeon in his anatomy classes. It has taken
    hundreds of years and millions of dissections to build up the
    detailed and accurate picture of the structure of the human
    body that enables the surgeon to know where to cut. A highly
    specialized sublanguage has evolved for the sole purpose of
    describing this structure. The surgeon had to learn this
    jargon of anatomy before the anatomical facts could be effec-
    tively transmitted to him. Thus, underlying the "effective
    action" of the surgeon is an "effective language."

Bross's illustration is convincing. It would be unimaginable to
learn certain fields without learning the special vocabulary developed for them. This does not mean that expertise is always
or only gained in this way. In many cases the expertise comes
first and the specialized vocabulary, if any, comes later.

    The education of the surgeon may be compared to the edu-
cation of children as they develop into adults. The "highly specialized" language they hear is really a distillation of generations
of human experience, and this knowledge is most effectively transmitted to children through this "adult jargon." The process is
cumulative. Learning new words enables children to conquer new
areas of knowledge, and these new areas enable them to learn
new words, and so on. Thus, a well-differentiated vocabulary
may be a crucial aid to children in becoming "experts"--adults.

Memory. It is in memory that language has been shown to influence thought most convincingly. In one well-known study by
Carmichael, Hogan, and Walter (1932), people were shown a series
of line drawings, each accompanied by one of two labels. For example, O——O was presented with either the label eyeglasses or
barbells. When later asked to reproduce the line drawings they
had seen, those who had seen the figure labeled eyeglasses tended
to distort the figure toward O O, and those who had seen the
figure labeled barbells tended to distort it toward O——O (see Herman, Lawless, and Marshall 1957; Glanzer and Clark 1964). Apparently, people remember the label along with some perceptual information and reconstruct the figure in part from the label and
what it denotes.

The mere presence of a label aids in the recall and recognition
of things. Santa and Ranken (1972) presented people with a large
number of so-called nonsense shapes--line drawings of random-
looking closed figures drawn from a number of line segments--
either with or without arbitrarily chosen labels. The people shown
the labeled figures recognized them better at a later time than the
ones who were shown the unlabeled ones. Labels help even more
when they make sense of a nonsense figure--as, for example, when
star labels a nonsense figure that looks roughly like a star (Ellis
1968). What the labels do apparently is help people distinguish
among the figures more completely and, if recall is required, help
them decide what figures to recall at what times.

Problem Solving. Labeling also affects the way people solve
problems. This is nicely illustrated in Duncker's (1945) classic
problem in which the solver has to overcome "functional fixedness."
In this problem people are presented with a candle, a box of tacks,
and two or three matches. Their problem is to fix the candle to a
wall in an upright position so that the candle won't drip. To solve
the problem, they must see that the box the tacks are kept in can
itself be used as a support for the candle when the box is tacked to
the wall. What makes the problem hard is that most people view
the box merely as a tack holder and fail to see its possible function
as a candle support. In a study by Glucksberg and Weisberg (1966),
people tried to solve the problem under one of two conditions: (a)
when the objects were each labeled (box, tacks, candle, matches)
or (b) where there were no labels. When there were labels people
averaged 0.61 minutes solving the problem, but when there were no
labels, they averaged nearly 9 minutes, almost fifteen times as
long. What the labels do, the explanation goes, is encourage people
to pay attention to each object separately. This in turn enables
them to see the box not merely as a holder but as an object that may
figure in the solution to the problem. Interestingly, people who

succeeded on the problem talked about <u>the box,</u> while those who
failed tended to talk about <u>the box of tacks.</u>

Although this was a demonstration within one language, in
principle it could be extended to compare two languages. Consider the ENGLISH <u>thimble</u> and its GERMAN translation <u>Finger-
hut,</u> literally "finger hat." In GERMAN the name itself expresses
the object's function as a finger cover, whereas in ENGLISH it
doesn't. A problem that required people to abandon the thimble's
function as a finger cover--just as the candle problem requires
people to abandon the box's function as a tack holder--may therefore be more difficult when the thimble is labeled <u>Fingerhut</u> than
<u>thimble.</u> Unfortunately, little work of this kind has been carried
out.

What can one conclude about the Sapir-Whorf hypothesis?
At present, very little. It is easy to find thought processes
in which language plays an important role, and we have examined
some of these. Certain facts are easier to learn in linguistic
than in visual or some other form. Certain visual forms are
easier to remember when labeled than when unlabeled. Certain
problems are solved more easily expressed one way rather than
another. Very generally, language is important whenever people
talk to themselves as they try to keep track of where they are
in a problem or in a list of things to do. Yet the main thrust of
the Sapir-Whorf hypothesis is that differences in languages affect
thought. Because one speaks ENGLISH, JAPANESE, or APACHE,
certain concepts are difficult, perhaps impossible, to deal with.
So far, however, no convincing examples of these differences
have turned up. On the contrary, languages can apparently be
stretched and adapted to fit the needs of virtually any group of
experts. What this suggests is that language differences reflect
the culture, and not the reverse.

BIBLIOGRAPHY

Adams, K.L. and N.F. Conklin. 1973. Toward a theory of natural
    classification. Papers from the Ninth Regional Meeting,
    Chicago Linguistic Society. 1-10.

Anderson, J.M. 1971. The grammar of case: Towards a localistic
    theory. Cambridge University Press.

Bartsch, R. and T. Vennemann. 1972. Semantic structures:
    A study in the relation between syntax and semantics.
    Frankfurt: Athenäum Verlag.

Berlin, B. 1968. Tzeltal numeral classifiers: A study in ethnographic semantics. The Hague: Mouton.

_____. 1972. Speculations on the growth of ethnobotanical
nomenclature. Language in Society 1. 51-86.

_____, D. E. Breedlove and P. H. Raven. 1968. Covert catego-
ries and folk taxonomies. American Anthropologist 70. 290-99.

_____, _____, _____. 1973. General principles of classi-
fication and nomenclature in folk biology. American Anthropologist 75. 214-42.

_____ and P. Kay. 1969. Basic color terms: Their universality
and evolution. Berkeley: University of California Press.

Bierwisch, M. 1967. Some semantic universals of German
adjectivals. Foundations of Language 3. 1-36.

Boas, Franz. 1911. Introduction. In Franz Boas (ed.), Handbook
of American Indian Languages, Part 1. 1-84. Washington, D.C.:
Government Printing Office.

Boring, E. G. 1942. Sensation and perception in the history of
experimental psychology. New York: Appleton-Century-Crofts.

Boucher, J. and C. E. Osgood. 1969. The Pollyanna hypothesis.
J. of Verbal Learning and Verbal Behavior 8. 1-8.

Boyd, J. and J. P. Thorne. 1969. The semantics of modal verbs.
J. of Linguistics 5. 57-74.

Bross, I. D. J. 1973. Languages in cancer research. In G. P.
Murphy, D. Pressman and E. A. Mirand (eds.), Perspectives in
cancer research and treatment. New York: Alan R. Liss. 213-21.

Brown, R. 1958. How shall a thing be called? Psychological
Review 65. 14-21.

_____ and E. H. Lenneberg. 1954. A study in language and
cognition. J. of Abnormal and Social Psychology 49. 454-62.

Burling, R. 1970. Man's many voices: Language in its cultural
context. New York: Holt, Rinehart and Winston.

Carmichael, L., H. P. Hogan and A. A. Walter. 1932. An experimental study of the effect of language on the reproduction of
visually perceived forms. J. Experimental Psychology 15. 73-86.

Chomsky, N. 1965. Aspects of the theory of syntax. Cambridge,
Mass.: M.I.T. Press.

_____. 1968. Language and mind. New York: Harcourt Brace Jovanovich.

Clark, E.V. 1970. Locationals: A study of 'existential,' 'locative,' and 'possessive' sentences. WPLU 3. L1-L36.

_____. 1974. Normal states and evaluative viewpoints. Language 50. 316-32.

_____. 1977a. Universal categories: On the semantics of classifiers and children's early word meanings. In A. Juilland (ed.) Linguistic studies offered to Joseph Greenberg on his sixtieth birthday, v. 1. Saratoga, Calif.: Anma Libri. 449-62.

_____. 1977b. From gesture to word: On the natural history of deixis in language acquisition. In J.S. Bruner and A. Garton (eds.) Human growth and development: Wolfson College lectures 1976. Oxford University Press.

Clark, H.H. 1973. Space, time, semantics, and the child. In T.E. Moore (ed.), Cognitive development and the acquisition of language. New York: Academic Press. 28-63.

_____. 1974. Semantics and comprehension. In T.A. Sebeok (ed.), Current trends in linguistics, v. 12: Linguistics and adjacent arts and sciences. The Hague: Mouton. 1291-1498.

_____ and H.H. Brownell. 1975. Judging up and down. J. Experimental Psychology: Human Perception and Performance 1. 339-52.

_____ and E.V. Clark. 1977. Psychology and language. New York: Harcourt Brace Jovanovich.

_____ and S.E. Haviland. 1977. Comprehension and the given-new contract. In R.O. Freedle (ed.), Discourse production and comprehension. Norwood, N.J.: Ablex. 1-40.

DeCamp, D. 1971. Introduction: The study of pidgin and creole languages. In D.H. Hymes (ed.), Pidginization and creolization of languages. Cambridge University Press. 13-39.

Decroly, O. and J. Degand. 1913. Observations relatives au développement de la notion du temps chez une petite fille. Archives de Psychologie 13. 113-161.

Denny, J.P. 1976. The "extendedness" variable in classifier semantics: Universal features and cultural variation. In M. Mathiot (ed.), Boas, Sapir, and Whorf revisited. International Journal of the Sociology of Language 3.

de Valois, R.L. and G.H. Jacobs. 1968. Primate color vision. Science 162. 533-40.

Dougherty, J.W.D. 1976. On the significance of a sequence in the acquisition of color vocabulary. Paper presented at NATO Conference on the Psychology of Language, University of Stirling.

Duncker, K. 1945. On problem-solving. Psychological Monographs 58 (5, whole no. 270).

Ellis, H.C. 1968. Transfer of stimulus predifferentiation to shape recognition and identification learning: Role of properties of verbal labels. J. Experimental Psychology 78. 401-09.

Farnham-Diggory, S. and M. Bermon. 1968. Verbal compensation, cognitive synthesis, and conservation. Merrill-Palmer Quarterly 14. 215-27.

Fillmore, C.J. 1968. The case for case. In E. Bach and R. T. Harms (eds.), Universals in linguistic theory. New York: Holt, Rinehart and Winston. 1-90.

Forchheimer, P. 1953. The category of person. Berlin: W.deGruyter.

Friedrich, P. 1970. Shape in grammar. Language 46. 379-407.

Ghent, L. 1960. Recognition by children of realistic figures in various orientations. Canadian J. of Psychology 14. 249-56.

_____. 1961. Form and its orientation: The child's-eye view. American J. of Psychology 74. 177-90.

Glanzer, M. and W.H. Clark. 1964. The verbal loop hypothesis: Conventional figures. American J. of Psychology 77. 621-26.

Glucksberg, S. and R.W. Weisberg. 1966. Verbal behavior and problem solving: Some effects of labelling in a functional fixedness problem. J. Experimental Psychology 71. 659-64.

Greenberg, J.H. 1963. Some universals of grammar with particular reference to the order of meaningful elements. In J. H. Greenberg (ed.), Universals of language. Cambridge, Mass.: M.I.T. Press. 58-90.

_____. 1966. Language universals. The Hague: Mouton.

_____. 1972. Numeral classifiers and substantival number: Problems in the genesis of a linguistic type. WPLU 9. 1-39.

_____. 1975. Dynamic aspects of word order in the numeral

classifier. In C.N. Li (ed.), Word order and word order change. Austin, Texas: University of Texas Press. 27-45.

Gruber, J.S. 1976. Lexical structures in syntax and semantics. North-Holland Linguistic Series 25. Amsterdam: North-Holland.

Harner, L. 1975. Yesterday and tomorrow: Development of early understanding of the terms. Developmental Psychology 11. 864-5.

Harvey, N. 1973. Does intermodal equivalence exist between heteromodal stimulus dimensions or between stimulus values in these dimensions? Quarterly J. of Experimental Psychology 25. 476-91.

Heider, E.R. 1971. "Focal" color areas and the development of color names. Developmental Psychology 4. 447-55.

_____. 1972. Universals in color naming and mastery. J. Experimental Psychology 93. 10-20.

_____ and D. Olivier. 1972. The structure of the color space in naming and memory for two languages. Cognitive Psychology 3. 337-54.

Hering, E. 1964. Outlines of a theory of the light sense. Cambridge, Mass.: Harvard University Press. [Orig. pub. 1920.]

Herman, D.T., R.H. Lawless and R.W. Marshall. 1957. Variables in the effect of language on the reproduction of visually perceived forms. Perceptual and Motor Skills 7, Monograph Suppl. 2. 171-86.

Hjelmslev, L. 1935. La catégorie de cas: Étude de grammaire générale. Acta Jutlandica 9.

Ingram, D. 1971. Typology and universals of personal pronouns. WPLU 5. P1-P35.

Jackendorf, R. 1976. Toward an explanatory semantic representation. Linguistic Inquiry 7. 89-150.

Jameson, D. and L.M. Hurvich. 1955. Some quantitative aspects of an opponent-colors theory: I. Chromatic responses and spectral saturation. J. Optical Society of America 45. 546-52.

Kay, P. 1975. Synchronic variability and diachronic changes in basic color terms. Language in Society 4. 257-70.

_____ and G. Sankoff. 1974. A language-universals approach to pidgins and creoles. In D. DeCamp and I.F. Hancock (eds.), Pidgins and creoles: Current trends and prospects. Washington, D.C.: Georgetown University Press. 61-72.

Keenan, E.L. 1976. Towards a universal definition of "subject." In C.N. Li (ed.), Subject and topic. New York: Academic Press. 303-33.

Kučera, H. and W.N. Francis. 1967. Computational analysis of present-day American English. Providence, R.I.: Brown U. Press.

Kuno, S. 1971. The position of locatives in existential sentences. Linguistic Inquiry 2. 333-78.

Kuryłowicz, J. 1964. The inflectional categories of Indo-European. Heidelberg: Carl Winter Universitätsverlag.

Langacker, R.W. 1974. Movement rules in functional perspective. Language 50. 630-64.

Lehmann, W.P. 1972. On converging theories in linguistics. Language 48. 266-75.

_____. 1973. A structural principle of language and its implications. Language 49. 47-66.

Lehrman, D.S. 1953. A critique of Konrad Lorenz's theory of instinctual behavior. Quarterly Review of Biology 28. 337-63.

Lenneberg, E.H. and J.M. Roberts. 1956. The language of experience: A study in methodology. IJAL, Memoir 13.

Levelt, W.J.M. 1975. What became of LAD? In Ut videam: Contributions to an understanding of linguistics, for Pieter Verburg on the occasion of his 70th birthday. Lisse: Peter de Ridder Press. 171-90.

Li, C.N. and S.A. Thompson. 1974. Historical change of word order: A case study and its implications. In J.M. Anderson and C. Jones (eds.), Historical linguistics I: Syntax, morphology, internal and comparative reconstruction. Amsterdam: North-Holland. 199-217.

Lumsden, E.A. and B.W.S. Poteat. 1968. The salience of the vertical dimension in the concept of "bigger" in five- and six-year-olds. J. of Verbal Learning and Verbal Behavior 7. 404-8.

Lyons, J. 1967. A note on possessive, existential, and locative sentences. Foundations of Language 3. 390-6.

MacKay, D.G. 1976. On the retrieval and lexical structure of verbs. J. of Verbal Learning and Verbal Behavior 15. 169-82.

McDaniel, C.K. 1974. Basic color terms: Their neurophysiological bases. Paper presented at the Annual Meeting of the American Anthropological Association, Mexico City.

Mervis, C.B., J.Catlin and E. Rosch. 1975. Development of the structure of color categories. Developmental Psychology 11. 54-60.

Miller, C. and K. Swift. 1976. Words and woman: New language in new times. New York: Doubleday.

Moravcsik, E.A. 1969. Determination. WPLU 1. 64-98.

_____. 1971. Agreement. WPLU 5. A1-A69.

Olson, G.M. and K.Laxar. 1973. Asymmetries in processing the terms 'right' and 'left.' J. Experimental Psychology 100. 284-90.

_____ and _____. 1974. Processing the terms 'right' and 'left.' J. Experimental Psychology 102. 1135-7.

Piaget, J. 1953. The origins of intelligence in the child. London: Routledge and Kegan Paul.

_____ and A. Szeminska. 1952. The child's conception of number. New York: Humanities Press.

Pullum, G.K. 1977. Word order universals and grammatical relations. In P. Cole and J.M. Sadock (eds.), Syntax and semantics, v. 8: Grammatical relations. New York: Academic Press. 249-77.

Rosch, E.H. 1973. On the internal structure of perceptual and semantic categories. In T.E. Moore (ed.), Cognitive development and the acquisition of language. New York: Academic Press. 111-44.

_____. 1974. Linguistic relativity. In A. Silverstein (ed.), Human communication: Theoretical perspectives. New York: Halstead. 95-121.

_____. 1977. Human categorization. In N. Warren (ed.), Advances in cross-cultural psychology, v. 1. London: Academic.

_____ and C.B. Mervis. 1975. Family resemblances: Studies in the internal structure of categories. Cognitive Psychology 7. 573-605.

_____, _____, W. Gray, D. Johnson and P. Boyes-Braem. 1976. Basic objects in natural categories. Cognitive Psychology 8. 382-439.

Rudel, R.G. and H.L. Teuber. 1963. Discrimination of the direction of lines by children. J. Comparative and Physiological Psychology 56. 892-98.

Sanders, G. 1975. On the explanation of constituent order universals. In C.N. Li (ed.), Word order and word order change. Austin, Texas: University of Texas Press. 389-436.

Sankoff, G. and P. Brown. 1976. The origins of syntax in discourse: A case study of Tok Pisin relatives. Language 52. 631-66.

Santa, J.L. and H.B. Ranken. 1972. Effects of verbal coding on recognition memory. J. Experimental Psychology 93. 268-78.

Schlesinger, I.M. 1967. A note on the relationship between psychological and linguistic theories. Foundations of Language 3. 397-402.

Slobin, D.I. 1973. Cognitive prerequisites for the acquisition of grammar. In C.A. Ferguson and D.I. Slobin (eds.), Studies of child language development. New York: Holt, Rinehart and Winston. 175-208.

_____. 1977. Language change in childhood and in history. In J. Macnamara (ed.), Language learning and thought. New York: Academic Press. 185-214.

Stern, C. and W. Stern. 1928. Die Kindersprache (2nd revised edition). Leipzig: Barth.

Stross, B. 1973. Acquisition of botanical terminology by Tzeltal children. In M.S. Edmonson (ed.), Meaning in Mayan languages. The Hague: Mouton. 107-41.

Sutherland, N.S. 1957. Visual discrimination of orientation and shape by Octopus. Nature 179. 505.

_____. 1960. Visual discrimination of orientation by Octopus: Mirror images. British J. of Psychology 51. 9-18.

Talmy, L. 1976. Semantic causative types. In M. Shibatani (ed.), Syntax and semantics, v. 6: The grammar of causative constructions. New York: Academic Press. 43-116.

Thorne, J.P. 1972. On the notion 'definite.' Foundations of Language 8. 562-8.

_____. 1974. Notes on 'Notes on "On the notion 'definite.'"' Foundations of language 11. 111-14.

Traugott, E.C. 1974. Explorations in linguistic elaboration: Language change, language acquisition, and the genesis of spatio-temporal terms. In J.M. Anderson and C. Jones (eds.), Historical linguistics I: Syntax, morphology, internal and comparative reconstruction. Amsterdam: North-Holland. 263-314.

_____. 1975. Spatial expressions of tense and temporal sequencing: A contribution to the study of semantic fields. Semiotica 15. 207-30.

Ultan, R. 1969. Some general characteristics of interrogative systems. WPLU 1. 41-63.

Vennemann, T. 1973. Explanation in syntax. In J. Kimball (ed.), Syntax and semantics, v. 2. New York: Seminar Press. 1-50.

_____. 1974. Topics, subjects, and word order: From SXV to SVX via TVX. In J.M. Anderson and C. Jones (eds.), Historical linguistics I: Syntax, morphology, internal and comparative reconstruction. Amsterdam: North-Holland. 339-76.

_____. 1975. An explanation of drift. In C.N. Li (ed.), Word order and word order change. Austin, Texas: University of Texas Press. 269-305.

Whorf, B.L. 1956. Science and linguistics. In J.B. Carroll (ed.), Language, thought, and reality: Selected writings of Benjamin Lee Whorf. Cambridge, Mass.: M.I.T. Press. 207-19.

Zajonc, R.B. 1968. Attitudinal effects of mere exposure. J. of Personality and Social Psychology, Monograph Supplement 9 (No. 2, part 2). 1-27.

Zimmer, K.E. 1964. Affixal negation in English and other languages: An investigation of restricted productivity. Word 20 (2, part 2).

Zipf, G.K. 1935. The psycho-biology of language. Boston, Mass.: Houghton-Mifflin.

_____. 1949. Human behavior and the principle of least effort. Cambridge, Mass.: Addison-Wesley.

Index of Languages

Index of Authors Cited